EXPATRIATE TAX AND INVESTMENT HANDBOOK

Seventh edition

**Andrew Wells, Nigel Eastaway
and Paul Gauntlett**

PEARSON EDUCATION LIMITED
London Office:
128 Long Acre, London WC2E 9AN
Tel: +44 (0)20 7447 2000
Fax: +44 (0)20 7240 5771
Website: www.pearsoned-ema.com

First published in Great Britain in 2000

ISBN 0 273 64176 X

British Library Cataloguing in Publication Data
A CIP catalogue record for this book can be obtained
from the British Library

Typeset by M Rules
Printed and bound in Great Britain by Biddles Ltd, Guildford and King's Lynn

*The Publishers' policy is to use paper manufactured
from sustainable forests.*

CONTENTS

ABBREVIATIONS

ACT	advance corporation tax
CGT	capital gains tax
CGTA 1979	Capital Gains Tax Act 1979
EEA	European Economic Area
ESC	Extra-Statutory Concession
EU	European Union
FA	Finance Act
FSA 1986	Financial Services Act 1986
IHT	inheritance tax
IHTA 1984	Inheritance Tax Act 1984
NICs	National Insurance Contributions
para	paragraph (of a Schedule to an Act)
s	section (of an Act)
Sched	Schedule (to an Act)
SP	Inland Revenue Statement of Practice
TA 1988	Income and Corporation Taxes Act 1988
TCGA 1992	Taxation of Chargeable Gains Act 1992
TMA 1970	Taxes Management Act 1970
VAT	value added tax
VATA 1983	Value Added Tax Act 1983

ACKNOWLEDGEMENTS

The central chapters of this new edition of the Handbook, with their updated exposition of UK tax legislation as it affects British expatriates, were provided by Andrew Wells, FTII of *BDO Stoy Hayward*, and by Nigel Eastaway, FCA, FTII of *WJB Chiltern plc*. The special chapter on the tax aspects of property in the United Kingdom owned by expatriates was originally written by P A Goodman, MA, ACI, ATII of *Wilkins Kennedy*, Chartered Accountants, but has been revised for this edition. The chapter on constructing an investment portfolio, based partly on earlier material contributed by Richard Sayer and Peter Ashton of *Allied Dunbar* has been revised with the addition of new material by Paul Gauntlett, ASFA, ATII, of *Advisory & Brokerage Services Ltd* who has also revised and updated the chapter on pensions originally contributed by Debbie Harrison, BA, and the chapter on exchange rate movements originally written by David Phillips, MA, DPhil. This edition of the Handbook has been edited by Andrew Wells, Nigel Eastaway and Paul Gauntlett.

INTRODUCTION

This Handbook is aimed primarily at professional advisers, and, as in previous editions, its core chapters update the detailed analysis of tax statutes, case law and Inland Revenue practice as they all bear upon the taxation of British expatriates. But many expatriates with no professional background in matters of tax and investment will find the book useful, especially as a guide to future action.

The basic fact that the April-to-April tax year, and not the calendar year, is the key to successful tax planning, and the expatriate's special situation in this regard combine to enforce the maxim that to be forewarned is to be forearmed.

This new edition covers the relevant changes introduced in the 1998 and 1999 Finance Acts. Some of these changes are far-reaching, as summarised below:

• Foreign earnings deduction	Abolished
• Indexation allowance for CGT	Frozen at 6 April 1998
• Taper relief for CGT	Introduced
• Re-entry charge for CGT	Introduced for temporary non-residents
• Anti-avoidance: offshore trusts	Introduced to catch existing trusts
• Special 'Schedule F' rates for dividends	Introduced (imputation system abolished)
• Married couples and other allowances	Relief reduced to 10 per cent

There are still reasons to think that further changes may follow; notably, inheritance tax (IHT) has hardly been altered at all by the Labour government and it has been a long held view in that Party that the present regime, which allows potentially exempt transfers (PETs) and other reliefs, is too generous.

Meanwhile, there has been much significant legislation to consider. In the last edition we reviewed Labour's main policy objectives and there have been significant moves towards some of these.

As regards residence, for the time being there is no change to the rules and capital gains tax (CGT) avoidance has simply been targeted by the introduction of a new 're-entry' charge for 'temporary non-residents'. Many commentators had been anticipating an exit charge. A charge on return to the United Kingdom does not crystallise an immediate gain as an exit charge might, and leaves the expatriate with the 'don't sell' option. No doubt the government believes that this will discourage some people from relatively short absences coinciding with disposals of gainful assets. Interestingly enough, the introduction of the new CGT taper relief is probably more likely to have this effect. Taper is a clever relief as it greatly reduces the tax payable, especially for business assets held long term, yet never completely eliminates the tax. In time, many people who would have considered emigration in the face of a potential CGT bill of 40 per cent will not consider this worthwhile, as taper will eventually reduce the effective rate of tax payable to as little as 10 per cent on current rates. Under proposals in the 1999 Autumn Statement, it may be that the qualifying period for cerain shareholdings representing business assets will be reduced to only five years.

In the meantime, the wisdom of the re-entry charge is questionable. Loopholes still exist, eg periods of residence in countries which have appropriate double taxation treaties may still lead to avoidance, although the choice of destination is now considerably narrower! Furthermore, a significant number of people who would have been willing to leave these shores for at least three years will be willing to extend this to five. It is difficult to see how it will benefit the UK economy to encourage a longer period of absence by wealthy people who, whilst overseas, have no great incentive to invest here. The Revenue have indicated that the five-year rule is not ideal but there has to be a cut-off point somewhere. Be that as it may, it is quite possible that the last has not been heard of new statutory residence rules, following the thought processes behind the 1988 Consultative Document.

The Chancellor has also delivered on his promise (or threat!) to target trusts. The two main thrusts are to introduce a charge on UK resident and domiciled settlors of pre-March 1991 'golden' trusts, which in some cases appears to have wiped out any hoped for tax advantage at a stroke, and to extend the beneficiary charge to trusts with non-resident or non-domiciled settlors. The latter change may not have been high on the agenda but following the extensive publicity surrounding the personal affairs of the then Paymaster General, himself reported to be a beneficiary of such an arrangement, the government apparently felt that it had to do something. Offshore trusts have been wounded but not fatally. They still have their uses.

On the other hand, the United Kingdom is still a tax haven for non-domiciliaries. So far Labour has not followed up its 1994 threats against those of foreign origin who come here to live, spend and invest and it is to be hoped that this reflects a maturing of attitude brought on by the experience of office as there has always been a strong economic case for retaining these incentives, disliked as they may be by some of our European neighbours. The case against would appear to be a purely political one and whilst projections can be prepared to anticipate increased yields from taxing the non-domiciled, these cannot properly predict how many would migrate in the face of unfriendly tax developments. Some material changes to the domicile rules could still be on Labour's shopping list, nevertheless.

Since the last edition of this handbook we have seen the proposals to introduce a general anti-avoidance rule (GAAR) shelved following a healthy consultation debate. There are those in the Inland Revenue and elsewhere who are not particularly happy about this and who have made noises about 'the return of the GAAR'. We might well have a GAAR of some sort in the United Kingdom at some time, even if it does not now seem imminent. Certainly the prospect of continuing evolution of essentially judge-made anti-avoidance case law is not a very satisfactory alternative to a GAAR. Here we have also seen developments. In particular it is notable that the *McGuckian* case has kept the 'substance versus form' debate wide open and no taxpayer should rely on a positive decision from the courts in a case involving schemes of an artificial nature.

Perhaps the most controversial development is the increasing tendency of Ministers and Revenue officials to fail to draw a proper distinction between tax avoidance (legal) and tax evasion (illegal). Until such time as tax avoidance becomes illegal, those who indulge in it should not be tarred with the same brush as fraudsters, however morally reprehensible the government may feel the practice is. Avoidance comes in many shapes and sizes, subtle and sophisticated or otherwise, but it is surely preferable to the activities of those who fabricate, conceal or mislead. If the distinction is lost, is there a danger that taxpayers who have been 'legal' if 'aggressive' in their planning will turn their thoughts to more dubious practices? Certainly the expatriate needs to be aware of toughening attitudes including a steady flow of recent prosecutions, not just against taxpayers but also their professional advisers, which have resulted in stiff jail sentences for those involved. Standards of advice must be higher than ever, and proper implementation is crucial.

Since the previous edition we have seen tax law getting ever more complex (FA 1998 had some 166 sections and 27 Schedules). The tax law rewrite project, which is designed to express the law in comprehensible terms, does not seem to be keeping pace with the deluge of new legislation, changing and complicating the tax system. This may turn out to be a hopeless quest – the fiscal equivalent of painting the Forth Bridge!

As well as updating all the taxation chapters, we have expanded the section on National Insurance contributions and revised the chapters on investment, life assurance and pensions and the chapter on exchange. The euro is now a reality and for the time being at least it is a foreign currency even though notes and coins are not yet changing hands in the shops. The euro has had an 'interesting' debut on the currency markets. In the meantime, UK inflation has fallen to a 30-year low and this is impinging on interest rates, investment returns and, in particular, likely returns on 'money-purchase' pension policies. Expatriates will, like everyone else, need to give serious thought to the adequacy of their pension arrangements, particularly since onshore pension providers are no longer going to enjoy the repayment of tax credits arising from UK stockmarket portfolios.

The editors have, as before, concentrated on areas likely to be of prime importance to expatriates. Even then, some of the laws are so complex that it is impossible to give in-depth analysis in a handbook. For more detailed explanations of UK tax legislation readers are referred, in the first instance, to the *Allied Dunbar Tax Handbook* and the *Allied Dunbar Pensions Handbook*. Ultimately, however, there is no substitute for detailed analysis of the relevant statutes and case law and expert professional advice. It is also vitally important for the expatriate to obtain advice on the taxation requirements of the host country in which he is based, as the rules may be very different from those of the United Kingdom and the consequences of failing to do so could have serious consequences for his wealth or even liberty.

Finally, throughout this book we refer to the individual expatriate as 'he', rather than 'he or she', but only in order to avoid bringing undue grammatical complexity into the treatment of topics that are already complicated enough for most readers' tastes.

1

PREPARING TO BE AN EXPATRIATE

1.1 INTRODUCTION

There is one major rule of expatriate life: plan ahead. This rule applies as much before departure from home as it does during the expatriate's absence from the United Kingdom; but it is particularly important in the tax year before the tax year of the expatriate's planned return home.

This chapter is intended as an introduction to the more detailed explanations to be found later in this handbook. It begins with a consideration of the necessary precautions to be taken before leaving the United Kingdom. It then covers a number of key factors involved in making the most of the time spent abroad, after which it deals with returning to the United Kingdom and what may happen thereafter. Finally, a number of basic terms and concepts that the expatriate may encounter are explained briefly. They will prove useful when reading subsequent chapters and other relevant material.

1.2 PREPARING FOR DEPARTURE

This process begins when the intending expatriate is either offered a job abroad or has reached a definite decision to retire or otherwise move abroad. In the case of working expatriates, reasons to accept the appointment may include a higher salary, professional advancement, or simply the positive effect that international experience is likely to have on one's CV and future employability.

Reasons not to accept may include the effect on family life or on one's children's education. Accompanying wives or husbands may have to give up jobs of their own, and will not usually be likely to find satisfactory work abroad. Because of the strains that are put on family life during expatriate assignments, it is important for both partners to attend any available predeparture briefing seminars. This is especially true if the move is to an area known for problems with crime or political instability.

Persons retiring abroad may be attracted by milder climates, milder tax regimes, and lower living costs. A pension denominated in pounds sterling may stretch further in a country with a relatively weak currency. On the other hand, there may be matters of health, access to medical care, personal security and a satisfactory social life (both now and following the possible death of a spouse) to be taken into consideration. It goes without saying that one should know the proposed location, in season and out of season, before committing oneself, and should always leave open the possibility of return. But it is not unknown for couples to decide on impulse to retire to a region that they hardly know, only to find themselves effectively stranded there, even though they would much rather be somewhere else. Some important decisions in life may be taken instinctively, but this is one where an element of calculation is certainly called for. A US subscription website (www.expatspouse.com) may be of interest.

1.2.1 Assessing the remuneration package

The salary offered to an expatriate typically comprises the gross salary that he would be offered for the same job in the United Kingdom (which is not necessarily the same as his present salary, because expatriation is generally treated as promotion) plus a foreign service allowance of between 5 per cent and 50 per cent (usually 10 per cent, unless the country in question is classified as a 'hardship posting'). This will be adjusted according to a cost-of-living comparison with the destination. Thus to go from an annual salary of, say, £50,000 in London to one of £75,000 in Tokyo would mean in effect taking a cut in pay, because ordinary living costs are more than twice as high in Tokyo as in London.

The salary offered should therefore be judged on the basis of living-cost comparisons such as those obtainable from Eurocost at 1 rue Emile Bian, L-1235, Luxembourg (tel: +352 40 48 06; fax: +352 49 57 13). The consultancy Employment Conditions Abroad (commonly known as ECA International) at Anchor House, 15 Britten Street, London SW3 3TY (tel: +44 (0)20 7351 5000; fax: +44 (0)20 7351 9396) sells *Country Profiles*. These contain data about the cost of living and other useful information. Useful websites include www.countrynet.com and www.cibfarnham.com (the Centre for International Briefings).

The salary offered will only be acceptable if it means a rise in pay even after cost-of-living adjustments and continues to be inflation linked. A simple way to establish whether there is scope to negotiate for more is to ask at interview whether other nationalities were considered for the job. British expatriates are widely regarded as costing relatively less than many other nationals in the international jobs market. If the salary budget in question was allocated to allow for, say, a Scandinavian, German or US successful candidate, the British applicant may be able to get the salary offer increased.

The salary should be paid either in sterling or in another strong international currency. If the salary is not paid in sterling, there may be exchange rate complications on returning to the United Kingdom. The remuneration package should include a range of non-salary benefits, such as regular paid leave, subsidised flights home, and contributions to medical insurance and company or personal pensions or pension type schemes (see Chapter 15, below). It may, however, be more tax efficient for a company to make specific payments to cover certain costs of life overseas than to structure an allowance in the remuneration package. Additional benefits may include the payment of local taxes, education for your children at an international school, good quality local accommodation, a company car (or equivalent compensation) and full reimbursement of removal costs.

Finally, the incidence of home and host country taxation must be considered. Employers that operate a tax 'equalisation' scheme will seek to put the employee in a 'no better, no worse' position based on net salary after taxation in the home country. Employers that operate tax 'protection' will offer opportunities for employees to benefit from assignments to low tax jurisdictions or havens, whilst protecting against higher taxes. Other employers may leave taxation entirely in the hands of the employee.

1.2.2 Job security and related questions

It is generally advisable, at this stage, to consider what career prospects will follow the period as an expatriate. Will the employer bring the expatriate home, or is it a question of a short-term contract overseas that will be renewable only by means of another similar short-term contract overseas?

Job security should also be considered. The contract of employment should be drawn up in English, or presented in a legally binding English translation, and the expatriate should have access to legal advice overseas that is independent of his employer. It is essential to know, too, in which jurisdiction any disputes that may possibly arise out of the contract will be settled (see also **2.2.26**).

It should be noted that an unexpected termination of the expatriate's employment overseas, usually entailing an unscheduled return to the United Kingdom, can jeopardise his tax position and the tax-efficiency of his financial arrangements.

It should not be overlooked, either, that many countries require an application for a work permit before the expatriate arrives there. If a partner, who is not taking up an appointment already contracted for, intends to seek paid employment in the new location, he or she should apply for a work permit before leaving the United Kingdom, and as far in advance as possible. Some countries may be reluctant to grant visas to partners who are not spouses (ie unmarried).

If the contract is one offered by the expatriate's present employer, repatriation should be discussed at the outset, rather than a short time before it occurs. An expatriate leaving a job to take up a post with another employer should bear in mind that the UK employment market may be quite unfamiliar by the time he returns to the United Kingdom, and old networking contacts may be out of date. Try, if you can, to talk to someone who has experienced this first hand.

1.2.3 Preliminary banking arrangements

Before leaving the United Kingdom, the intending expatriate should open a local banking account in the new country. This can be done through his UK bank. It will often be advisable for him to transfer the bulk of his financial affairs offshore, ie to a bank in a third jurisdiction (see **2.2.9**, 'Offshore'), perhaps to an offshore bank or subsidiary of his UK bank, and to have his salary paid into this offshore account. In any case, an expatriate should have banking facilities in each of the currencies in which he may have liabilities. Multicurrency cheque accounts are useful in this respect.

Both the local bank and the offshore bank should be in receipt of any relevant and necessary authority to enable them to act on telephoned, faxed, e-mailed or posted instructions. Ideally, the local bank account should hold a balance equivalent to at least one month's salary. The expatriate should also have at least one credit card denominated in an internationally acceptable currency: many expatriates prefer US dollars for this purpose. The spending limit on at least one card should exceed the cost of a flight home at short notice for the whole expatriate family.

The expatriate should aim to minimise income from sources in the United Kingdom. UK tax allowances are retained even by a non-resident, and the expatriate may therefore choose to retain a minimal balance in a United Kingdom-based bank account in order to facilitate the handling of any UK liabilities. It is also worth considering briefing a friend or relative (or, more formally, a solicitor or accountant) on anything that might need handling in the United Kingdom while the expatriate is away.

1.2.4 Tax planning priorities

The UK tax laws are so complex, and individual circumstances so varied, that there is no question of drawing up an overall plan that could be generally applied to expatriates. Questions of tax are treated exhaustively in the central chapters of this Handbook, and implicit or explicit in this detailed treatment are many points of tax planning. But it is probably helpful at this point to signpost a few basic, preliminary steps.

To begin with, the intending expatriate should request a form P85 from his tax office, complete it, and return it. This provides the information by reference to which the Inland Revenue will decide whether the intending expatriate is eligible or not for non-resident tax status.

The expatriate may be eligible for a PAYE repayment for part of the tax year in which he will go overseas. This will require submission of parts 2 and 3 of the expatriate's form P45 to the tax inspector.

The expatriate owning any investments on which losses can be realised in order to reduce the liability to capital gains tax (CGT) on disposal of other assets should realise such losses before becoming non-resident for tax purposes. Losses may be offset against any tax liability on future gains, but obviously this is only relevant if they occur at a time when the investor is liable to CGT. Conversely, the realisation of capital gains on assets acquired before departure should, if possible, be deferred until five tax years of qualifying non-residence have elapsed since departure, at which time the investor is no longer subject to UK CGT. Otherwise any chargeable gains realised whilst overseas will be charged to CGT on resuming UK tax residence.

If the contract of employment abroad is due to begin shortly after the beginning of a UK tax year (on 6 April), the expatriate should ask whether it can be brought forward. The point here is that non-resident tax status is provisional until completion of the first full tax year of non-residence.

It is also advisable to find out the basis of the expatriate's tax liability, if any, in the destination country. A list of internationally competent advisers who can help with this question may be obtained from the Institute of Chartered Accountants in England and Wales at Chartered Accountants Hall, Moorgate Place, Moorgate, London EC2 2BJ (tel: +44 (0)20 7920 8100; fax: (0)20 7920 0547) or from the Chartered Institute of Taxation, 12 Upper Belgrave Street, London SW1X 8BB (tel: +44 (0)20 7235 9381; fax: (0)20 7235 2562).

1.2.5 Last minute preparations

The expatriate should not leave the United Kingdom without the address and telephone number of a friend or colleague in the overseas destination, who can provide assistance, if necessary, when the newcomer arrives. In an emergency, without such help, it is best to get to an international hotel, and handle things from there. It may also be useful to be forearmed with the address and telephone number of the local British embassy or consulate, if there is one, although these offices should quite literally be regarded as a last resort.

1.3 RETURNING TO THE UNITED KINGDOM

This subject is treated in detail in Chapter 12, but here we simply outline some of the basic problems that may arise.

The first question which arises here is: 'is the expatriate returning for good, or merely temporarily before taking up another assignment overseas?' If it is the latter, the expatriate may find himself able to retain his non-resident status for tax purposes if his stay in the United Kingdom does not contravene the 183-day rule (see **2.2.22** for details). Even if this rule is contravened, however, the former expatriate may qualify for resident but not ordinarily resident status, in which case he may be liable for UK taxation on the remittance basis (see **12.1.1**).

Imminent return to the United Kingdom throws up a number of planning points, and these should ideally be addressed in the tax year before the tax year of return.

1.3.1 Tax planning for return

The expatriate should notify the authorities in his host country that he will be leaving for the United Kingdom, and he should find out what tax clearance procedures, if any, have to be gone through before he can export any of the assets he has in that country. It is often the case that expatriates have more local assets than they suppose. In most expatriate centres there is a thriving market in the second-hand and non-portable goods of departing expatriates, whose successors may well be among the prospective buyers.

The Inland Revenue should also be notified of the intention to return. The expatriate who has not been completing an annual UK tax return during his absence should take his accountant's advice on how to do this. As he will be likely to be a self-assessment taxpayer after his return, he should assemble detailed records of his financial and tax affairs during his absence (including records relating to payments of tax overseas).

If a sufficient period of non-UK tax residence has elapsed (see **1.2.4**) the long-term expatriate should realise any substantial capital gains in the tax year before that of his return. In this context, he should remember that gains made on currency transactions may also be subject to CGT.

It is also worth noting that salary payments made in respect of terminal leave will be subject to UK tax if the terminal leave is spent in the United Kingdom.

The date at which the expatriate returns to the United Kingdom is the date on which he should consider UK tax efficiency, so it may be convenient to ensure access to enough cash for investment in Individual Savings Accounts, National Savings Certificates, and so on. These are all explained in detail in the *Allied Dunbar Investment and Savings Handbook 1999–00*.

Some forms of life assurance offer a degree of tax efficiency to the returning British expatriate. An expatriate holding a life assurance policy issued by an insurer in a jurisdiction other than the United Kingdom is advised to find out whether it will be tax efficient once he is UK resident again, or whether it can be transferred into an insurance contract that is tax efficient.

Expatriates holding 'personal portfolio bonds' will be well advised to consider their encashment before re-entering the UK tax system, as offshore policies within that class are now heavily penalised for resident taxpayers.

2

KEY TERMS AND CONCEPTS IN THE EXPATRIATE WORLD

2.1 INTRODUCTION

Table 2.1 Terms and rules explained in this chapter

United Kingdom	Domicile of origin
UK Finance Acts and Taxes Acts	Domicile of depenence
Extra-Statutory Concessions	Domicile of choice
UK tax year	Deemed domicile
Self-assessment	Residence
Double taxation agreement	Dual residence
Taxpayers' rights and obligations	The six-month rule
Tax clearance certificate	The three-month rule
Offshore	Available accommodation
Non-resident trusts	Working abroad
Designated territories	Overseas employment contracts
Offshore fund	Accompanying spouse or partner
UCITS	Emigration
Home and host currency	Ordinary residence
Domicile	

Any person leaving the United Kingdom to spend a prolonged period overseas will soon be obliged to add a whole battery of new terms to his or her vocabulary, or at the very least, new meanings to familiar expressions. Some of these terms crop up frequently in the context of tax and investment, where they are not only specially defined but tend to have specific legal implications.

As these terms are fundamental to an understanding of the topics covered by this book, we review them at the outset. Inextricably bound up with these terms, and indeed often forming a decisive part of their definition, are a number of rules applied in practice by the Inland Revenue to determine the tax status of UK expatriates. Here we also review some of the more far-reaching of these rules.

2.2 KEY TERMS AND RULES

2.2.1 United Kingdom ('The United Kingdom of Great Britain and Northern Ireland')

The United Kingdom was originally established by the Union of Great Britain and Ireland in 1801, and took its present form in 1921 when the Irish Free State (since 1949, the Republic of Ireland) was created.

The United Kingdom now consists of England, Wales and Scotland (which make up Great Britain), and Northern Ireland (Ulster). It does not include the Channel Islands or the Isle of Man, which have their own legislative assemblies and their own tax laws. For the purposes of tax residence, the United Kingdom includes the territorial waters – a range of up to 12 nautical miles.

2.2.2 UK Finance Acts and Taxes Acts

The Finance Act is the annual enactment of a Bill put before Parliament by the government of the day concerning the raising of finance by taxation. It incorporates the measures proposed by the Chancellor of the Exchequer in his Budget, after they have been considered in committee.

Taxes Acts either introduce a new tax, such as inheritance tax (IHT) in 1984, or consolidate previous enactments relating to a particular tax or taxes – a recent example is the Income and Corporation Taxes Act 1988 (TA 1988).

The Financial Services Act 1986 (FSA 1986) is an act of a different kind. Its purpose was to regulate the carrying on of investment business, and to make provisions concerning insurance and stock market dealings. The Act is of interest to expatriates not only because it establishes the framework of investor protection in the United Kingdom, but because it also contains provision for the recognition by the Secretary of State of collective investment schemes (unitised funds) in member states of the European Union (EU) and in other states recognised as 'designated countries or territories'.

2.2.3 Extra-Statutory Concessions

These are detailed modifications to the various taxing statutes applied in general practice by the Inland Revenue. The concessions are frequently revised and consolidated as booklet IR 1, and there may be subsequent press releases introducing new concessions. Details may be obtained from HMSO Publications Centre, 51 Nine Elms Lane, London SW8 5DR, www.hmso.gov.uk, any tax inquiry centre, tax office or the Public Enquiry Room, West Wing, Somerset House, Strand, London WC2R 1LB. A great deal of information is available on the Inland Revenue website www.inlandrevenue.gov.uk.

2.2.4 UK tax year

As a consequence of the reform of the calendar in 1752, the tax year in the United Kingdom runs from 6 April one year to 5 April the next. British expatriates should be aware, however, that the tax year in their host country may be on a different basis – usually coinciding with the calendar year.

2.2.5 Self-assessment and the keeping of records

The United Kingdom's self-assessment tax regime is dealt with in detail at **5.2**. Prospective expatriates should note that potential as well as actual self-assessment taxpayers are now legally requied to keep detailed records of their tax matters, with neglect to do so incurring possible stiff penalties. In the event of any dispute with the Inland Revenue, either during or after a period of absence overseas, the expatriate's case will be damaged if he cannot show detailed tax records.

2.2.6 Double taxation agreement

A double taxation agreement or double taxation treaty is a legal arrangement between two sovereign countries to eliminate or at least reduce the individual taxpayer's liability to tax at the same time and on the same income in both countries. Under such an agreement, the taxpayer will receive credit for the tax paid in one country when his liability in the other country is determined. A detailed treatment of double taxation agreements and their impact on income tax, capital gains tax (CGT), inheritance tax (IHT) and on other matters is given in Chapter 11. Double taxation agreements usually contain an exchange of information article authorising the treaty parties to exchange tax information.

2.2.7 Taxpayers' rights and obligations

Taxpayers' statutory rights and obligations vary in detail from country to country, but in most countries they conform with certain globally recognised general principles. Thus in the 29 member countries of the Organisation for Economic Co-operation and Development (the United Kingdom, the United States, Australia, New Zealand, Japan, Korea,

Mexico and most countries in continental Europe, including Turkey) taxpayers generally have the following *rights*:

(1) to have up-to-date information on the operation of the tax system and the basis of assessment;
(2) to be able to appeal against any decision of the tax authorities;
(3) not to have to pay more than the correct amount of tax;
(4) to have a high degree of certainty as to the tax consequences of their actions;
(5) to enjoy privacy (ie very strict limits on the entry into the taxpayer's dwelling or business premises); and
(6) to be guaranteed confidentiality and secrecy (ie the information made available to the tax authorities will be used only for the purposes specified in the tax legislation, including its exchange with treaty parties under a double taxation agreement).

Taxpayers also have certain *obligations* enforceable by law, the chief of which is to file an annual return. In many countries taxpayers must supply additional information or specified documentation on the request of the authorities. In some countries there is a specific legal obligation to report on a change in the taxpayer's situation, such as the formation of a partnership, initiation of some professional activity, acquisition of a new source of income, or even on certain construction contracts.

2.2.8 Tax clearance certificate

Many countries require the departing expatriate to obtain a tax clearance certificate before permitting him to export capital at the end of his stay. Such a certificate will show that he has complied with any local tax liabilities, and also that any money he may have imported into the country was imported legally. Obtaining tax clearance can take time, and this may be regarded as another reason to leave money offshore rather than take it with one to the overseas destination.

2.2.9 Offshore

An asset, such as a bank deposit or shares in an investment fund, or a liability, such as a bank loan, is said to be offshore when it is in a jurisdiction at least one remove from that of the individual holding the asset or incurring the liability. In spite of its legal implications, however, the term is not a legal term as such, but simply one of ordinary (particularly expatriate) discourse. It usually refers to a jurisdiction which, from the investor's (or borrower's) point of view, offers opportunities to mitigate tax liabilities.

Popular usage defines an offshore centre as generally small, and generally adjacent to a larger jurisdiction from which it derives much of its business. Thus, the Channel Islands and the Isle of Man are 'offshore-UK', while the Caribbean islands are 'offshore-US'. Luxembourg, one of the few landlocked offshore centres (although Switzerland and Liechtenstein also come into this category), could originally have been considered 'offshore Belgium', but nowadays draws more business from Germany. But in practice, thanks to the progress of telecommunications, offshore centres attract business from around the world, irrespective of where they are situated.

For a British expatriate, an offshore centre ideally provides a location for his financial affairs that is beyond the reach of the tax authorities in both the United Kingdom and the country where he is living. Many UK banks and financial institutions have subsidiaries located in offshore centres.

2.2.10 Non-resident trusts

Non-resident trusts are treated in detail at **9.5.7**. Otherwise known as offshore trusts or foreign trusts, they can generally be treated as such for purposes of UK taxation if all the trustees are non-resident and the trust is administered and managed overseas. Tight anti-tax avoidance provisions relating to non-resident trusts have been introduced in the United Kingdom in recent years and these were further tightened in the Finance Bill 2000.

2.2.11 Designated territories

Designated territories are offshore jurisdictions, such as the Channel Islands and the Isle of Man, that are authorised by the UK Department of Trade and Industry to promote and sell certain investment funds and insurance policies in the United Kingdom, on the grounds that their own investor protection rules and regulations are as stringent as those in force in the United Kingdom.

2.2.12 Offshore fund

An offshore fund is an open-ended fund that is registered and administered outside (and therefore often said to be domiciled outside) the United Kingdom (although in some cases the fund's assets may be managed – ie the investment decisions regarding them taken – in the United Kingdom). Such funds are not subject to UK taxation, and many are based in jurisdictions where they are subject to minimal local taxation, or to no taxation at all. For example, it is often the case that no withholding tax is imposed on distribution of income to investors (more detail on offshore funds is given at **7.11** and **13.8**.

2.2.13 UCITs

UCITs are undertakings for collective investments in transferable securities, and take their name from an EU Directive, allowing publicly offered open-ended funds such as unit trusts and OEICs in the United Kingdom and Sicavs (investment companies with a variable capital) in France, Belgium and Luxembourg, which have been authorised in one EU member state to be sold without further authorisation in any or all of the other member states. Legally speaking, UCITs may take contractual, corporate or trust form, but the practical implications for the investor are hardly dependent on which legal form the collective vehicle takes (see **13.8** for further details).

2.2.14 Home and host currency

A British expatriate's home currency is sterling. The currency of the country in which he lives as an expatriate is his host currency. The hazards of exchange rate movements and some practical measures to cope with them are explained in Chapter 16.

2.2.15 Domicile

In 1987 the Law Commission and the Scottish Law Commission presented a report to Parliament recommending changes in the present laws concerning domicile. As far as British expatriates are concerned the proposed changes could be important, in so far as they would make it easier to establish a domicile of choice (see **2.2.18**). Interest in the Law Commission's recommendations was rekindled towards the end of 1991, when in reply to a parliamentary question the Attorney General said that the government had accepted the recommendations and would introduce legislation when a suitable opportunity arose. In 1993 the Prime Minister confirmed that the then government had no immediate plans to introduce legislation and, indeed, no changes were legislated before the general election on 1 May 1997. This is an area which may well be revisited by the Labour government. A 1994 Tribune Report, which emanated from Gordon Brown, now Chancellor of the Exchequer, said 'Britain's tax regimes for the super-rich are now recognised as so lax as to constitute a tax haven'. The document then goes on to identify the 'savings' from 'ending the abuse of non-domiciled status, offshore and onshore trusts and changing the definition of residence' as amounting to 'almost a billion'.

What follows immediately below sets out the rules in force at the time of this Handbook's publication.

Domicile is a long-established concept rooted in English common law. It is the fundamental concept determining an individual's rights and duties. It can be defined as the legal relationship between an individual and a territory subject to a distinctive legal system. Strictly speaking, therefore, a person has a domicile in, for example, England and Wales, Scotland or Northern Ireland rather than the United Kingdom but for most purposes the term UK domicile is used. The courts of that territory may then invoke that system as the individual's personal law (relevant, for instance, to marriage and divorce, and what lawyers refer to as 'succession' – inheritance, in another word). The point about the courts is important, because many expatriates are under the misapprehension that they individually, and not the courts, are able to determine their domicile.

Put more practically, if somewhat less accurately, domicile refers to the country to which an individual belongs, the country which is his natural home in which he resides and intends to remain permanently or indefinitely, or, if absent, the country to which he intends ultimately to return. Important as it is in UK law, domicile is not a universal concept of private international law. Outside the British Commonwealth, only the United States, Denmark, Norway and Brazil use domicile as the connecting link between an individual and the system of law to which he is subject. Most European countries use nationality as the test determining personal law.

For British expatriates, the question of domicile is significant for reasons of tax. It is particularly important in regard to IHT, but it can also have a bearing on an individual's liability to other taxes, as we explain in later chapters.

2.2.16 Domicile of origin

While it is perfectly possible for an individual to be without a fiscal residence at any time, he cannot be without a domicile. A domicile of origin is established at birth. For legitimate children this is the domicile of the father. An illegitimate child, or a legitimate child whose father dies before his birth, takes the domicile of the mother at the time of birth unless the child is adopted in which case the domicile of origin becomes that of the adoptive father. The parent's domicile will prevail regardless of where the child is born, despite any effect the place of birth may have on the child's nationality or citizenship. A child will retain this domicile of origin until he can establish an independent domicile of choice or until his father (or mother in the case of illegitimate children) himself acquires a new domicile of choice. In the latter case the child will also acquire the new domicile but this will be a domicile of dependence, not a domicile of choice.

2.2.17 Domicile of dependence

Dependency on the domicile of the parent will continue until the child reaches the age of 16 or marries, whichever is earlier (Domicile and Matrimonial Proceedings Act 1973). This does not, however, apply in Scotland where a boy can acquire an independent domicile at age 14 and a girl at age 12. Where the parents of a child under 16 (or the respective ages in Scotland) are living apart, the child's dependent domicile is that of his mother if he lives with her and does not have a home with his father.

Until 1973, a woman acquired her husband's domicile on marriage. Any woman married before 1 January 1974 will therefore have had a domicile of dependence, but she will now (following the Act of 1973 just quoted) be considered to have that domicile as one of choice if it is not also her domicile of origin. Since the beginning of 1974, a married woman has been treated as an independent person in matters of domicile and will retain her domicile of origin on marriage on or after 1 January 1974 unless she establishes her own new domicile of choice.

2.2.18 Domicile of choice

The third form of domicile, the domicile of choice, is the one which can be of greatest interest to expatriates and which can cause the most problems. It can be very difficult to convince the courts that a new domicile has been acquired. The basic requirements are that the person should reside in the new country and that he should intend to stay there permanently or indefinitely. The residence part can be simply established; the length of that residence is not necessarily material, so that if, for example, a person dies shortly after arrival, he may none the less have satisfied the test of residence. Providing evidence of the intention to remain is more complex.

Some of the indicators of intent which will be considered on the advancement of any claim to a change of domicile include the following:

(1) a period of residence in the new country;
(2) purchase of a home there;
(3) disposal of property in the old country;
(4) development of business, social, religious and political interests in the new country;
(5) burial arrangements there;
(6) local education of children;
(7) the making of a new will according to local laws;
(8) application for citizenship of the new country;
(9) severance of all formal ties with the old country.

It is invariably difficult to prove an intention; the best that can be hoped for is that the circumstantial evidence will be sufficient for the authorities to be convinced.

If a domicile of choice is abandoned then the domicile of origin revives until such time as a new domicile of choice is acquired. It would be open to the authorities to claim that on the facts of the abandonment of a purported new domicile, it did not exist. This can have serious effects for IHT if the revived domicile of origin is considered as never having been lost.

2.2.19 Deemed domicile

The 'deemed domicile' provisions contained in the Inheritance Tax Act 1984 (IHTA 1984), s 267 have no counterpart in the income tax or CGT legislation. The effect of this section is to treat as UK domiciled anyone who emigrates from the United Kingdom having been previously domiciled there or who had been a long-term resident. This deeming provision endures for a period of at least three years following departure.

The section treats an individual as domiciled in the United Kingdom if:

(1) he was domiciled in the United Kingdom within the three years immediately preceding the relevant time; or
(2) he was resident in the United Kingdom in not less than 17 out of the 20 income tax years ending with the income tax year in which the relevant time falls.

The 'relevant time' referred to above is the time at which a transfer of value takes place.

For the person domiciled initially within the United Kingdom, item (1) means there is a period of at least three calendar years from the acquisition of a new domicile during which time liability for IHT remains. For the long-term UK resident who is not domiciled here, there must be an absence of three complete income tax years before he can be free of IHT. Double taxation agreements which cover IHT may affect this provision: see Chapter 11 and Chapter 7.

2.2.20 Residence

Whatever meanings may be given to the words 'residence' and 'resident' in everyday discourse, we are concerned here only with their use in the context of UK taxation. In that context, the expressions 'ordinarily resident', 'dual residence' and 'non-resident' are also frequently used, and are defined below. None of these terms is explicitly defined in the various Taxes Acts, and the Inland Revenue state that they use the terms 'resident' and 'ordinarily resident' in their everyday sense without giving them any special or technical meaning. For the purposes of National Insurance Contributions (NICs), the Inland Revenue Contributions Agency will normally do the same, and certainly accepted meanings for tax purposes would carry great weight for NICs as well.

Nevertheless, the terms have been explained in a number of court decisions, going back at least as far as 1875; and the Inland Revenue in practice apply a number of rules to their application, which are set out in some detail in their booklet IR 20: 'Residents and Non-residents – Liability to Tax in the United Kingdom'. Most, if not all of these rules are subject to exceptions; some (but not all) of them have statutory force; while others embody certain concessions that are allowed in practice by the Inland Revenue, although not specified in the Taxes Acts. These are the so-called Extra-Statutory Concessions (see **2.2.3**).

The booklet IR 20 points out that the terms 'resident' and 'ordinarily resident', while not defined in the UK Taxes Acts, are always used to describe a situation arising in a tax year (ie from 6 April to 5 April in the following year), and not in relation to some longer or shorter period. The question that generally has to be decided is whether or not a person is resident (or ordinarily resident) in the United Kingdom in a particular tax year. That is not to say that a tax year cannot be split between periods of residence and non-residence, but the practice of so doing is non-statutory and only available in specific circumstances such as at the beginning or end of an overseas employment.

The residence of a married woman is determined independently from that of her spouse. The income of a married woman has been taxed independently from that of her spouse since 1990/91. There is, nonetheless, a concession allowing the residence status of a husband or wife of someone who leaves the United Kingdom to work full-time abroad to be treated in the same way as that of their spouse in certain circumstances (see **3.6**).

2.2.21 Dual residence

An individual who is resident for tax purposes in the United Kingdom is not precluded from also being resident elsewhere, and a claim to non-residence cannot be sustained simply on the grounds of being resident in another state. A person may be resident in two or more states in the same tax year or, indeed, resident in none. Where dual residence gives rise to a double charge to tax then special provisions may exist in a tax treaty between the states which can overrule the purely domestic regulations on residence. See Chapter 11.

Finally, before going on to a discussion of the current practice, it should also be pointed out that *force majeure* will be ignored in any decision as to whether or not an individual is resident in the United Kingdom under the six-month rule (see **2.2.22**). Illness, military service, or even, in borderline cases, the cancellation of a flight, can sufficiently extend a stay so as to render the otherwise non-resident person resident for a particular tax year. However, for the three-month rule (see **2.2.23**) any days spent in the United Kingdom because of exceptional circumstances beyond the taxpayer's control, eg illness of the taxpayer or a member of his family, are not normally counted.

2.2.22 Physical presence: the six-month rule

If an individual is to be regarded as resident in the United Kingdom for a given tax year he must normally be physically present in the country for at least part of that year. *He will always be resident if he is in the United Kingdom for six months or more in the tax year.* **There are no exceptions to this rule** (the Inland Revenue's use of bold type), although a double taxation treaty may treat the taxpayer as non-resident for income and gains covered by the treaty. Six months is regarded as equivalent to 183 days. For this purpose a count is made of the total number of days spent in the United Kingdom during the year, whether the stay consists of one period only or a succession of visits. Under present Inland Revenue practice days of arrival and days of departure are normally ignored. Note the word 'normally'. There may be circumstances in which this practice is not followed, eg if there are regular and frequent arrivals and departures. For the purposes of NICs the opposite is true, and days of arrival and departure are normally counted. Still different tests may apply for establishing residence under a tie-breaker clause in a double taxation treaty.

In spite of the words in bold type in the previous paragraph, the rule they refer to is subject to qualification in the case of an individual leaving the United Kingdom permanently, or leaving to take up full-time employment abroad for a period which includes one complete tax year. Such an individual, or his spouse, may be treated as non-resident and not ordinarily resident (see below for an explanation of this expression) from the day following his departure. This treatment can be applied regardless of when during the tax year the individual leaves. If, for example, he leaves on 5 January, he will have been resident for nine months, but will be treated as non-resident for the three remaining months. This treatment is purely concessionary, but is an Inland Revenue practice of some long standing, although it is no longer normally available for CGT.

The converse of the six-month rule does not generally apply. That is to say that an individual who is not physically present in the United Kingdom for six months is not necessarily to be treated as non-resident for tax purposes.

An individual's residence is what lawyers call 'a question of fact'. That is to say, a question of actual circumstances. But a permanent or semi-permanent abode is not necessary to establish residence. In various court cases, the availability of a yacht, a shooting lodge and a hunting box have been held as establishing that their occupants were resident in the United Kingdom. But in other cases, living in hotels or with friends in the United Kingdom was not enough to render the individuals concerned resident for tax purposes. If an individual is physically present in the United Kingdom for less than six months, the Inland Revenue's decision as to whether or not he is resident for tax purposes depends on other circumstances.

A final point to be made about physical presence is that under TA 1988, s 334, a British subject or a citizen of the Republic of Ireland whose ordinary residence (see **2.2.29**) is in the United Kingdom will continue to be taxed as resident if he is abroad for the purpose of occasional residence only.

2.2.23 The three-month rule

Under this rule a person may become resident if he makes regular lengthy visits to the United Kingdom. Where the visits are made every year for four consecutive years, and the average length of stay over those four years is 91 days or more a year, then the visitor will be considered as resident in the United Kingdom. Where the pattern of visits is irregular or cannot be foreseen then the residence status will apply after the fourth year. If, on the other hand, the pattern is known and admitted then residence will start from the original date of arrival. If a decision to make regular visits is taken and carried out before the end of the year, residence commences from the preceding 6 April.

When calculating the number of days, days of arrival or departure would normally not be counted, however frequent the visits. It would, however, seem prudent if this rule jeopardises non-resident status to keep visits to no more than 90 days per annum on average.

2.2.24 Available accommodation

If a person goes abroad permanently but has accommodation (eg a house or apartment) available for his use in the United Kingdom, he was, prior to 1993/94 regarded as resident here for any tax year in which he visited the United Kingdom, however short the visits were. From 1993/94 available accommodation in the United Kingdom is ignored in the case of a short-term visitor to the United Kingdom, ie a person who does not intend to stay more than three months a year in the United Kingdom. As regards a long-term visitor, Inland Revenue booklet IR 20 indicates that a person could be treated as resident merely because he owns or leases accommodation in the

United Kingdom in the year of arrival. This implies that, for example, the existence of let property would be taken into account. It is not considered that this is the Inland Revenue's actual view.

According to IR 20, para 3.11, an individual will be regarded as ordinarily resident in circumstances where accommodation is available if he comes to 'and remains in' the United Kingdom. What is meant by 'remains in' is not defined, but it must require the visit to have a settled purpose to accord with case law.

Booklet IR 20 now indicates that someone who comes to the United Kingdom for a specific purpose such as employment for two years (rather than three) may be regarded as resident from the date of arrival. The latest version of IR 20, published in December 1999 (the 2000 version) is updated to deal with temporary non-residence for capital gains tax; to delete the references to 'available accommodation' which ceased to have a relevance in 1993; and to include a chapter on National Insurance Contributions.

2.2.25 Working abroad

A person who leaves the United Kingdom to work full-time abroad under a contract of employment is treated as not resident and not ordinarily resident from the day following departure if the absence and the employment will both last for at least a complete tax year and any visits to the United Kingdom do not breach the six-month or three-month rules described above. UK residence would be acquired on the day of arrival in the United Kingdom following the end of the employment.

An Inland Revenue booklet IR 58 'Going to Work Abroad' answers many of the questions asked about tax where a UK resident works abroad as an employee. The Department of Social Security leaflet NI 132 gives information about NICs.

2.2.26 Overseas employment contracts

The terms and conditions of overseas employment contracts vary according to the jurisdiction under whose rules they are drawn up. Broadly speaking, the greatest job security is offered where the expatriate is sent overseas by a UK employer, and the least where the employer is an individual person in the overseas location. The expatriate should know which jurisdiction governs his contract, and he should have access to legal advice independent of any that may be made available by his employer.

The Law Society at 113 Chancery Lane, London, WC2A 1PL (tel: +44 (0)20 7242 1222) will supply a list of lawyers in the destination country.

2.2.27 Accompanying spouse or partner

A non-employed accompanying spouse will be granted the same status for UK tax purposes as the working spouse, subject to the same conditions on absence as those applying to the working spouse. Where the non-employed accompanying partner is not married to the working expatriate, the Inland Revenue will look for other evidence of full-time *de facto* absence. Such evidence might include the abandonment of UK accommodation and commitment to overseas accommodation, participation in any pre-departure briefing courses taken by the working partner, transfer of bank accounts and other financial operations offshore, and so on. Each case is dealt with on its merits, and non-resident status will tend to be granted provisionally for the first year.

2.2.28 Emigration

A person who leaves the United Kingdom permanently is provisionally treated as not resident and not ordinarily resident from the day following departure if he can provide evidence that his emigration is permanent. Normally this provisional ruling is confirmed after the taxpayer has lived abroad for a whole tax year, provided that the six-month or three-month rules are not breached. Evidence might, for example, include the sale of UK property and the acquisition of property abroad. In the absence of such evidence or a settled purpose the taxpayer remains provisionally resident in the United Kingdom for up to three years. If on a final analysis the six-month or three-month rules have not been broken the taxpayer is normally reclassified as not resident from the day of departure and his tax liabilities adjusted accordingly.

Table 2.2   Residence summary

A person who is resident in the United Kingdom will usually have a liability for UK income tax on his worldwide income and would also be liable for capital gains on any chargeable gains.

In essence, a person will be considered resident in the United Kingdom if:

(1) he is physically present in the United Kingdom for six months or more in the tax year, given that six months are equivalent to 183 days and days of arrival and departure are ignored; or

(2) he makes substantial and habitual visits to the United Kingdom; 'substantial' is taken to mean an average of three months or more each year and visits are considered 'habitual' after four consecutive years; or

(3) being a British subject (or citizen of the Republic of Ireland) he has left the United Kingdom for the purpose only of occasional residence abroad (TA 1988, s 334).

2.2.29 **Ordinary residence**

Whereas the term 'residence' is mainly concerned with individual tax years, the term 'ordinary residence' (more often encountered in the adjectival form 'ordinarily resident') implies a greater degree of continuity. Again the term is not defined in any statute, but in some relevant cases the courts have held ordinary residence to be the converse of occasional or casual residence. It has been referred to as 'a man's abode in a particular place or country which he has adopted voluntarily and for settled purposes as part of the regular order of his life for the time being, whether of short or long duration'.

An individual who becomes resident in the United Kingdom under the three-month rule (see **2.2.23**) will also be considered ordinarily resident.

It is quite possible to be resident but not ordinarily resident in the United Kingdom for a tax year. Whether it is possible to be not resident but ordinarily resident is less clear. There is arguably precedent in case law for the proposition that a person must be resident to be ordinarily resident. However, the Inland Revenue take a contrary view. In Inland Revenue booklet IR 20 it is stated that 'you may be ordinarily resident but not resident for a tax year if, for example, you usually live in the UK but have gone abroad for a long holiday and do not set foot in the UK during that year'. Clearly if ordinary residence is relevant to a tax liability, as it will be for CGT (see Chapter 7), considerable care will be needed if absences are short and do not fall squarely within the circumstances described in IR 20 in relation to working abroad.

For the purposes of NICs it is possible for an individual to be ordinarily resident at a time when he is not ordinarily resident for tax purposes, and the converse, although unlikely, is also possible in theory.

3

CATEGORIES OF EXPATRIATE

3.1 INTRODUCTION

Statistically speaking, British expatriates are a fairly representative sample of the UK population at large, except that for obvious reasons their age distribution is different. In ordinary commonsense terms, therefore, expatriates come in all forms and guises, and it is a mistake to think that they conform to any kind of stereotype. So in this chapter when speaking of categories of expatriate, we mean to refer only to their various situations or functions that determine their tax status in the eyes of the Inland Revenue. This, we believe, is to adopt the individual's own point of view. Because in seeking a thread to guide him through the ghastly British tax labyrinth, the individual expatriate is likely to begin by defining his own situation in terms of his functional reasons for being overseas in the first place – ie whether he is working abroad and, if so, for how long and under what terms and conditions; whether he has retired abroad; whether he intends to return to the United Kingdom, and, if he does, when; or whether he has decided (or more or less decided) to emigrate permanently.

From this point on, our Handbook inevitably becomes more technical, and in particular we are obliged to resort to the use of abbreviations when referring to the various Taxes Acts and Finance Acts, not to mention the occasional Inland Revenue Statement of Practice or its Extra-Statutory Concessions. For an explanation of these abbreviations the reader is referred to the list on page ix.

Table 3.1, summarising the scope of UK income tax in relation to earnings based on various permutations of residence, ordinary residence and domicile is on page 31.

3.2 SHORT-TERM WORKING ABROAD: THE EXPATRIATE WHO REMAINS UK RESIDENT

The previous chapter explained the terms 'resident' and 'non-resident' and it was pointed out that most working expatriates would achieve non-resident status if their overseas work was for a period that included at least one complete tax year. There are, however, many people who, although abroad for more than 12 months, are not in fact overseas from 6 April to the following 5 April and who do not, therefore, qualify for non-resident treatment.

Although the expression is, literally, a contradiction in terms, we refer here to persons in this category as 'resident' (ie not non-resident) expatriates. A person in this category might, for example, have an 18-month contract commencing in June 1998; his return in December 1999 means that he has spent part of two tax years abroad but not one complete year. Indeed, he may have spent less than 183 days in the United Kingdom in one or both of the tax years concerned. Then there is the case of the person whose UK job entails much foreign travel, perhaps for months on end, but whose duties in the United Kingdom cannot be described as merely incidental to his duties abroad. This category might include seamen whose voyages start or finish in the United Kingdom but who travel the world in between times (see **3.9.3**). Finally, among the group of people who are abroad often but either not often enough, or not for long enough to qualify as non-resident for UK tax purposes, are travelling salesmen, consultants, airline pilots and the like.

What these 'semi-expatriates' have in common is that they cannot obtain the tax benefits of the non-resident expatriate proper. They remain liable for UK income tax on their worldwide income. In the 'export or die' atmosphere of the 1970s, the importance of the semi-expatriate to the country's economic well-being was recognised and new legislation was introduced to counter the disincentive effect of domestic taxation for these people, ironically by a Labour government. The legislation relating to what became known as the Foreign Earnings Deduction (FED) was mainly contained in the Income and Corporation Taxes Act 1988 (TA 1988), s 193 and Sched 12. In essence, this Schedule provides for total exemption from UK income tax for earnings from work done overseas provided that certain conditions are satisfied, as described at **3.3**. The resident expatriate who cannot qualify for relief remains liable in the United Kingdom.

Prior to 17 March 1998, this relief was available to any employee who met the complex qualifying tests. However, in 1998 the government saw fit to remove the relief from everyone except seafarers in relation to qualifying periods beginning on or after that date. Whilst there was a transitional relief for periods commencing before 17 March 1998 that had not, by that time, amounted to 365 days' absence, no relief is available for later periods. The legislation contained rules to counter the artificial attribution of emoluments to earlier periods.

The government initially announced this change under the heading 'measures to prevent avoidance' as there had been some reports in the media of entertainers and sporting personalities arranging their affairs to rely on the FED to avoid large amounts of tax. Even if this important tax relief was being abused by a small number of the rich and famous, it was highly controversial to announce its complete and immediate abolition as a counter-measure. Following an intensive lobbying campaign on behalf of multinationals and their employees, the Inland Revenue drafted a stock response which attempted to justify abolition on economic grounds. The stock response stated that the FED was introduced to create employment by boosting exports, yet 'in practice, buyers travelling abroad to source for import . . . benefited to the same extent – but to the opposite effect'. It went on to recognise that having employees immune from tax 'can make them less expensive' which is 'welcome to employers'. However, the most revealing statement is reproduced below:

> 'The Government is committed to protecting ordinary taxpayers by developing a modern system that is fair for all. Ministers did not consider it fair that those working abroad have been able to escape tax on their income – leaving others to pay their dues for them. The Chancellor gave an explicit warning in his first Budget that the Government would be relentless in its war against tax avoidance. This means the closing of loopholes. Withdrawal of the FED was part of this process.'

Abuse can be targeted by anti-avoidance measures rather than the abolition of a relief, penalising many thousands of short- to medium-term UK resident expatriates. Moreover, it is disingenuous to describe the withdrawal of a statutory tax relief as 'the closing of loopholes'. Finally, one might ask why, if the tax system is to be fair for all, the government is willing to continue to allow seafarers to be subsidised by 'the main body' of taxpayers!

The lack of relief can be particularly distressing for someone who leaves the United Kingdom in expectation of establishing non-resident status but has to return prematurely for whatever reason, only to find the Inland Revenue ready to welcome him with a large tax demand. In these circumstances a double taxation treaty may be of some assistance if applicable, but otehwise double taxation may arise and the expatriate can only rely on the unilateral relief which the Inland Revenue may grant under TA 1988, s 790 (see **11.17**).

Subject to double taxation relief, we now have a situation in which the timing of overseas assignments is all important, as the following example shows.

Example

> Mr B and Ms P are both sent to work full time overseas by their employer. Mr B leaves on 31 March 1998 and returns on 1 May 1999. Ms P leaves on 1 May 1998 and returns on 31 March 2000. Neither of them visits the United Kingdom during these periods.
>
> Mr B is absent for just 13 months but he will not be liable for UK tax on his earnings from work performed outside the United Kingdom or on other non-UK income as he is not resident.
>
> Ms P is absent for 23 months but she will not establish non-resident status and her earnings and any other non-UK income will remain fully taxable in the United Kingdom.
>
> The above situation might seem strange enough. However, consider Mr B's position if he is prematurely recalled to the United Kingdom (as does happen in practice) on 4 April 1999. He may have obtained an NT (no tax) PAYE coding and have paid nothing. He will nevertheless be expected to file a self-assessment tax return for 1998/99 and pay over his tax by 31 January 2000.

Following the withdrawal of the FED, the Inland Revenue have elaborated on their practice concerning premature terminations and will look 'sympathetically' at *bona fide* cases as long as there is not perceived to be any abuse. Strictly, for non-resident status to be attained, an overseas employment must last for a complete tax year. However, the Revenue's practice is that if an employee loses the overseas job having been employed overseas for the 'preponderant part' of the tax year, the employee may be treated as if the employment had continued for the whole of the tax year provided that he remains abroad. It is still necessary to apply the 183-day and 91-day tests (see **2.2.22** and **2.2.23**) but the period abroad may consist of time spent in different countries or employment with different employers. Therefore, in the example, if Mr B had been able to take a couple of days off before returning to the United Kingdom, he might have been able to rely on this practice.

3.3 SEAFARERS

Employment as a 'seafarer' consists of the performance of duties on a ship, excluding offshore installations such as oil rigs. The relief for seafarers is dealt with in TA 1988, s 152A.

Relief under this category may be obtained against earnings from an employment the duties of which are performed wholly or partly outside the United Kingdom, when the employee remains resident and ordinarily resident in the United Kingdom. The relief does not apply to a seafarer who is resident but not ordinarily resident as a 'remittance basis' will apply to the non-UK earnings of such a person (see Table 3.1 and section **12.1.1**). Any duties performed abroad which are merely incidental to those performed at home will be treated as being performed in the United Kingdom and will not be taken into account for the purposes of this relief. In order to qualify for relief, a seafarer must perform the duties of his employment in the course of a qualifying period of at least 365 qualifying days. A qualifying period is not restricted by tax years and may span two or more years. For example, a qualifying period may run from September 1999 to December 2000. In that case the Schedule E assessments for 1999/00 and 2000/01 would take account of the emoluments for that part of the qualifying period in each year of assessment and grant the relief accordingly. The amount of the relief is equal to 100 per cent of the emoluments covered by it. A period of non-residence does not count as part of a qualifying period from 6 April 1992. Therefore pay for terminal leave spent in the United Kingdom following a period of non-residence would be taxable (Inland Revenue Statement of Practice SP18/91). However, terminal leave abroad following a qualifying period can be covered by the relief (see booklet IR 58).

A qualifying period consists either of days of absence from the United Kingdom or partly of such days and partly of days in the United Kingdom. In the former case, the situation is quite straightforward. The seafarer performing the duties of his employment wholly abroad for at least 365 days will obtain the relief. Given that the legislation refers to 'in the course of a qualifying period' there does not seem to be a requirement that the employment must subsist for the whole period. Therefore, an absence of 365 days made up of six months' work interspersed with six months' overseas holiday would still be a qualifying period but not six months' work followed by six months' holiday (*Robins v Durkin* [1988] STC 588). A day will be considered as a day of absence for the purpose of this relief if the person is outside the United Kingdom at the end of the day, ie at midnight (*Hoye v Forsdyke* [1981] STC 711). This can be contrasted with the normal test of days for considering residence (see **2.2.22**).

The alternative definition of a qualifying period, ie where there are some days spent in the United Kingdom, contains restrictions on the length of time which can be spent in the United Kingdom. Between any two periods of absence, the time spent in the United Kingdom must not exceed 183 consecutive days. Thus a seafarer abroad for two periods of 155 days with a 60-day break between them will achieve a qualifying period of 370 days and qualify for the relief. In addition, the number of intervening days in the United Kingdom must not exceed one-half of the total number of days in the period under consideration (TA 1988, Sched 12, para 3 (2)).

3.3.1 Qualifying periods – illustrative example

Going on from the simple case of the single return visit, qualifying periods may be built up from a series of overseas spells interspersed by returns to the United Kingdom. But what is vital with this regime is to keep a close check on the length of each stay both at home and overseas. This build-up of qualifying periods to a length sufficient to entitle the employee to obtain the tax relief is best illustrated by an example.

The qualifying period tests have to be applied after every overseas period. An expatriate in this situation must keep a very close watch on his visits to the United Kingdom. This had particular relevance before 17 March 1998, when an employee may have been able to choose between a late flight or an early flight on the following morning in marginal cases; some expatriates got into the habit of arriving in the United Kingdom on morning flights and leaving on evening ones.

A particular source of difficulty is that the expatriate may not know how long he can afford to spend in the United Kingdom unless he knows for certain exactly when his next return visit will begin. Previous editions of this Handbook contained a worked example of the relief prior to 17 March 1998.

There are special rules covering the usual payments that may afford tax relief where the payment is referable to an overseas tour of duty, in whole or in part, but the payment is made at a time when it would otherwise be taxable. The 1996 case of *Nichols v Gibson* ([1996] STC 1008) confirmed that a severance payment is assessable even though it may not come within any of the cases of Schedule E, because the taxpayer was neither resident, ordinarily resident, nor in employment at the time of payment. This is because terminal payments are taxed under TA 1988, s 187, an independent charging provision.

3.3.2 Apportionment of emoluments

The earnings or emoluments which qualify for relief are those which are attributable to the period of overseas work. Thus someone who works solely abroad may obtain exemption for all his emoluments. Where a person works partly abroad and partly in the United Kingdom (where the UK duties are not merely incidental to the overseas duties) then there is provision for the emoluments to be apportioned between the respective duties (TA 1988, Sched 12, para 2). Since the abolition of the relief for all but seafarers, this is likely to be of academic interest only.

Apportionment apart, relievable emoluments include salaries, bonuses and allowances, benefits in kind and so on.

For employees of companies based in the United Kingdom which operate PAYE, the relief is normally obtained by the issue of a 'No Tax' (NT) code if it is clear that the 100 per cent relief will be due, otherwise it will be necessary to claim a refund of the PAYE after the relevant year-end.

3.4 FOREIGN EMOLUMENTS

This term is used to describe the emoluments of a person *not domiciled in the United Kingdom* from an employment with a person or concern which is resident outside the United Kingdom. Thus, for example, an American working for an American corporation would be in receipt of foreign emoluments. Whether, and to what extent, foreign emoluments are taxable in the United Kingdom depends both on the residence position of the individual and the place in which he carries out the duties of his employment.

Duties performed in the United Kingdom are chargeable on the basis of income arising regardless of the residence status of the individual concerned. Where the duties are performed abroad the individual's residence is crucial. If he is non-resident then there is no liability for emoluments earned outside the United Kingdom. If he is resident but not ordinarily resident in the United Kingdom, then foreign emoluments for duties performed abroad will be chargeable on the remittance basis. If he is both resident and ordinarily resident in the United Kingdom, then the emoluments will be charged on the arising basis unless the duties of the employment are carried out wholly abroad. In this latter case the remittance basis is applied. It is quickly apparent that it is desirable for foreign-domiciled employees in receipt of foreign emoluments to have separate employment contracts covering UK and non-UK duties in order to ensure that the remittance basis is applicable if they become ordinarily resident in the United Kingdom.

3.5 OTHER RELIEFS FOR RESIDENT EXPATRIATES

The normal rules which apply to relief for expenses, ie that they are incurred wholly, exclusively and necessarily in the performance of the duties of the employment, apply to duties which extend overseas and to the emoluments therefrom. In the usual way the expenses would be deductible from the gross emoluments. However, for employments which involve working overseas, certain expenses are allowable which would not be so in purely domestic circumstances. In addition, certain benefits which would be taxable in the UK employment are available with no tax penalty for overseas work.

It has already been mentioned that emoluments cover all benefits in kind. These often form a significant part of an expatriate remuneration package. There are special rules relating to travel costs, board and lodging of the overseas worker and to travel costs of the employee or his family during his spell abroad.

These rules are contained in TA 1988, ss 193, 194 and cover the following situations. In each case the employee is resident and ordinarily resident in the United Kingdom and his emoluments are not foreign emoluments:

(1) If the duties of the employment are performed wholly outside the United Kingdom then travelling expenses incurred by the employee to take up the employment and to return at the end of that employment are allowable as a deduction.

(2) If the cost of board and lodging is provided or reimbursed by the employer this will not be assessable in the case of wholly overseas employment.

(3) Where there are two or more employments and at least one of them is performed wholly or partly outside the United Kingdom, then travelling expenses incurred by the employee getting from one place of employment to another, where either or both places are outside the United Kingdom, are deductible against the emoluments of the second employment.

Where the expenses described above are not incurred wholly in the performance of the duties of the employment(s), they may be apportioned with relief restricted to that part related to the employment.

(4) Travel expenses for an unlimited number of outward and return journeys to the United Kingdom by the employee are to be allowed tax free in the hands of the employee if paid for by the employer.

(5) Where an employee is absent from the United Kingdom for a continuous period of 60 days or more, certain travel facilities will not attract any UK tax liability. These facilities are for travel by the employee's spouse and/or children under the age of 18 between the United Kingdom and the place where the duties are performed and include any accompanying journey at the beginning of the period, or an interim visit; and any return journey. These travel facilities will be tax exempt for up to two outward and return journeys by any person in any one tax year if provided by the employer or reimbursed by him.

An employee who is temporarily absent from his normal place of work may claim a deduction for accommodation costs and subsistence. This is of greater importance for a larger number of employees following the abolition of the FED and the period which may be regarded as temporary

Table 3.1

Employees Not in Receipt of Foreign Emoluments

UK Residence Status	Employment Performed Wholly or Partly in UK		Employment Performed *Wholly Abroad*
	UK Duties	Overseas Duties	
Resident and Ordinarily Resident	*Case I* Earnings arising (less 100% deduction where appropriate)	*Case I* Earnings arising (less 100% deduction where appropriate)	*Case I* Earnings arising (less 100% deduction where appropriate)
Resident but Not Ordinarily Resident	*Case II* Earnings arising	*Case III* Earnings remitted to or received in UK	*Case III* Earnings remitted to or received in UK
Not Resident	*Case II* Earnings arising	Exempt	Exempt

Foreign-domiciled Employees Working for Foreign Employers

UK Residence Status	Employment Performed Wholly or Partly in UK		Employment Performed *Wholly Abroad*
	UK Duties	Overseas Duties	
Resident and Ordinarily Resident	*Case I* Earnings arising (less 100% deduction where appropriate)	*Case I* Earnings arising (less 100% deduction where appropriate)	*Case III* Earnings remitted to or received in UK
Resident but Not Ordinarily Resident	*Case II* Earnings arising	*Case III* Earnings remitted to or received in UK	*Case III* Earnings remitted to or received in UK
Not Resident	*Case II* Earnings arising	Exempt	Exempt

has now been increased from 12 months to 24 months to coincide with the withdrawal of the FED. In some cases it may be beneficial to agree *per diem* allowances at a tax-free level with the inspector of taxes. In considering such matters, the tax consequences in the host country should always be considered as well, as part of the complex process of planning expatriate remuneration packages.

Travel facilities for members of HM Forces going on leave are specifically exempted from tax.

Several points must be noted about the reliefs described above. First, in the case of board and lodgings and the family travel facilities, the relief extends only to cases where the cost is met directly or by reimbursement by the employer. There is no relief available for the employee against his emoluments if he bears these costs himself. Secondly, the relief for travel facilities is restricted to travel to and from the place where the duties are actually performed. There is no allowance, for example, for a family reunion at any halfway house. Thus Mr Green who is working in Australia for three months could not obtain relief for a trip for himself and his family to meet up in Singapore, say. Neither his travel nor that of his family would qualify.

There are also special expenses rules for non-UK domiciled employees working in the United Kingdom which exempt reimbursement of the cost of certain travel facilities for up to five years from the date of arrival in the United Kingdom to perform the duties.

3.6 LONG-TERM WORKING ABROAD: THE NON-RESIDENT

In our discussion of the terms 'resident' and 'ordinarily resident' in Chapter 2, we pointed out that these terms are not explicitly defined in any of the Taxes Acts, but that the Inland Revenue claim to use them in an everyday, non-technical sense. Chapter 2 also indicated, however, that the way the Inland Revenue apply these categories in practice depends on rather complex rules.

For all that, the rules applying to the expatriate who has gone abroad to work as an employee for an extended period are to some extent simpler than those concerning other categories of expatriate. Perhaps the definition of 'long-term' is the most arbitrary part of it, because it means not simply longer than a year, but covering a complete tax year (6 April one year to 5 April the following year).

We can therefore repeat from Chapter 2 our designation of the expatriate who leaves the United Kingdom to work full-time abroad under a contract of employment, and which will last for a period including at least one complete tax year, as a person who will normally be treated by the Inland Revenue for income tax purposes as not resident and not ordinarily resident from the day following his departure. This treatment remains provisional until the individual in question has actually remained abroad for a full tax year and, in that tax year, has not infringed any of the other residence rules explained in Chapter 2.

Although the treatment is provisional it does not normally prevent the Inland Revenue from making a tax repayment on departure if, for example, only part of the individual's personal allowances have been granted under PAYE. Where the year is split in this way into a resident part and a non-resident part, full allowances are due. There is no apportionment. The expatriate should obtain the tax repayment claim form P85 and submit it shortly before or soon after departure. An accompanying spouse is normally given similar treatment under Extra-Statutory Concession ESC A78.

The main tax consequences of having the status of not resident and not ordinarily resident in the United Kingdom concern UK income tax and CGT, and are explained in detail later on in this Handbook. But broadly speaking, as far as income tax is concerned, the non-resident whose earnings arise from trade or employment carried on wholly overseas will have no UK liability on those earnings.

3.7 THE SHORT-TERM SELF-EMPLOYED EXPATRIATE

The rules governing self-employed expatriates are not so straightforward as those applying to expatriates under a full-time contract to an overseas employer. But here again we can usefully distinguish between those who remain UK resident under the rules and those who succeed in acquiring non-resident status.

Where the individual remains UK resident and carries on a trade or profession wholly overseas, his profits from that trade or profession are subject to UK income tax under Schedule D, Case V (see Chapter 5 for an explanation of the schedular system).

The profits of a trade or profession carried out partly in the United Kingdom and partly overseas by a UK resident are assessable under Case I or Case II in the same way as those of a purely domestic business. The remittance basis applies to Schedule D, Case V income of a non-UK domiciliary but not to Schedule D, Cases I or II.

Where an individual carries on a trade, profession or vocation wholly or partly outside the United Kingdom, he will be taxed on a change of residence as if the trade, profession or vocation had permanently discontinued and immediately recommenced. This not only allows overlap and loss relief to apply as for a real cessation but enables the non-resident to be taxed only on his UK income and the resident on his worldwide income. Losses before the change may be carried forward and set against profits or gains arising on UK income after the change. For these purposes there is a change of residence when a non-resident becomes resident in the UK, or where a UK resident ceases to be resident under TA 1988, s 110A.

The object is to tax a resident individual on his worldwide income, but a non-resident only on income arising in the United Kingdom. There is no deemed cessation on becoming non-resident before 6 April 1997 where the business has existed prior to 6 April 1994.

ESC A11 which splits a fiscal year for tax purposes where the individual becomes resident or non-resident during that year will continue to apply. The strict position is that an individual resident for part of a fiscal year is resident for the entire year (*Neubergh v IRC* [1958] STC 181; *Gubay v Kington* [1984] STC 99). If the taxpayer wished to claim the strict legal position, the deemed cessation and commencement would take place on 6 April in the year in which the non-resident became UK resident and on 5 April in the year in which a UK resident ceased to be so resident. This could be important where losses arose which it was desired to set against other income under TA 1988, s 380. It could also be relevant for a non-resident becoming UK resident if losses were to be claimed under TA 1988, s 381 for the first four years of the trade following the deemed commencement.

Self-employed expatriates also receive travel and subsistence reliefs comparable to those for UK resident employees working abroad.

3.7.1 Claims for relief

Under the self-assessment rules, claims must normally be quantified and included in the self-assessment tax return under the Taxes Management Act 1970 (TMA 1970), s 42 or in an amended return submitted within 12 months of the normal filing date, which is 31 January following the end of the tax year. Where a claim cannot be included in a tax return or amended return it may be made as a stand-alone claim under TMA 1970, Sched 1A.

Time limits for making claims are usually either within one year ten months after the end of the tax year or, for personal allowances or carry forward of losses, etc and where not otherwise specified, within five years ten months after the end of the tax year to which they relate.

3.8 THE LONG-TERM SELF-EMPLOYED EXPATRIATE

In the case of expatriates who leave with no employment arranged overseas or with the intention of establishing themselves in self-employment overseas in the full sense, the Inland Revenue in effect take a 'wait and see' attitude. Formerly there was clearly a different attitude displayed by the Inland Revenue to self-employed persons in circumstances otherwise entirely comparable to those of an employee which many felt was unfair. The most recent revision of booklet IR 20 redresses this and acknowledges, at para 2.4, that when circumstances are similar, similar treatment will be afforded so that, for example, a self-employed consultant with a contract for services which covers a full tax year should be treated as not resident and not ordinarily resident from the date of departure as would an employee.

The treatment for income tax purposes as non-resident from the day following the day of departure is concessionary (ESC A11), and the Inland Revenue reserve the right not to apply it in certain cases. Wherever a concession gives rise to a significant loss of tax to the Revenue, its application is in doubt. The split-year treatment is not usually available for capital gains (see Chapter 7).

3.9 EXPATRIATES WITH A SPECIAL STATUS

There are certain classes of expatriates who, although actually working overseas, may be deemed to be performing their duties in the United Kingdom. These include Crown servants and members of the armed forces, seafarers and airmen, and persons employed in oil and gas exploration or exploitation activities in a designated area under the Continental Shelf Act 1964, s 1(7). The special circumstances of these individuals are described below.

3.9.1 Crown servants

The duties of an office or employment under the Crown are deemed to be duties performed in the United Kingdom irrespective of where they are, in fact, performed. The effect of this is to render the emoluments from such an employment liable to UK income tax under Case II of Schedule E if the employee is not resident and under Case I, but without any of the special reliefs, if the employee is resident. It must be stressed that this deeming provision (TA 1988, s 132(4)(a)) does not, of itself, affect the individual's residence position. If the Crown servant can otherwise satisfy the conditions for non-residence then the other advantages, such as no liability on overseas investment income or to CGT, will still accrue. In addition, certain allowances which are certified as representing compensation for the extra costs involved in living overseas are payable tax free. Under TA 1988, s 278 certain classes of non-resident, including Crown servants, are entitled to some or all of the normal UK personal allowances (for full details see Chapter 5 – Income arising in the United Kingdom). In practice, the Crown servant will be taxed under PAYE with an appropriate code for the personal allowances.

One exception to the UK tax liability of Crown servants concerns locally recruited staff overseas. If they are unestablished staff who are not UK resident and the maximum pay for their grade is less than that of an executive officer in the United Kingdom on the Inner London rate, then no tax will be payable (ESC A25).

3.9.2 Armed forces

In general terms, members of the armed forces on overseas duty are treated in the same way as other Crown servants. There is, however, one special relief available to members of the armed forces or their spouses. Such individuals will be treated as resident in the United Kingdom for the purpose of obtaining relief on qualifying life assurance premiums or policies issued before 13 March 1984.

3.9.3 Seafarers and airmen

Duties by seafarers and members of aircraft crews are deemed to be performed in the United Kingdom if the voyage does not extend to a port outside the United Kingdom or if the person concerned is a resident of the United Kingdom and part of the voyage or flight begins or ends here (TA 1988, s 132(4)(*b*)). This provision is now subject to TA 1988, Sched 12, para 5. This latter provision provides that seamen and aircrew engaged on voyages outside the United Kingdom are entitled to the special 100 per cent deduction for long absences (see **3.3**) in respect of the proportion of voyages or flights spent outside the United Kingdom. The legislation covers two types of voyage or flight: one which begins or ends outside the United Kingdom, and any part beginning or ending outside the United Kingdom of a journey which begins and ends in the United Kingdom.

In a letter dated 22 July 1980, reproduced in *Butterworth's Yellow Tax Handbook*, the Inland Revenue expanded on the meaning of this provision, by quoting an example concerning the following voyages. A voyage from Tilbury to Antwerp would qualify as being carried out overseas; a voyage from Newcastle to Tilbury to Antwerp would qualify for the Tilbury–Antwerp portion; a round trip Tilbury–Antwerp–Tilbury would also qualify and that portion of a Newcastle–Tilbury–Antwerp–Tilbury–Newcastle trip would likewise be considered as overseas working. The Inland Revenue practice is that a voyage containing a scheduled call at an overseas port will have an overseas portion, but if there is no such scheduled call, then the voyage will not qualify as constituting overseas working. For the purposes of calculating the number of qualifying days for the 100 per cent relief, a person will be considered as leaving the United Kingdom when a ship leaves its berth for a foreign port or prior to 17 March 1998, when an aircraft takes off.

3.9.4 Oil rig workers

For tax purposes, the territorial sea of the United Kingdom is deemed to be part of the United Kingdom under FA 1973, s 38. This area is further extended in the case of employments in designated areas concerned with oil and gas exploration or exploitation activities. Generally this means that persons employed in the British sectors of the North and Celtic Seas will be treated as working in the United Kingdom. 'Designated areas' are those designated by Order in Council under the Continental Shelf Act 1964, s 1(7). Apart from the rig workers themselves, this extension of the United Kingdom is also of interest to the crews of ships and aircraft servicing the offshore installations. Flights or voyages to the installations will not constitute overseas working.

3.10 THE EXPATRIATE FAMILY

Some aspects of UK tax law treat the family effectively as a single unit. Thus, minor children's income inasmuch as it derives from a parental gift or settlement is treated as the income of the parent. This unified treatment does not apply to questions of residence and domicile. Not only is it the case that the residence or domicile of one spouse does not necessarily affect the residence or domicile of the other, but children are capable of having a residence status quite independent of their parents.

Because each member of a family is considered individually there is some scope for intra-family tax planning. There can also be some pitfalls if this is not done properly.

It is not unknown for the husband (in the majority of cases) to be treated as not resident in the United Kingdom from the day following departure on account of his full-time overseas employment, but his accompanying wife remains classified as a UK resident because of breaching the three-monthly rule on return visits to the United Kingdom.

It is possible for an expatriate wife to have part-time employment abroad and in the United Kingdom this is taxable, if she remains resident for tax purposes. It may also be taxable overseas (see Chapter 11 on double taxation).

The expatriate wife with no income of her own, either earnings or investment, is unaffected by her residence status. But if her husband has investment income arising in the United Kingdom which is liable to tax, eg income from letting the family home, there may be scope for transferring that income to the wife. It should be noted that the resident wife of a non-resident husband is entitled to the single personal allowance. This means that her allowance can be used to offset investment income, resulting perhaps in a repayment of income tax deducted at source. It is usually simpler to ensure that income-producing assets are held in the name of the non-resident. A joint bank deposit account where one of the parties is resident will produce interest half of which is not liable to tax in the hands of the non-resident under FA 1995, s 128. The presumption, in TA 1988, s 282A, that jointly held property is owned equally can be countered by a declaration under TA 1988, s 282B given to the inspector on form 17, that the beneficial interest in the income is in a specified proportion. It is possible, therefore, to elect that the non-resident spouse is entitled to, say, 100 per cent of the income arising after submission of the election but 50 per cent of the capital. Such a non-resident can register with the bank on form R85 to have the interest credited gross (TA 1988, s 481(5)(*k*)).

Interest in UK government securities (gilts) is paid gross and is exempt from tax in the hands of a non-resident unless the gilts form part of a trade carried on in the United Kingdom.

The general rule is that UK assets producing taxable income should be held by the resident spouse and UK assets producing an income exempt in the hands of a non-resident and non-UK assets should be held by the non-resident spouse.

Spouses are also treated separately for CGT, each having an annual exemption (£7,200 for 2000/01). Assets may be transferred between resident spouses who are living together or are not separated in circumstances likely to remain permanent. It follows that there is scope for planning disposals of capital assets where one spouse is both non-resident and not ordinarily resident (see Chapter 7 and section **12.2**) although great care will be needed to avoid IHT if one spouse is domiciled in the UK, whilst one is not (see section **8.15**).

Children who remain resident in the United Kingdom, perhaps staying at a boarding school, are also entitled to a personal allowance. Where the parents are resident in the United Kingdom this personal allowance of the children is rarely of significant benefit unless the child has a substantial income from a non-parental source. Gifts from parents to minor children are treated as settlements and any income arising therefrom is treated as if it were the parent's income (TA 1988, s 660B), although this does not catch gifts from grandparents to grandchildren or between other family members.

3.11 EXPATRIATES RETIRING ABROAD OR PERMANENTLY EMIGRATING

The Inland Revenue treatment of persons retiring abroad or otherwise permanently emigrating is very much the same as that given to a temporary expatriate taking up overseas employment and the non-resident status remains conditional until a complete tax year has been spent abroad and any visits have been kept within the limits described in Chapter 2. Confirmation of the non-resident status is sometimes not given, unless the emigrant has cause to continue to complete UK tax returns because of continuing UK income sources such as pensions. Although an enquiry might be made of the emigrant to determine whether or not he remains non-resident after the first tax year, as often as not this is a futile enquiry and his tax office file will eventually become a dead file. The Inland Revenue do, however, have remarkable powers of recovering files, if not the individuals they relate to, from limbo. The dead file will normally be traced should the emigrant decide to return to the United Kingdom and, with this in mind, departing expatriates should be prepared to explain significant variations in their wealth should they return to the United Kingdom to re-establish residence.

It would be normal for most people leaving permanently to sell their home in the United Kingdom and this is considered as quite firm evidence of intent by the Inland Revenue. It is by no means crucial for the emigrant who has *bona fide* employment arranged in his new country, because he will in any case be treated as any other overseas employed expatriate. When a home is retained as an investment (ie for letting) or because market conditions do not favour a sale, it may still be possible to demonstrate that emigration is with permanent intent.

3.11.1 The retired expatriate

In the case of a retired emigrant, failure to divest himself of his property in this country will mean that he will continue to be regarded provisionally as resident and ordinarily resident for up to three years after departure. A decision on his residence status will be made retrospectively in the light of what has actually happened in the meantime. During the three intervening years, his tax liability will be provisionally computed on the basis that he remains resident in the United Kingdom. Such a person will also have a provisional entitlement to personal allowances (since he is provisionally resident) and these will be reflected in any PAYE code operated, eg against a company pension, or may form the basis of a tax repayment claim if tax is deducted, or effectively deducted in the form of tax credits, from interest, dividends (until April 1999), or other sources of income.

If after three years the emigrant has not broken the rules, then his non-resident, non-ordinarily resident status will normally be backdated to the day following his departure. Any tax paid in the meantime because of his provisionally resident treatment which would not have been payable in the case of a non-resident will then be repaid.

GUIDE TO DOMICILE AND RESIDENCE: THE TAX CONSEQUENCES

4.1 INTRODUCTION

This chapter is intended as a schematic guide to the tax and investment planning chapters that follow it. In using this guide, it is important **to check the status of each spouse separately**, in order to identify the relevant category.

4.2 USING THE GUIDE

Step 1: establish domicile

Use Domicile Chart as guide.

For inheritance tax (IHT) purposes only, it is possible for the Inland Revenue to **deem** an individual UK domiciled (such action does not disturb the legal domicile).

Step 2: establish where resident for tax purposes

Use:

Residence Chart 1 for non-UK domiciled individuals
Residence Chart 2 for working UK expatriates
Residence Chart 3 for non-working UK expatriates.

Step 3: check tax and investment considerations

Having decided domicile and residence category, use:

(1) UK Taxation Chart to check planned actions for tax effectiveness
(2) UK Taxation – Effect on Investment, to check overall financial strategy, but ensure no conflict with sensible tax and investment planning.

The symbols on this latter chart can be regarded as:

☺   Usually harmless, or even good!

⑦   May well be harmless, but take care to double check

①   Check – there could be disadvantages

🛑   Check carefully – there will usually be major disadvantages

Category: A

Applies to someone who is:

- non-UK domiciled;
- non-UK resident; and
- non-UK ordinarily resident.

Basic strategy:

Can invest in the United Kingdom provided local legal and exchange controls permit. To minimise risk of IHT on UK assets, should:

(1) restrict UK assets below IHT zero-rated band;
(2) take advantage of UK government exempt stocks;
(3) ensure any 'portable' assets are held outside the United Kingdom;
(4) consider alternative structures for major investments in the United Kingdom.

Also, should take advantage of investments offered by offshore subsidiaries of UK institutions, which can offer investments free of UK taxation other than that deducted at source. A similar effect can be achieved through a non-UK private investment company.

Category: B

Applies to someone who is:

- non-UK domiciled;
- UK resident; and/or
- UK ordinarily resident.

Basic strategy:

To minimise UK income tax and CGT liabilities should keep all assets and accumulated gains/income outside the United Kingdom, remitting to the United Kingdom **only** the absolute minimum. If remittance, eg to cover living expenses, is unavoidable, individuals should create separate offshore accounts to contain and identify:

(1) income arising outside the United Kingdom;
(2) gain-laden capital from asset disposal; and
(3) capital untainted by income or gain.

Once these accounts have been established and their nature verified, the preferred strategy is to remit from account:

(1) up to the level of available personal tax allowances for the tax year, assuming no taxable income arising in the United Kingdom;
(2) up to the level of the available CGT exempt amount for individuals for the tax year, assuming no gains arising in the United Kingdom;
(3) any balance required in the United Kingdom.

If remittances are made at such a level that the balance on account (3) is getting low, there are valid techniques for 'capitalising' amounts held on account (1) and professional help should be sought to arrange this.

To minimise UK IHT exposure, UK assets may be held by offshore trusts and/or companies.

Category: C

Applies to someone who is:

- UK domiciled;
- non-UK resident; and
- non-UK ordinarily resident.

Basic strategy:

Invest in offshore subsidiaries of UK institutions, to retain investment qualities without unnecessary UK tax implications. Ensure spare capital is working for capital growth as well as income, and realise all accumulated capital gains while still non-UK ordinarily resident, and preferably before the beginning of the tax year in which a return to the United Kingdom is planned (but check the re-entry charge – see Chapter 7). Generally the best timing for a disposal is towards the end of a tax year, as unforeseen circumstances can sometimes necessitate a premature return.

Still liable to UK IHT on worldwide assets, check local estate or gift taxes rules, including laws of succession.

Take care to maintain a realistic level of health insurance and life cover and keep equal cover for a spouse running the UK family base, if appropriate.

If one spouse remains UK resident, take care to avoid **joint** assets, as the income/gain on the asset will be assessable to UK taxes.

Note:
Where the Inland Revenue may try to assert that the individual is non-

resident but ordinarily resident in the United Kingdom, he may remain liable to CGT on his worldwide assets, even if the re-entry charge does not apply.

Category: D

Applies to someone who is:

- UK domiciled (but claiming a new domicile of choice);
- non-UK resident; and
- non-UK ordinarily resident.

Basic strategy:

As part of the exercise to replace UK domicile with a new domicile of choice, the individual concerned must show that all formal ties with the United Kingdom have been severed. Because of the deemed domicile rules for IHT, it is recommended that these steps are taken as soon as a decision not to return is made. Single ties, eg a banking service, an investment in a UK equity, etc will not individually prevent a successful claim to non-UK domicile, but together could convince the UK authorities that the individual retains British roots.

The individual should, therefore, move everything possible offshore and use UK facilities only if quite sure it will not damage non-domicile claim.

It may be possible to enter into a transaction on which domicile would have a bearing to provide a means of testing the water. Otherwise the Inland Revenue will not rule on this until they become aware of a potential occasion of charge to IHT (eg death).

It may be a wise precaution to plan for eventual IHT liability, on the assumption that the claim may eventually fail.

Note:

A UK expatriate will in any event be treated as deemed domiciled (for IHT purposes only) if he was domiciled in the United Kingdom within the three years immediately preceding the relevant time (IHTA 1984, s 267(1)(*a*)). This means he will be treated as deemed domiciled for at least three years following departure.

This provision causes problems as the deeming test refers to legal domicile and this will not necessarily have changed on the date of departure. If, for example, an expatriate did not make up his mind to stay overseas permanently and establish his domicile of choice elsewhere until after he had left, the three years could not begin to accrue until that decision had been made. This point is often overlooked and it is unsafe to assume that the deeming rule has no effect after three years of non-residence.

4.3 DOMICILE CHART

UK domiciled or non-UK domiciled?

Note: If 'domicile of choice' is not **actively** established, domicile
will be either 'domicile of origin' or 'domicile of
dependence'.

Note:*   If parents were married (to each other!) at
time of birth, take father as relevant parent:
otherwise, take mother as relevant parent.

Note:⁑   Except in Scotland, where the
relevant age is 14 for males
and 12 for females.

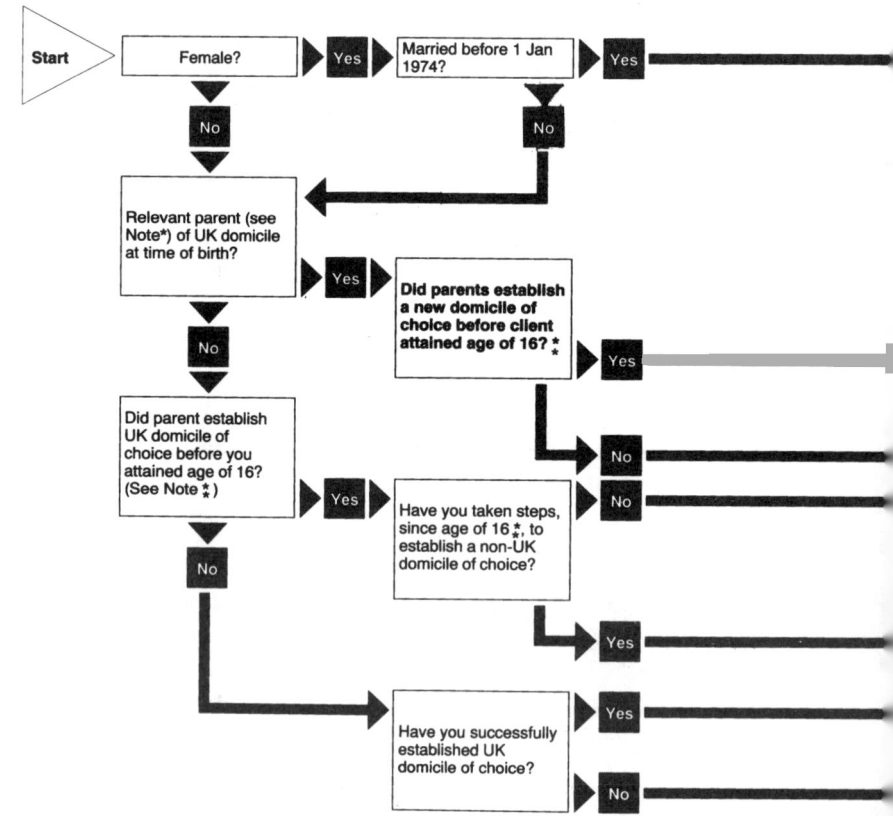

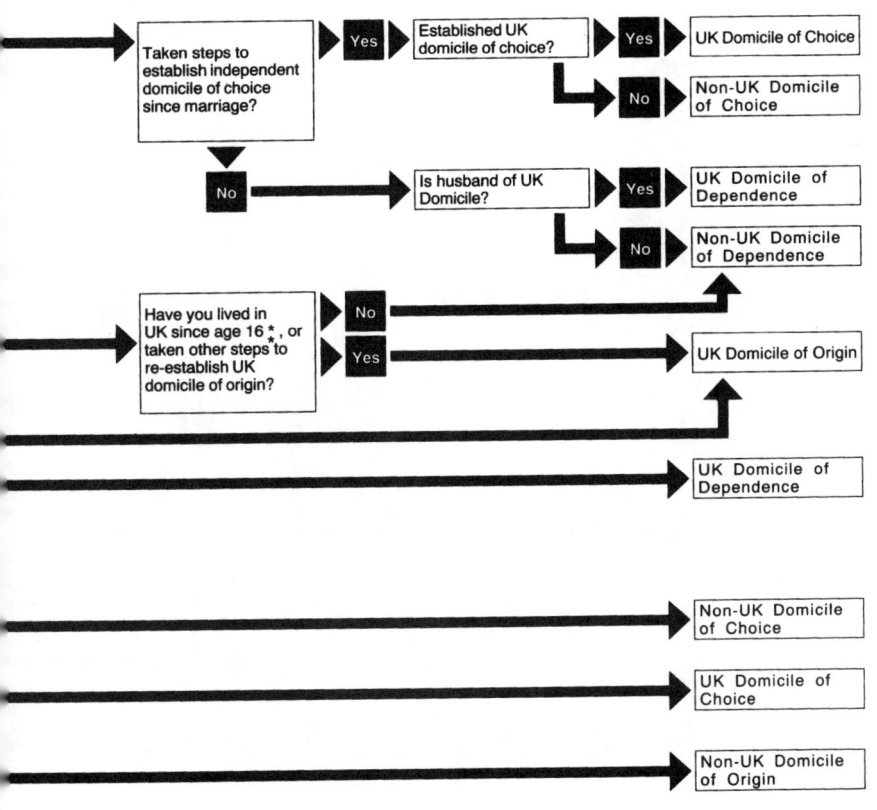

4.4 RESIDENCE CHARTS

Residence Chart 1 (non-UK domicile)

Non-UK domiciled

(see **4.3**) ie roots, parentage, etc outside UK

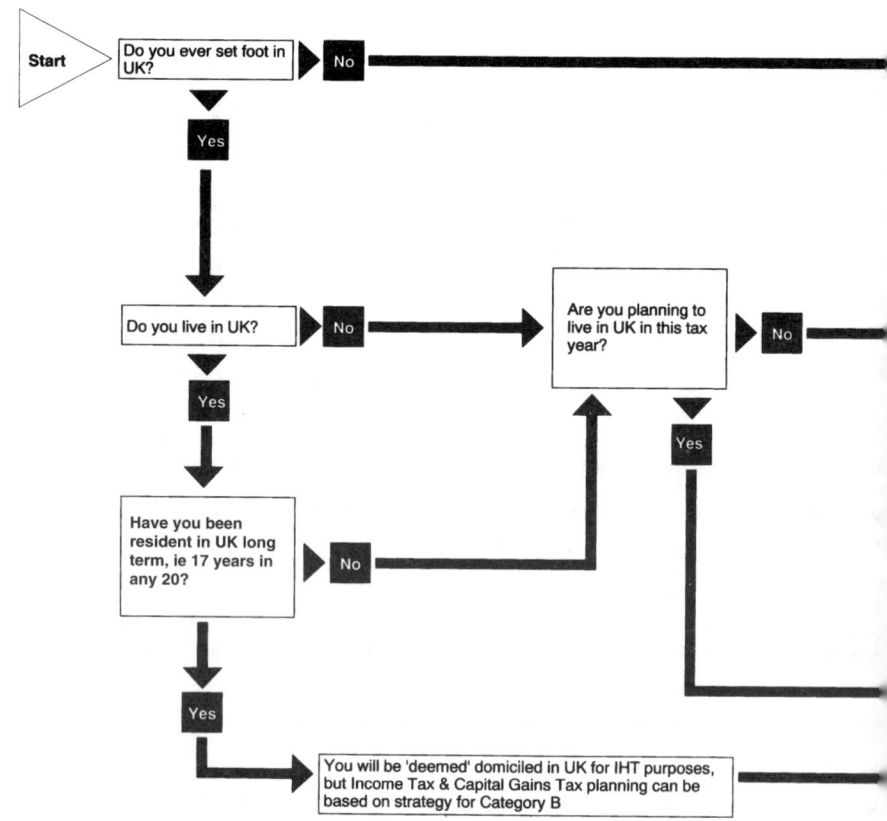

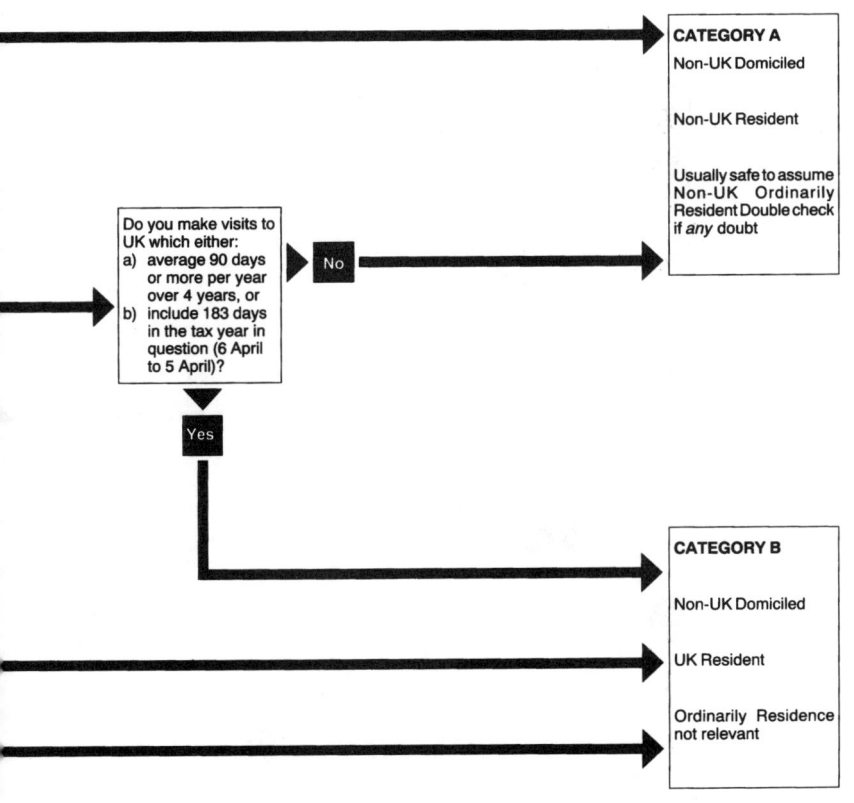

Residence Chart 2 (UK domicile – employed)

UK domiciled working abroad

ie roots, parentage etc (domicile) in UK, and in
full-time gainful occupation outside UK.

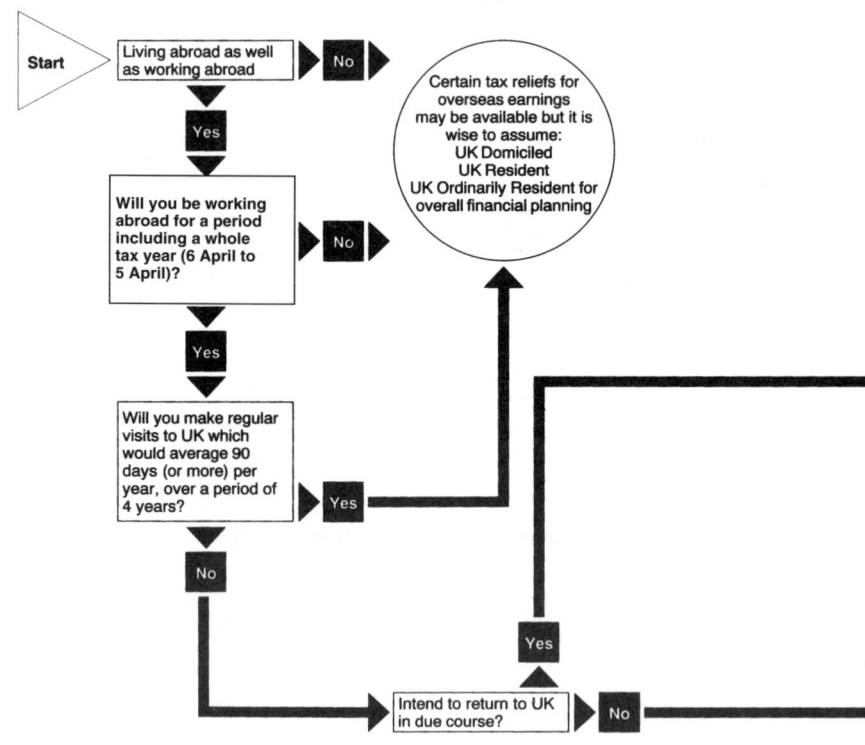

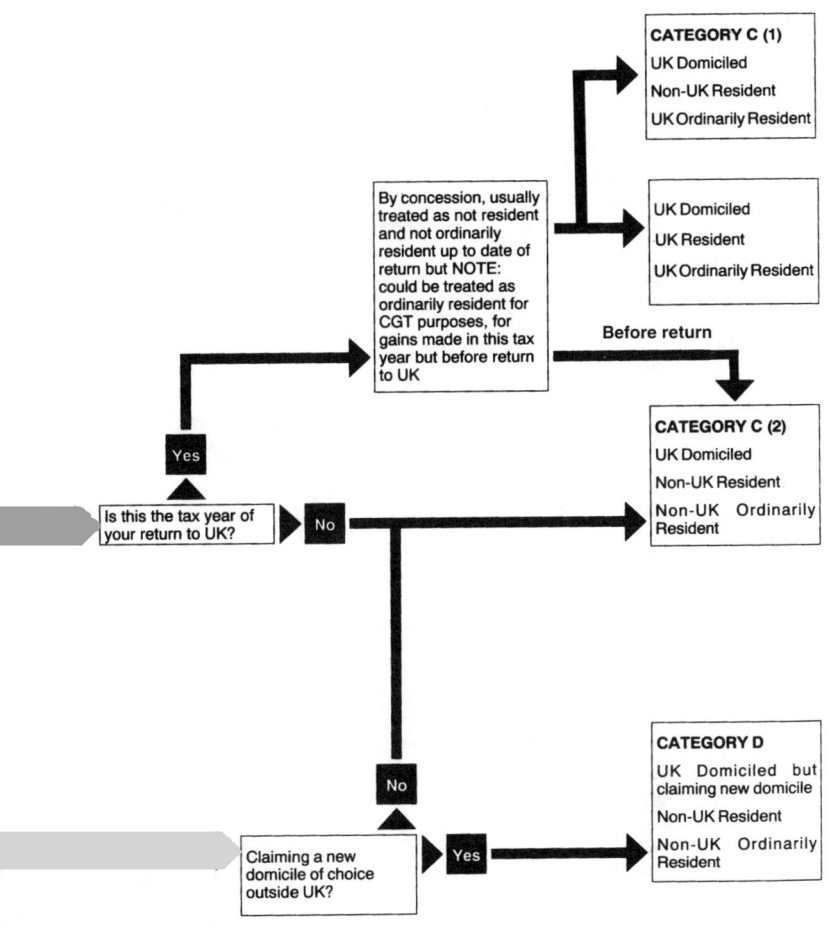

Residence Chart 3 (UK domicile – not employed)

UK domiciled living abroad

ie roots, parentage etc (domicile) in UK, living
outside UK, but not in full-time gainful occupation.

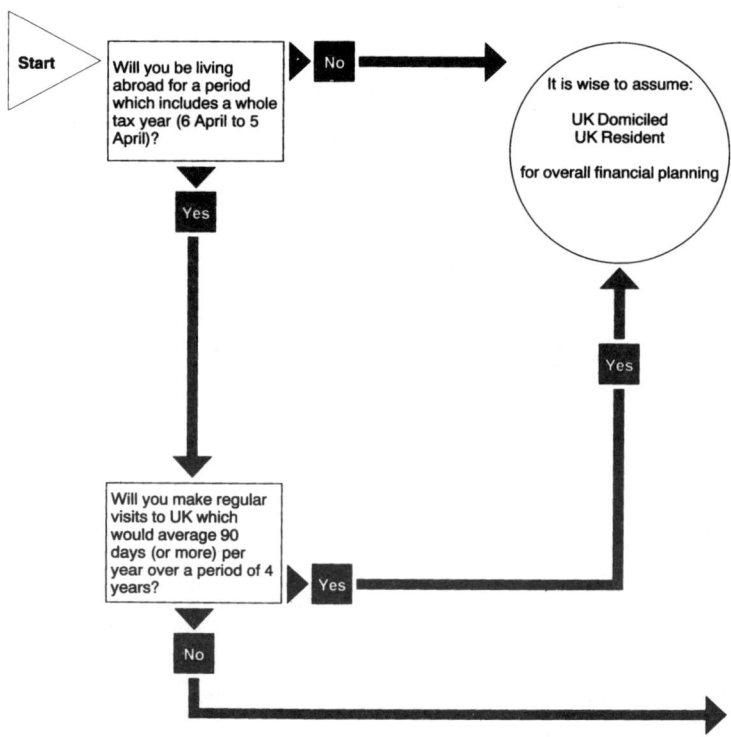

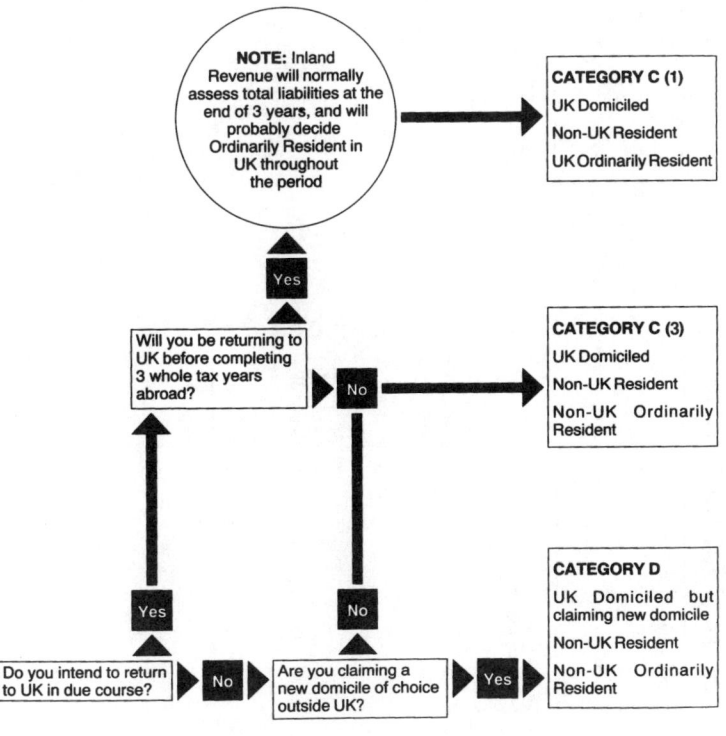

4.5 UK TAXATION CHART

Client category	A	B	C1	C2	D
	Non-UK domicile Non-UK resident and/or Non-UK ordinarily resident	Non-UK domicile UK resident UK ordinarily resident	UK domicile Non-UK resident UK ordinarily resident	UK domicile Non-UK resident Non-UK ordinarily resident	Claiming non-UK domicile of choice Non-UK resident Non-UK ordinarily resident
UK income tax – *income arising in UK*	• May apply for UK source interest to be paid gross • Overseas dividends collected in UK can be passed on gross of UK tax to non-residents • Some UK government stocks (exempt gilts): interest and bank and building society interest can be paid gross if non-UK ordinarily resident • UK personal reliefs and allowances may be available depending on citizenship and/or status	Liable on all income arising in UK Able to claim normal UK personal reliefs and exemptions	As for Category A (but gilt exemptions do not apply while still ordinarily resident in UK) Bank and building society interest liable to deduction of tax at source at rate applicable for time being: 20% from 1996/97	As for Category A	As for Category A
– *income arising abroad*	No liability, but may be subject to local taxes	Liable on any income remitted to the UK (income arising and retained outside UK is not assessed unless and until remitted to UK)	No liability, but may be subject to local taxes	No liability, but may be subject to local taxes	No liability, but may be subject to local taxes

Client category	A	B	C1	C2	D
UK capital gains tax					
– *assets in UK*	No liability – except perhaps on business property in UK (TCGA 1992 s 10) unless re-entry charge applies (TCGA 1992 s 10A)	Liable on gains realised in UK while UK resident and/or ordinarily resident	Liable on worldwide gains while still ordinarily UK resident	As for Category A	As for Category A
– *assets abroad*	No liability unless re-entry charge applies (TCGA 1992 s 10A)	Liable on any gain remitted to the UK (gains realised and retained outside UK are not assessed unless and until remitted to UK)			
UK inheritance tax					
– *assets in UK*	Liability can arise on assets held in UK. Gilts exempt under IHTA 1984 s 6(2) if non-UK ordinarily resident	As for Category A	Liable on worldwide assets	Liable on worldwide assets	Liable on worldwide assets
– *assets abroad*	No liability	As for Category A (but may become liable if ever becomes deemed UK domiciled)	Liable on worldwide assets	Liable on worldwide assets	Liable on worldwide assets (if successfully establishes a non-UK domicile of choice, liability will be as for Category A)

4.6 UK TAXATION – EFFECT ON INVESTMENTS CHART

Client category	A Non-UK domicile Non-UK resident and/or non-UK ordinarily resident	B Non-UK domicile UK resident UK ordinarily resident	C1 UK domicile Non-UK resident UK ordinarily resident	C2 UK domicile Non-UK resident Non-UK ordinarily resident	D Claiming non-UK domicile of choice Non-UK resident Non-UK ordinarily resident
UK equities, UK loan stocks, UK unit trusts, etc	(!) Beware IHT and UK withholding tax – although investment advantages may outweigh tax disadvantages	(!) Beware IHT and CGT, plus: • Income will be paid in UK net of withholding tax or basic rate tax • Prefer offshore alternatives, with income paid gross, and assets outside UK for CGT and IHT purposes • Income remitted to the UK is taxable	(!) Beware UK withholding tax – prefer offshore alternatives with less, or no, withholding taxes on income distribution (offshore funds are usually cheaper to invest in than dealing directly with foreign markets)	(!) Beware UK withholding tax – prefer offshore alternatives with less, or no, withholding taxes on income distribution (offshore funds are usually cheaper to invest in than dealing directly with foreign markets)	(!) Apart from the tax disadvantages as described in C, the investment will form a UK connection which may damage the domicile claim – prefer offshore alternatives
UK government stocks	(:)) Interest paid gross and asset is exempt from IHT		(?) Strictly, cannot claim interest gross until no longer ordinarily UK resident. Income will be paid net in the interim	(:)) Interest paid gross. (CARE if making claim to UK personal reliefs under TA 1988, s 278)	(?) If non-UK domicile is established, will be as for A, but in the interim a UK asset and a UK connection
UK taxation – effect on investments *– UK bank and building society deposits*	(!) Can request interest paid gross of basic rate tax if non-ordinarily resident – but beware IHT		(?) Cannot claim interest gross of UK basic rate tax until no longer ordinarily UK resident (will receive any income net in interim)	(:)) Can claim interest gross of UK basic rate tax as not ordinarily UK resident. Care if making claim to UK personal reliefs under TA 1988, s 278 – prefer offshore alternatives	(STOP) UK banking could be regarded as a strong remaining tie with UK and taken together with other UK links, invalidate non-domicile claim – prefer offshore bank services

Client category	A	B	C1	C2	D
UK taxation – effect on investments – *continued* – *Joint holdings with spouse who is UK resident for tax purposes*	[STOP] Could expose income and gains to UK tax liability	[?] No immediate disadvantage while both UK resident	[STOP] Any assets held jointly with resident spouse are assessable to UK taxes. (Each spouse should maintain separate bank account, investments and other assets in own sole name)	[STOP] Any assets held jointly with resident spouse are assessable to UK taxes. (Each spouse should maintain separate bank account, investments and other assets in own sole name)	[STOP] Non-domicile claim would be rare if spouse remains in UK – joint assets with resident spouse would almost certainly defeat any non-UK domicile claim
UK taxation – effect on money movement – *Overseas income remitted to UK*			[?] Remitting to UK will not incur a tax liability in itself – but it usually makes more practical sense to send all 'spare' income direct to offshore investment to save time, postage and paper	[?] Remitting to UK will not incur a tax liability in itself – but it usually makes more practical sense to send all 'spare' income direct to offshore investment to save time, postage and paper	[?] Remittance of income to UK may serve to reinforce UK links and increase UK assets
– *Capital gains arising in UK*	[:)] No tax implications to prevent free movement of money into UK (CARE if increasing UK assets – beware IHT) (If previously UK resident, beware CGT re-entry charge if will be resident in future)	[STOP] Will incur UK income tax if remitted to UK. Retain offshore [!] Delay realisation of any UK gains until tax year after leaving UK if possible. Gains realised while resident will incur CGT	[STOP] Will incur CGT liability if realised while still ordinarily UK resident whether remitted to UK or not – delay until not ordinarily resident	[!] If not NR/NOR before 17 March 1998, beware re-entry charge if returning to UK before five tax years have elapsed	[:)] This would mark a disposal of UK assets and therefore severing of UK ties. Helpful in decreasing UK assets in event of non-domicile claim being successful
– *Overseas capital gains remitted to UK*		[STOP] Will incur CGT if remitted. Retain offshore and only remit to limit of annual CGT exemption			[?] Remittance of capital to UK may serve to reinforce UK links and increase UK assets

55

5

INCOME ARISING IN THE UNITED KINGDOM

5.1 INTRODUCTION

In this and the following five chapters we look in more detail at the impact of UK taxes of various kinds on the British expatriate, and in the subsequent chapter we describe some of the principles determining his liability to tax in another jurisdiction, particularly that of his overseas residence. The UK tax system is extremely complex by itself. Interaction with taxes elsewhere in the world adds considerably to these complexities. Nevertheless, to be forewarned is the only way to be forearmed in one's dealings with the tax administration in any country; and to act as far as possible in advance will in many cases save not only a great deal of time and trouble but considerable amounts of money as well.

Tax legislation is complex because it tries by means of general measures to apply equity to numberless individual cases. Anyone who deals professionally with the tax matters of expatriates soon becomes aware of the enormous variation in their individual circumstances: in fact at times it seems that no two sets of circumstances are exactly alike. For this reason, if for no other, a Handbook of this kind cannot provide all the answers. To obtain a complete picture, the expatriate must in any case consider any local taxation which applies in his country of residence and the provisions of any double taxation agreement between that country and the United Kingdom. But even when this has been done, in many cases the complications are such and the sums of money potentially involved so large that it is essential to seek individual professional advice.

For most British expatriates the source of their earnings will be outside the United Kingdom. But many will receive an income from one source or another in the United Kingdom itself. Many who were previously resident will already have investments in the United Kingdom, and many more will wish to invest there. It may also be the case that an expatriate will receive earnings from UK business or draw a pension from an earlier employment.

In any of these circumstances, a UK source of income will have a tax consequence, but the British tax system is such that the tax consequence may be different for every type of income. Earnings from employment are treated differently from pensions, which in turn are treated differently from business profits. Earned income is treated in a different manner from investment income, and different types of investment give rise to different methods of taxation.

This chapter looks in some detail at the UK taxation consequences attaching to the major types of income originating in the United Kingdom. Income from letting UK property is considered separately in Chapter 6, and further chapters deal with capital gains tax (CGT) and inheritance tax (IHT).

5.2 THE UK SCHEDULAR SYSTEM OF INCOME TAX

An unusual feature of the UK income tax system is that different sources of income have historically been assessed in different ways.

The tax schedules, as they are known, corresponding to each distinct source of income, originated in Addington's Act of 1803 which, by taxing each source separately with deduction of tax at source where possible, avoided the need for a return of total income. No UK taxpayer had to make such a return until Lloyd George introduced supertax on incomes over £3,000 in his 1909 'people's Budget'.

The sources of income covered by each of the Schedules are broadly as follows:

Schedule A: rents from land
Schedule D:
    Case I: profits from trades and businesses (self-employment)
      II: profits from professions and vocations (self-employment)
     III: interest on investments
     IV: interest on overseas securities, eg mortgages
      V: income from overseas possessions, ie other investments
     VI: casual profits
Schedule E: income from employment and pension
Schedule F: income from dividends and distributions paid by UK companies and unit trusts
Schedule B: (annual value of commercial woodlands) was abolished in 1988.

Schedule C: (interest on government securities) was brought into Schedule D, Case III in 1996.

Until 1997, a UK taxpayer with several sources of income had to deal with several tax offices. As a general rule, Schedule E income was dealt with by the tax office for the area where the salary or pension is paid, and Schedule D, Cases I and II profits were dealt with by the tax office covering the business address. Other income was dealt with by the tax office covering the taxpayer's home address.

With effect from 6 April 1997, the system has been radically reformed. The schedular system is still in existence, but individual taxpayers are required to file their own tax returns to a single tax office and self-assess their liabilities. If a return is filed by 30 September, the Inland Revenue will calculate the liability. Otherwise, the filing date is the 31 January following the end of the tax year, and that is also the date on which the balance of the tax liability is to be paid in respect of all sources of income for the year ended on the previous 5 April. Failure to file a return on time attracts an automatic penalty, and interest runs automatically on any tax overpaid or underpaid at 31 January. As an incentive to accurate payment, the Inland Revenue benefit from an interest rate differential based on rates available to borrowers and net of tax to depositors, and there are surcharges for tax remaining unpaid more than 28 days and again more than six months after the due date for payment.

The Inland Revenue have produced various explanatory leaflets, including:

- SA/BK1 – A general guide;
- SA/BK2 – A guide for the self-employed;
- SA/BK3 – A guide to keeping records for the self-employed;
- SA/BK4 – A general guide to keeping records.

There is no specific guide to self-assessment for expatriates, although the Inland Revenue *Tax Bulletin* of August 1995 contains a summary of the rules for taxing various types of income for non-residents at page 237.

5.3 INTEREST FROM BANK AND BUILDING SOCIETY DEPOSITS

Income accruing to a UK deposit account was strictly speaking taxable as income arising in the United Kingdom under Schedule D, Case III, up to 5 April 1995.

However, where the beneficial owner of the account was not resident in the United Kingdom and certain other conditions were fulfilled, then under Extra-Statutory Concession ESC B13 no action was taken to pursue that tax charge on bank deposits or building society interest or from certificates of deposit, deep gain securities, or client account deposits. From 6 April 1995, the Finance Act 1995 (FA 1995), s 128 limits UK tax on such income to any tax deducted at source.

The provisions relating to deduction of tax at source on bank interest do not apply to a non-resident, provided that he has declared in writing to the deposit taker liable to pay interest that at the time of the declaration he is beneficially entitled to the interest and is not ordinarily resident in the United Kingdom. The declaration contains an undertaking that if the depositor becomes ordinarily resident in the United Kingdom he will notify the deposit taker accordingly and must be in the form prescribed by the Board of Inland Revenue and contain such information as they may reasonably require (Income and Corporation Taxes Act 1988 (TA 1988), ss 481(5)(*k*), 482(2)).

Where, exceptionally, a declaration does not incorporate the address of the person making it, it needs to be supported by a certificate from the deposit taker. In such a case, the deposit taker needs to certify that, to the best of his knowledge and belief, the persons to whom the declaration relates are not ordinarily resident in the United Kingdom; that the person making the declaration has undertaken to notify him of a relevant change in residence status; and that if he receives information indicating that any of the persons concerned are ordinarily resident in the United Kingdom, he will deduct tax. In addition the Revenue are empowered to prescribe or authorise the form of the declarations and certificates under SI 1992 No 14.

5.3.1 Excluded income

From 6 April 1995 the UK tax liability of a non-resident is limited except in the case of income from a trade or profession carried on through a branch or agent, or under Schedule A, to the tax deducted at source if any. This is achieved by taking out of charge the excluded income and also ignoring the personal allowances given under a double taxation treaty or to Commonwealth citizens or citizens of the Republic of Ireland and certain others under TA 1988, s 278. Effectively, the personal allowances are set against the excluded investment income, although any balance of allowances in excess of this income could then be claimed against chargeable income assessed on a UK representative or under Schedule A.

Excluded income is defined in FA 1995, s 128, but does not include income charged on a UK representative as a trade or profession carried on through a branch or agent in the United Kingdom.

The excluded income, which is only subject to UK tax in the hands of a non-resident if, and to the extent that, it is subject to deduction of tax at source, is:

(1) income from government securities, deposit interest and other income taxable under Schedule D, Case III and dividends taxable under Schedule F, ie investment income other than from land in the United Kingdom;

(2) transactions in deposits taxable under Schedule D, Case VI under TA 1988, s 56;

(3) social security benefits taxable under Schedule E under TA 1988, s 150 or s 617 and incapacity benefits taxable under FA 1994, s 139, including state pension;

(4) income received through a broker or investment manager that meets the requisite conditions for exemption in FA 1995, s 114, previously excluded by ESC B40, other than underwriting profits of a Lloyd's name; and

(5) any other income that may be designated by the Treasury by statutory instrument.

Excluded income taxed at source includes income where tax is deducted or treated as deducted, which is paid or treated as paid, or in respect of which there is a tax credit. The amount of tax is the amount deducted, paid or credited as appropriate.

A non-resident trust does not qualify for exemption where there is a UK ordinarily resident individual or UK resident company as a relevant beneficiary, which mirrors the exclusion in ESC B13 and for authorised unit trusts under SI 1994 No 2318. A relevant beneficiary is defined by reference to entitlement to income, current or prospective.

Joint accounts, where one party is resident and the other is non-resident, as is often the case with married expatriates, are wholly taxable (regardless of whether the account is with a UK bank or offshore) because the interest is generally not apportioned between the two individuals but accrues to them jointly and can be drawn by either of them. This is a point missed by many expatriates.

In general, UK bank and building society deposit accounts are to be avoided. If it is desired to maintain a deposit account with a British bank, it should be made with an offshore branch or subsidiary of the bank, eg in the Isle of Man. In that way it will be beyond the reach of the UK legislation and attract no UK tax.

5.4 INTEREST FROM GOVERNMENT, LOCAL AUTHORITY AND CORPORATE STOCKS

Government stocks

From 6 April 1998, all gilt-edged securities issued prior to that date are treated as 'FOTRA' securities (free of tax for residents abroad), that is to say that the profits or gains arising from the securities are exempt from tax provided they are beneficially owned by persons not ordinarily resident in the United Kingdom. Before 6 April 1998, only certain securities qualified for this treatment.

Although not strictly a FOTRA security, the 3½ per cent War Loan is treated in the same way under its original terms of issue.

This exemption does not override any anti-avoidance legislation which may deem the income to be taxable on a UK resident person. Neither does the exemption apply if the interest forms part of the profits of a UK trade.

From 6 April 1998, the interest on gilts is paid without deduction of tax (F(No 2)A 1997, s 37). Prior to that date, non-ordinarily resident individuals had to apply for gross payment in most cases.

Exempt stocks have long been a mainstay for the appropriate portion of the British expatriate investor's portfolio because of their competitive yield and high security. They also form the basis of a large offshore gilt fund industry and both direct and fund investment can form part of a sound investment portfolio.

For more information, the Bank of England's Gilt-Edged and Money Markets Division may be contacted on +44 (0) 20 7601 4540.

Local authority stocks

Interest from local authority stocks is generally paid after deduction of tax. The only exception to this is where the stock was issued for borrowing in a foreign currency. In that case, and subject to Treasury direction, the interest may be paid gross and be exempt from income tax if the stockholder is not resident in the United Kingdom.

Corporate stocks – debentures, etc

These, too, are generally paid effectively net of income tax at the basic rate, although arrangements can be made for interest to be paid gross under a double taxation agreement (see Chapter 11).

Any other interest

Subject to the exceptions described above and to the specific provisions of double taxation treaties (see below) all interest payments made to non-residents should be paid net of UK income tax at the basic rate.

Double taxation agreements

Where there is a double taxation treaty in force between the United Kingdom and the country of residence of the recipient, then the treatment of interest may be covered therein. It is normal in these cases for interest to be payable gross and tax to be payable in the country of residence. Many agreements, however, have provision for a withholding tax in the source country. The appropriate agreement must be checked.

5.4.1 Dividends

Pre-6 April 1999

Dividends paid by UK companies are technically paid gross, ie there is no income tax deducted at source. However, alongside the dividend there was, prior to 6 April 1999, an associated tax credit equal to one-quarter of the net dividend. So far as the payer is concerned, this tax credit was accounted for and paid to the Inland Revenue as advance corporation tax (ACT). This ACT could be used to offset the payer's final or mainstream corporation tax liability. So far as the payee is concerned the tax credit could be treated as analogous to income tax deducted at source. For the UK resident non-taxpayer, the credit could be paid to him, but for the non-resident taxpayer, the dividend counts as excluded income from 6 April 1995, and there is no further UK tax charge (FA 1995 s 128). Previously the quantum of dividend income on which any higher rate tax was calculated was the sum of the dividend plus tax credit, TA 1988, s 207A.

Thus, where a person received a dividend of £400, there would have been a tax credit associated with the dividend of £100. For the non-taxpayer, this £100 could have been repaid (until April 1999). If the recipient of the dividend had a marginal tax rate of 40 per cent, however, then there would have been additional tax of £100 due on his dividend income:

	£
Dividend	400
Tax credit	100
	£500
Tax @ 40%	200
Less: tax credit	100
Additional tax due	£100

No tax credit was payable in respect of dividends or distributions which are foreign income dividends within TA 1988, Part VI, Ch VA.

Post-6 April 1999

Tax credits related to dividends payable to individuals and most other recipients, other than, to a limited extent, charities, cease to be repayable from 6 April 1999. From 1999/00 onwards, the tax credit is a fixed proportion (one-ninth for 1999/00) of the dividend. A UK resident is assessable on the sum of the net dividend plus the tax credit at a special Schedule F rate of tax. For basic and lower rate taxpayers no further tax is payable but for those liable for the higher rate of tax the special 'dividend rate' is 32.5 per cent for 1999/00. The tax credit can be set against this liability, leaving the UK resident taxpayer in the same net position as he was before 6 April 1999:

	£	£
Dividend	400.00	
Tax credit(⅑)	44.44	
	£444.44	
Tax @ 32.5%		144.44
Less: tax credit		44.44
Additional tax due		£100.00

Non-residents still receive the dividend paid (£400 in this example) with no payable credit and no UK tax liability.

5.5 LIFE ASSURANCE POLICIES

The benefits payable under UK life assurance policies are liable to UK tax for non-residents and residents alike. For tax purposes, policies are classified as 'qualifying' or 'non-qualifying'. A qualifying policy must be held for ten years, or three-quarters of the original term agreed, and the premiums must be paid regularly, at least once a year, and must be spread evenly throughout the duration of the policy. For a qualifying policy normally there will be no tax liability where the proceeds are payable to the original policyholder or to somebody to whom the policy has been given. In the case of a non-qualifying policy, tax may be payable on the proceeds. (For a single premium bond, for example, the permitted annual withdrawal is a cumulative 5 per cent per annum, which, if taken, could be for a maximum period of up to 20 years.) Tax is payable only by higher rate taxpayers – which includes those who are moved into the higher rate when any gain on total surrender or excess withdrawal is added to their annual taxable income – and is charged at the difference between the basic and the higher rate of tax (17 per cent for the 1999/00 tax year). For non-UK residents without other significant amounts of UK income, this will generally mean that there is no tax due.

It is important to bear in mind though, that this seemingly beneficial tax treatment is granted to take into account the tax that is paid by UK life assurance companies on the profits and gains within policy funds. Currently, franked income (that from UK equities and gilt edged securities) is taxed at 25 per cent, all other income (eg from foreign equities and Eurobonds) and capital gains are taxed at 30 per cent but of course the allowance available to individuals to offset the first £7,200 (2000/01) of gain, is not applicable. For non-UK residents 'offshore policies' may prove to be a better investment. An 'offshore policy' is one issued by a life assurance company resident in a tax haven where policy funds pay little or no tax on income and gains and the policy proceeds are similarly free of tax.

Expatriates returning to the United Kingdom should note that the proceeds of policies effected after 17 November 1983 may be fully liable to tax on the accrued profits, ie without the benefit of the basic rate tax credit, although the profit will be apportioned in direct relation to the periods of residence and non-residence during the policy term and only that portion relating to the period of UK residence will be subject to tax. (The proceeds of offshore policies taken out before 18 November 1983 continue to be free of liability to UK taxation.)

These comments refer only to UK taxation of UK policies, and non-UK residents must also take account of any local tax liability that may be due on policy proceeds.

Where life assurance premium relief is available (for a qualifying policy issued on or before 13 March 1984) the premiums may be paid net of the relief – currently 12½ per cent of the premium. The policyholder is eligible for relief if the policy is written on his life or that of his spouse, if either of them pays the premiums, and if the person paying is resident in the United Kingdom for tax purposes. Where the policyholder and his spouse will both be non-resident for the whole of a tax year the premiums must be paid gross, but net payments may be resumed when they again take up UK residence.

Non-residents are not charged to tax if the proceeds of a policy are not payable in the United Kingdom and the policy or contract was made outside the United Kingdom by a non-resident insurance company or an overseas branch of a resident insurance company.

With effect from 6 April 1999, the Treasury has power to impose a yearly charge in relation to 'personal portfolio bonds', in addition to any charge under the above provisions. A personal portfolio bond is a policy under the terms of which:

(1) some or all of the benefits are determined by reference to the value of or income from any description of property or fluctuations in, or an index of, the value of such property; and

(2) some or all of the property, or such an index, may be selected by or on behalf of the holder of the policy or a connected person.

The annual charge will be on a deemed gain equal to 15 per cent of the sum of the total premiums paid up to the end of each policy year and the total of deemed gains of earlier years. A deemed gain also arises on termination of the policy. The tax charge renders personal portfolio bonds unattractive as an investment for UK resident individuals with effect from 6 April 1999.

5.6 NATIONAL SAVINGS

Most of the investments offered by the Department for National Savings are tax free both for residents and non-residents. But the yield from these investments largely reflects this, in that greater yields can often be obtained elsewhere. As with other 'tax-free' investments there is no guarantee that the proceeds will remain so overseas.

The main taxable National Savings investments are the National Savings Bank investment account, income bonds and capital bonds which usually offer very competitive interest returns. Interest on all of these is always paid without deduction of income tax. The first £70 of interest on the National Savings Ordinary Account is exempt under TA 1988, s 325. Premium Savings Bond prizes are exempt from income tax and CGT.

5.7 PENSIONS

Many expatriates will, whether now or later, receive pension income from the United Kingdom and for tax purposes this income may be divided into three separate groups:

(1) State pensions – these include Retirement Pension and the State Earnings Related Pension Scheme.

(2) Private pensions – such as an occupational pension payable by a UK employer or self-employed and personal pensions (including Personal Pension Plans which became available from 1 July 1988).

(3) Government pensions – pensions arising from UK government

service: eg an armed services pension, an NHS pension, a teacher's pension, etc.

State pensions are always paid gross and can be paid in any country. The pensioner may be liable for tax in the country where he is resident, but where he receives any other pension taxable in the United Kingdom (see below), the State Retirement Pension will usually be taxed alongside that other pension. This is carried out either by a reduction of allowances or by the use of the higher rate of taxation in addition to the basic rate.

Private pensions continue to be liable to tax in the United Kingdom – they are likely also to be liable for tax in the country in which the expatriate is resident. Fortunately the United Kingdom has double taxation treaties with more than 100 countries, including those where expatriate Britons are most commonly to be found. Most of these treaties include an article covering private pensions and provide for the pension to be paid gross in the United Kingdom and taxable only in the country of residence. This usually requires authorisation by a competent authority in the country of residence which should serve to ensure that the pension does actually suffer tax there!

Government and local authority pensions are always taxable in the United Kingdom and, like private pensions, they are likely also to be liable for tax in the country of residence. Once again, relief is available where there is a double taxation agreement in force – this will normally provide for government pensions to be taxable only in the United Kingdom, so that a claim for exemption would need to be filed in the country of residence. Such claims usually require authorisation by a competent authority in the United Kingdom. (More information on double taxation agreements may be found in Chapter 11.)

Non-residents in receipt of a UK pension will often qualify for UK personal allowances (TA 1988, s 278) and these allowances should be claimed.

5.8 EMPLOYMENTS

The taxation treatment of employments which are carried on partly within and partly outside the United Kingdom is fully described in Chapter 3. Some non-residents do, however, have employments which are carried on wholly in the United Kingdom. Commonly, these are directorships where the non-resident does not work full-time in the employment but attends board meetings, etc in the United Kingdom. The whole of the remuneration from an entirely domestic employment is liable to UK income tax. Taxable too are benefits in kind and travelling expenses from the overseas home to the United Kingdom received or incurred in the performance of such employments, unless they are wholly, exclusively and necessarily incurred in the performance of the duties; TA 1988, s 198, *Taylor v Provan* [1974] STC 168.

Where a non-UK domiciled individual comes to work in the United Kingdom and was not resident in the United Kingdom during either of the two preceding tax years or was not present in the United Kingdom at any time during the two years up to the date of his arrival, he is entitled to relief for travel between the United Kingdom and his normal place of abode abroad for a period of five years, so long as the cost is borne or reimbursed by the employer. The journey includes travel from the home in the United Kingdom to the home overseas. Where the employee is in the United Kingdom for a continuous period of 60 days or more, he is entitled to relief for two visits a year by his spouse and minor children so long as the expenses are paid for or reimbursed by the employer. Apportionment is possible in cases of duality of purpose. There are provisions to prevent double allowances. Expenses incurred by the employee and not reimbursed are not deductible (TA 1988, s 195).

Where it can be shown that some of the duties of the employment are carried out overseas then part of the remuneration should be exempt from tax.

5.9 TRADES AND PROFESSIONS

Where a non-resident has trading or professional income arising in the United Kingdom this will normally be liable to UK income tax under Schedule D, Cases I or II. It is important, however, to consider the nature of the trade, where it is actually carried on, and whether or not an agent is involved.

A trade *with* the United Kingdom should not be confused with a trade *within* the United Kingdom. The latter is certainly taxable but the former may not be. A non-resident trader may have a representative office or an advertising department within the United Kingdom, he may even have a sales agent in the United Kingdom, without incurring any income tax liability. But care must be taken with agents, as discussed below. An advertising or representative office will not be trading in the United Kingdom if, for example, the contracts for the sale of goods, or for services, are in fact made overseas directly with the trader. This would constitute trading *with* the United Kingdom. But if the overseas trade was represented by a UK sales office, for example, where orders were taken and paid for locally, then this would constitute trading *within* the United Kingdom.

In the simple cases of sale of goods and services, the position is fairly clear-cut, but if the trade involves both manufacturing and selling in different countries then the situation becomes more complex. The introduction of self-assessment in the United Kingdom from 1996/97 required changes in the taxation of non-residents trading in the United Kingdom. Up until 5 April 1996, where only selling took place in the United Kingdom, the profit assessed could be limited to the merchanting profit under the Taxes Management Act 1970 (TMA 1970), s 81. Where UK branch profits did not appear to show the true profit, a proportion of the total worldwide profit could be charged in the United Kingdom based on the turnover in the United Kingdom, under TMA 1970, s 80. Such a situation allowed for tax avoidance by arranging for profits to be realised in the least onerous fiscal regime. Needless to say, this was counteracted by anti-avoidance legislation such as the transfer pricing rules contained in TA 1988, ss 770–773. Under self-assessment, the taxpayer is responsible for establishing whether those transfer pricing rules could apply and will suffer penalties and interest and surcharges if this is wrong. Therefore careful disclosure of material facts is advisable and liable persons may be well advised to file their returns by 30 September each year – in which case the Inland Revenue will undertake to calculate the assessment.

Where a non-resident trades within the United Kingdom he will be liable to tax, but collecting that tax is another matter, given that courts will not normally enforce foreign tax debts. TMA 1970, ss 78 and 79 attempt to get around this by providing that a non-resident trading in the United Kingdom will be chargeable in the name of any branch or agent in the United Kingdom. Thus the UK sales office mentioned above could be a taxable or chargeable entity in that case. The only exception to this is where the agent is an independent broker or general commission agent carrying on a *bona fide* brokerage or commission agency in its own right.

Up until 1995/96 trades and professions were assessed on a preceding year basis of assessment, on the adjusted profits of the accounting year ending in the preceding fiscal year. From 1997/98 (or 1994/95 for new businesses commenced after 6 April 1994) the assessment is on the adjusted profits of the accounting year ended in the fiscal year (the current year basis). The financial year 1996/97 was a transitional year normally based on the average adjusted profits for the two accounting years ending in 1996/97. There are complex provisions for commencement and cessation and on a change of accounting date as well as the seemingly inevitable anti-avoidance provisions.

The provisions in FA 1995, s 126, which apply from 6 April 1996, relating to income from trading in the United Kingdom through a branch or agent, sought to replace and clarify the provisions of Part VIII of the TMA 1970, ss 78–85, and re-enact the legislation for self-assessment without intending to change the established practice any more than is necessary. The Revenue have decided not to introduce legislation on the basic principles which have been established through case law and practice over many years. It is clear that the profits of a trade carried on wholly or partly in the United Kingdom are assessable under Schedule D, Case I (*Ogilvie v Kitton* (1908) 5 TC 538; *Spiers v MacKinnon* (1929) 14 TC 386; *San Paulo (Brazilian) Railway Co Ltd v Carter* (1985) 3 TC 407; *Denver Hotel Co Ltd v Andrews* (1895) 3 TC 356; *Grove v Elliots & Parkinson* (1896) 3 TC 481; *London Bank of Mexico v Apthorpe* (1891) 3 TC 143). Where the trade is carried on wholly abroad the profits are assessable under Schedule D, Case V (*Colquhoun v Brooks* (1889) 2 TC 490; *Trustees of Ferguson Deceased v Donovan* [1929] IR 489), which is assessable on similar lines to Schedule D, Cases I and II, although in this case a non-resident would not be liable.

Trading in the United Kingdom, broadly means that economic activities from which the profits are derived are carried on in the United Kingdom. This has been established by a series of cases, including: *Erichsen v Last* (1881) 1 TC 351; *Tischler v Apthorpe* (1885) 2 TC 89; *Pommery & Greno v Apthorpe* (1886) 2 TC 182; *Werle & Co v Colquhoun* (1888) 2 TC 402; *Grainger & Son v Gough* (1896) 3 TC 311; *Sulley v Attorney General* (1860) 2 TC 149; *Smidth & Co v Greenwood* (1992) 8 TC 193; *Firestone Tyre & Rubber Co Ltd (as agents for Firestone Co of USA) v Lewellin* (1957) 37 TC 111.

Where a non-resident carries on a trade partly in the United Kingdom and partly outside the United Kingdom, the charge is limited to the profits from the part of the trade carried on in the United Kingdom (*Pommery & Greno v Apthorpe* (1886) 2 TC 182 at 189).

In order to arrive at the measure of profits chargeable in such circumstances, the Revenue will adopt the internationally accepted arm's length principle set out in Art 7(2) and (3) of the OECD model double taxation convention. Trades carried on in the United Kingdom but not through a branch or agency rarely occur and present no special problems in determining the profits, which would be subject to taxation in the United Kingdom, unless exempted under a double tax treaty.

The Inland Revenue consider that profits can be measured on the arm's length principle set out in the OECD model double taxation convention even when there is no treaty governing the position. The decision in the case of *Pommery and Greno v Apthorpe* (2 TC 189) is cited as support for this view in the *Tax Bulletin* article of 18 August 1995, which was agreed with members of the Self Assessment Consultative Committee.

A branch or agent in the United Kingdom through which a non-resident carries on, whether solely or in partnership, any trade, profession or vocation, is made the non-resident's UK representative for income and corporation tax purposes in relation to:

(1) the income from the trade, profession or vocation arising directly or indirectly from the branch or agency;

(2) income from property or rights such as patents copyright, etc which are used by or held by the branch or agency; and

(3) capital gains on assets situated in the United Kingdom used for the purpose of a trade, profession or vocation or by the branch or agency within the Taxation of Chargeable Gains Act 1992 (TCGA 1992), s 10.

The non-resident's UK representative remains the representative for the income or capital gains which he has received even though he ceases to be the branch or agent and is treated as a separate and distinct person from the non-resident, which allows notices to be served on him and tax collected from him, etc.

Where the non-resident is carrying on the trade or profession through a branch or agency in the United Kingdom as a partner in a partnership, the trade or profession carried on through the branch or agency includes the deemed trade or profession arising from the non-resident's share in the partnership under TA 1988, ss 111–114.

Where the non-resident is carrying on a trade in the United Kingdom through a partnership where there is a UK resident partner, the changes brought about by the self-assessment regime ensure that a non-resident partner is taxed only on his share of profits earned in the United Kingdom. UK resident partners remain liable in respect of worldwide profits. The partnership is treated as a 'branch or agent' of the non-resident partner so as to make UK resident partners jointly liable in the event of difficulties arising over collection (FA 1995, s 126(7)). This has the effect of retaining the liability of UK resident partners for the tax liabilities of non-resident partners, even though the joint liability no longer applies under self-assessment for a UK resident partner in respect of the tax liabilities of his partners, in view of TA 1988, s 111.

5.10 ROYALTIES AND PATENTS

Copyright royalties paid to a person whose usual place of abode is outside the United Kingdom and UK patent royalties paid to non-residents normally have income tax deducted at source by the payer (see, however, Chapter 11). The payer is assessable even if he fails to deduct the tax. The sale of a patent in the United Kingdom by a non-resident vendor involves the deduction of basic rate tax by the purchaser from the consideration paid, under TA 1988, s 524(3).

Where copyright royalties are paid through a third party that party may be liable on the net sum, ie the royalty less commission, TA 1988, s 536(3), (4). Royalties paid to an author resident outside the United Kingdom are not subject to withholding tax, *Hansard* 10 November 1969, Vol 791, col 31.

5.11 MAINTENANCE PAYMENTS

Maintenance payments under a pre-15 March 1988 UK court order were, until 5 April 1989, paid subject to deduction of tax at source unless within the small payment limits of TA 1988, s 351.

For payments after 5 April 1989 and before 6 April 2000 under pre-15 March 1988 arrangements:

(1) the payer gets tax relief on payments up to the level for which he got relief for 1988/89; and
(2) an amount equal to that received in 1988/89 is treated as part of the recipient's total income;
(3) however, an amount which historically has been equivalent to the married couples' allowance (for the relevant year of assessment) is exempt from tax in the recipient's hands (FA 1988, s 38).

All payments of maintenance are paid gross – without tax deducted by the payer.

Payers under the old rules may have switched to the rules mentioned below. These rules applied to the recipient as well. An election, which applied for a whole tax year, could be made at any time during the year and up to 12 months after (FA 1988, s 39). An election was beneficial if payments increased, and the limit for relief 'pegged' at the 1988/89 level was below the maximum amount of relief available under the new rules.

For court orders and maintenance agreements made on or after 15 March 1988 the rules, up to 1999/00, are:

(1) the recipient is not liable to tax on any payments received;
(2) where one divorced or separated spouse is required to make payments to the other, the payer qualifies for tax relief (20 per cent for 1994/95 and 15 per cent for 1995/96 to 1998/99 inclusive and further reduced to 10 per cent thereafter) for payments up to a limit equal to the amount of the married couples' tax allowance until the recipient remarries;
(3) there is no tax relief for other new maintenance or alimony payments; and
(4) payments are made gross (ie without deduction of tax).

From 6 April 2000 the 10 per cent relief for maintenance payments is abolished unless one of the partners is aged 65 or over on 5 April 2000, in which case the 10 per cent relief on £1,970 continues (FA 1999, s 36). Substantial maintenance payments made under pre-15 March 1988 agreements may need to be renegotiated.

The married couples allowance itself is terminated from 6 April 2000 and replaced by a children's tax credit from 6 April 2001 (FA 1999, s 30 and Sched 3).

5.12 TRUST AND ESTATE INCOME

Where the administration of an estate is completed after 5 April 1995, under TA 1988, s 695 as amended by FA 1995, Sched 18, any amount which remains payable to a beneficiary with a limited interest in the residue of the estate on completion, ie one who is entitled only to the income, is deemed for tax purposes to have been paid out as an income distribution in the year of assessment in which the administration period ends. Where the interest ceased, eg on the death of the beneficiary before the end of the administration, any final payment is deemed to be paid for the last year of assessment in which the limited interest existed, eg the year of the beneficiary's death.

Where a person is entitled to a limited interest in the residue of a deceased's estate he is taxed on the grossed-up equivalent of any actual payments made as income distributions in the administration period. The personal representatives should issue a form R185 to the beneficiaries in respect of income distributions. Each payment has to be grossed up for tax purposes at the applicable rate. From 6 April 1999 the gross-up will be at the basic, lower, or 'Schedule F' (dividend) rate as appropriate.

Where a taxpayer has an absolute interest in the residue of a deceased's estate, ie he is entitled to both the income and capital of the residue, he is, in the first instance, taxed on the grossed-up equivalent of amounts paid to him as income of the year of assessment in which it is paid.

In the case of trust income a life tenant of a UK trust would receive income subject to tax at the basic rate, whereas the beneficiary of a discretionary UK trust would receive his share of income less UK tax at the rate applicable to trusts, ie currently 34 per cent, under TA 1988, s 687. Again, any overpayment of UK tax may be recovered and any underpayment of higher rate liability remains payable.

By concession, a residuary legatee or legatee with a limited interest, who is not resident or not ordinarily resident in the United Kingdom, may claim to have his tax liability on estate income adjusted to what it would be if such income had accrued to him directly from the relevant sources. There are time limits for making such a claim (Inland Revenue Concession A14). Where the non-resident resides in a jurisdiction with which the United Kingdom has a double taxation treaty, the income may be covered under, for example, an 'other income' article, in which case a UK refund may be obtained if the conditions are met.

5.13 AVOIDANCE OF HIGHER RATE LIABILITY

Where UK investment income received before 5 April 1995 was sufficient, the non-resident could find that he had an individual liability to higher rate taxation in addition to any basic rate tax that may have been withheld at source. In many cases the tax charge could be limited to the basic rate by transferring investments to an overseas holding company in an appropriate tax haven. For example, if investments were held by an investment company in Jersey with directors in, say, Hong Kong, it would be an exempt company subject to a flat rate of tax of only £600. As a non-UK resident company, the liability to tax on its UK investment income would be limited under TA 1988, s 1 to basic rate only. As most UK investment income other than Schedule A income from property is now excluded income as explained at **5.3.1**, it is unlikely in most cases that such companies will be necessary for income tax purposes but they could still have advantages for IHT in the hands of a non-UK domiciled person as the shares would be non-UK property and excluded property.

Despite the attractions, expatriates considering this route should first indulge in some careful consideration. The costs involved in establishing and running an offshore company can be sizeable and nowadays the savings to be made are much less than in previous years, the maximum income tax saving is now 17 per cent. Transferring the ownership of assets into an offshore company can also be a costly business especially where there is stamp duty to be taken into account: share transfers are charged at $\frac{1}{2}$ per cent and conveyances of land and buildings are charged at between 1 and 4 per cent.

Where it is calculated that the tax saving is likely to outweigh the costs involved, there are still a couple of factors to be borne in mind before proceeding. First, in view of the anti-avoidance provisions of TA 1988, s 739 the offshore investment company route should only be considered by individuals not ordinarily resident in the United Kingdom and the company should be wound up before UK residence is resumed.

This means that the procedure is only suitable as a means of tax limitation for the long-term non-resident, who has or has acquired a non-UK domicile.

Secondly, care is required because, as in all tax matters, if there is a pre-ordained series of transactions and steps have been inserted which have no business purpose apart from avoidance of tax, the inserted steps may be ignored for tax purposes: see *Craven v White* [1988] STC 476.

5.14 LLOYD'S UNDERWRITERS

The taxation of Lloyd's Underwriters is a specialist subject and the comments here are confined to areas of particular interest to non-resident names.

Lloyd's income arises in the United Kingdom and is classified as a trade carried on in the United Kingdom subject to UK tax. It is normally desirable for Lloyd's deposits to be arranged by way of letter of credit or bank guarantee as, for example, exempt gilts held as part of Lloyd's deposits or reserves remain UK taxable as connected with a business carried on in the United Kingdom (*Owen v Sassoon* (1950) 32 TC 101) (apart from $3\frac{1}{2}$ per cent War Loan). The CGT and IHT exemptions, however, continue to apply.

The basis of assessment for Lloyd's investment income may not be followed by the overseas Revenue which might, for example, assess the investment income as it arises even though it is not distributed until the account is closed. United States tax paid which would be refunded to a UK resident is treated as an expense so far as a non-resident is concerned and merely reduces the gross income. Transfers to a special reserve fund would not normally have any effect for foreign tax purposes, although they would affect the UK tax payable and therefore the amount available for credit. Where the UK tax is fully relieved overseas there is no advantage in a transfer to the special reserve fund, although care has to be taken to ensure that foreign tax credits are not inadvertently lost.

There are special rules in certain countries for Lloyd's Names, in particular the United States and Canada.

5.15 NON-RESIDENT'S ENTITLEMENT TO UK PERSONAL ALLOWANCES

Certain classes of non-residents may obtain relief against UK assessable income through entitlement to the normal personal allowances under TA 1988, s 278.

The classes of individuals to which the relief applies include the following:

(1) Commonwealth citizens and citizens of the Republic of Ireland;
(2) for 1996/97 onwards, nationals of states within the European Economic Area (EEA);
(3) persons who are or who have been in the service of the Crown;
(4) missionaries;
(5) servants of British Protectorates;
(6) residents of the Isle of Man or Channel Islands;
(7) persons abroad for health reasons after residence in the United Kingdom;
(8) widows of Crown servants; and
(9) residents of countries where relief is given under a double taxation treaty.

This tax relief is useful where the non-resident has a significant income taxable in the United Kingdom. Where the UK income is small, it may not be worth the trouble of claiming on an annual basis but possibly every few years (the time limit for the claim is six years).

5.16 ENTERTAINERS AND SPORTSMEN

Any person who makes a payment for or in respect of the performance of a relevant activity performed in the United Kingdom by an entertainer or sportsman, who is not resident in the United Kingdom in the relevant tax year, is required to deduct and account to the Inland Revenue for income tax on the payment. A relevant activity is performed in the United Kingdom by the entertainer or sportsman in his character as such or in connection with a commercial occasion or event as defined. Royalties are not included as these are taxable as described in **5.10**.

Where a payment is made within these provisions, the relevant activity is treated as being performed in the course of a trade, profession or vocation exercised in the United Kingdom and chargeable to tax as such under Schedule D, Case I or II and the tax deducted and accounted for by the payer is treated as a payment on account of the final liability.

6

TAX ASPECTS OF UK PROPERTY

Expatriates often retain property in the United Kingdom which is let during the period of absence overseas. The retention of such property ensures that the expatriate has a place to live in the United Kingdom on the completion of his overseas work, and may be a protection against rises in house prices during the period of absence.

Before entering into letting arrangements, the expatriate needs to give careful consideration to the proposed tenancy arrangements, with particular attention being given to rights of possession. Standard tenancy arrangements may create difficulties at a future date, and consequently advice should be sought from experienced professional advisers in relation to UK landlord and tenant law.

6.1 RENTAL INCOME

Taxation matters in connection with lettings also need careful review. Income from UK property, being income arising from a source in the United Kingdom, is chargeable to UK tax at lower, basic and, where applicable, higher rates. For fiscal years up to and including 1994/95 assessment to tax was under either Schedule A (Unfurnished Lettings) or Schedule D, Case VI (Furnished Lettings). With effect from 6 April 1995, all income from property (furnished or unfurnished) is pooled and taxed as Schedule A. Expatriates resident in a country which has a double tax treaty with the United Kingdom will find that it is normally the case that the treaty provides for rental income to be taxed by the country in which the property is situated.

For 1996–97 and subsequent years, if a landlord is non-resident, tax must be deducted at source from rental payments either by the rental collection agent or, if there is no agent, by the tenant, although the landlord may be eligible to apply for gross payments to be made under the non-resident landlords' scheme (see **6.3**). If the Inland Revenue authorise gross payments, the non-resident landlord must undertake to self-assess the liability on a timely basis.

A statement of rental income and expenditure will need to be prepared. Tax agents should liaise closely with letting agents. The rental income statement should be prepared in accordance with normal commercial accounting practice, matching income with expenditure in the chargeable period, and making provision for accruals and prepayments. By concession (see Inland Revenue booklet IR 150, paras 90–92) a cash basis may be used where gross annual receipts do not exceed £15,000. The cash basis must be used consistently and the result must be reasonable and must not differ substantially from the strict earnings basis.

Expenses associated with letting may include:

(1) water rates;

(2) agents' commission or other costs of rent collection;

(3) building and contents insurance, and valuation fees for insurance purposes;

(4) service charges and ground rent;

(5) repairs and maintenance (but not capital expenditure, eg central heating/double glazing installation);

(6) professional charges for preparing the letting statement;

(7) advertising;

(8) Extra-Statutory Concession (ESC) B47 provides for a wear and tear allowance (for furnished residential lettings only – being 10 per cent of gross rent receivable less council tax or water rates paid by the landlord. Alternatively a renewals allowance can be claimed for the net cost of replacing a particular item but not the cost of the original purchase. Whichever basis is adopted, it should be applied consistently;

(9) cleaning;

(10) garden upkeep;

(11) expenditure incurred for the benefit of tenants on private roads, common parts, etc;

(12) capital allowances in respect of certain eligible plant or machinery (but note that relief is not given for plant let for use in a dwelling house – Capital Allowances Act 1990, s 61(2));

(13) inventory check-in/check-out costs;

(14) tenancy agreement charges;

(15) interest (see **6.2**).

Additionally, personal allowances should be specifically claimed when available (see **5.15**). Losses incurred in a fiscal year are available to be carried forward to be set off against future income from property. On the cessation of the letting activity, unused losses will not be available for future carry forward.

6.2 LOAN INTEREST

For fiscal years 1995/96 onwards loan interest payable is an allowable expense in arriving at net rental income. Any payment of loan interest is capable of qualifying for tax relief, whether taken from a bank or individual in the United Kingdom or elsewhere, provided the loan was advanced to purchase the land or property or to fund repairs, improvements or alterations to the UK property.

For loans taken from an overseas lender, care needs to be taken in relation to the legislation covering withholding of tax at source from interest payments. The relevant provisions state that interest paid on a UK-source loan to a person whose place of abode is outside the United Kingdom must be under deduction of income tax. However, certain double tax treaties provide exemption from this rule.

In November 1993 the Inland Revenue published in their *Tax Bulletin* the following factors which they regard as most important in determining the source of a loan:

(1) the residence of the debtor, ie the place in which the debt will be enforced;
(2) the source from which the interest is paid;
(3) where the interest is paid; and
(4) the nature and location of the security for the debt.

If all of these are located in the United Kingdom, then it is likely that the interest will have a UK source. In addition, the Inland Revenue have commented that the precise tax treatment in each case will depend on 'all the factors and on exactly how the transactions are in fact carried out'.

The United Kingdom also has an anti-avoidance rule which disallows interest relief if at any time a scheme has been effected or arrangements made, such that the sole or main benefit expected to accrue was a reduction in tax liability by means of the relief (Income and Corporation Taxes Act 1988 (TA 1988), s 787). The Inland Revenue do not normally seek to apply this rule when interest is paid at a commercial rate on a mortgage.

6.3 ADMINISTRATION AND COLLECTION OF TAX

This is a complex area which can create a great deal of confusion for the expatriate. Where rents are paid direct by the tenant to the expatriate whose usual place of abode is outside the United Kingdom, then basic rate tax must be deducted from gross rents and paid to the Inland

Revenue by the tenant (TA 1988, s 42A). Payment of rent into a UK bank account held by the expatriate does not avoid the obligation of the tenant to deduct tax at source. It is important to note that, even if basic rate tax has been deducted by the tenant in these circumstances, it is still necessary to provide the Inland Revenue with a statement of rental income for each tax year, by way of a self-assessment tax return, in order that the correct income tax liability can be calculated. The expatriate will usually be keen to do this as it will be the only way to recover excess tax deductions and obtain relief for expenses. There is an exemption for tenants who pay less than £100 per week in rent, although the Inland Revenue may in certain circumstances still ask them to deduct tax.

Letting agents and tenants required to operate the non-resident landlords' scheme must pay tax at the basic rate to the Inland Revenue each quarter. This is calculated on a non-resident landlord's rental income less known allowable expenses and deductions. The non-resident must be given an annual certificate showing details of the tax deducted. The tax shown on the certificate may be set off against the final liability arising on the landlord's self-assessment.

Applications for rents to be received gross may be filed under the non-resident landlords' scheme provided that:

(1) the landlord's tax affairs are all up to date; or
(2) the landlord has never previously had any obligation in relation to UK tax; or
(3) the landlord does not expect to be liable for UK tax; and
(4) the landlord also undertakes to comply with any UK tax obligations in the future.

If approval is withheld or withdrawn there will usually be an obvious reason, but there is an appeal procedure if this is not the case.

The regulations, which are contained in SI 1995 No 2902, list the information requirements and penalties for non-compliance.

Inland Revenue booklet IR 140 'Non-resident landlords, their agents and tenants' sets out the details. Further guidance and assistance can be obtained from FICO Non-resident Landlords at St John's House, Merton Road, Bootle, Merseyside L69 9BB (tel: 0151-472 6000).

6.4 BEFORE SELF-ASSESSMENT

For years up to and including 1995/96 tax on lettings income was normally payable on 1 January in the year of assessment, and the tax was collected by assessment. Initially an assessment was based on the previous year's net income and this would be revised when an income and expenditure statement had been submitted and agreed with the Inland Revenue. Interest would begin to accrue on any unpaid balance of tax from 1 July following the year of assessment, although interest on an overpayment would not begin to accrue until the following 5 April. In this respect, the cash flow of the landlord who is registered under the non-resident landlords' scheme is better under self-assessment and the interest position is certainly fairer.

Moreover, the previous system under which agents and tenants were obliged to deduct tax from rents is now clearer, and before April 1996 there was no mechanism for gross payments, which often caused great problems for tenants who might well have been making payments in blissful ignorance of the rules. The Inland Revenue had the right to assess them notwithstanding that they might have paid gross rents to their landlord. All in all the current system is definitely an improvement.

6.5 FURNISHED HOLIDAY LETTINGS

Letting furnished property in the United Kingdom as holiday accommodation within the terms of the legislation may secure a beneficial tax treatment of expatriates with other UK-source income. Furnished holiday lettings are treated in the same way as a trade if the following conditions are met:

(1) the accommodation must be in the United Kingdom and let furnished on a commercial basis with a reasonable expectation of making a profit;
(2) it must be available for letting to the public at large for at least 140 days in any tax year;
(3) actual lettings must be at least 70 days in the tax year (although in the first and last years in which the trade is carried on the rules are modified);
(4) in a seven-month period, including the months that the property is let, no single let should normally be longer than 31 days.

The main income tax benefit to derive from the treatment of the activity as a trade is the ability to relieve losses against other UK income. There is no change to the administration and collection of income tax as described above. For capital gains tax (CGT) purposes expatriates may, in certain circumstances, and especially if a spouse remains resident and has an interest in the property, derive a benefit from the availability of roll-over relief and retirement relief relating to business assets. (Retirement relief is, however, being phased out over the fiscal years 1999/00–2002/03.)

6.6 MORTGAGE INTEREST RELIEF AT SOURCE (MIRAS)

MIRAS was introduced in April 1983, enabling UK interest payments to be made net of income tax relief to qualifying lenders. The loan on which interest payments arise must have been taken out for the purchase (or improvement, before 6 April 1988) of a property in the United Kingdom which is used wholly or to a substantial extent as the only or main residence of the borrower, his spouse (or before April 1988 a dependent relative or a former or separated spouse). MIRAS applied only to the first £30,000 of a loan which satisfied these conditions, and expatriates were not, as a class, excluded from MIRAS relief. Tax relief was at the rate of 10 per cent for 1999/00 but was abolished with effect from 6 April 2000. In many cases the tax advantage to be gained from deducting interest against rental income was greater than could be obtained under MIRAS, and the expatriate had to choose which form of tax relief to take. MIRAS, however, was given regardless of whether the borrower would otherwise have any tax liability in the United Kingdom and was effectively a government-sponsored mortgage subsidy. Qualifying lenders included most UK building societies, banks, insurance companies and specialised mortgage funding schemes. (From 6 April this is only of academic interest.)

6.6.1 Expatriates who do not let their property while overseas

An expatriate working full-time overseas may be unable to satisfy the conditions that any UK property retained is used 'wholly or to a substantial extent' as his only or main residence. 'Substantial' is not defined in the tax legislation, but it is understood that the Inland Revenue regard this as six months or more in the year. If the expatriate's spouse and family continue to live in the UK property, then the conditions may be satisfied. Additionally, ESC A27 allows temporary absences of up to a year to be ignored in determining whether a property is used as an only or main residence. When the absence is for purposes of employment this period is extended to four years. For Crown servants the period of absence is without time limit.

MIRAS continued to apply to mortgage interest payments until 5 April 2000 in respect of a loan for the purchase of a property used as an only or main residence before working overseas, provided this property could reasonably be expected to be used again as such on the expatriate's return. Relief was not given beyond a period of four years, but if there was a further temporary absence after the property had been reoccupied for a minimum period of three months, the four-year test applied to the new absence without regard to the previous absence.

It should be noted that if arrangements are entered into to take advantage of a concession for tax-avoidance purposes, it is likely that the Inland Revenue will deny the application of the concession (*R v IRC, ex p Fulford Dobson* [1987] STC 344). A warning is contained in Inland Revenue booklet IR 1.

If an expatriate on an overseas tour of duty purchased a property in the United Kingdom in the course of a leave period, and used that property as an only or main residence for a period of not less than three months before his return to the place of his overseas employment, he would be regarded as satisfying the condition that the property was being used as his only or main residence before he went away, and MIRAS would have been applied until its abolition with effect from 6 April 2000.

6.6.2 Expatriates who let their property while overseas

Where a loan was within MIRAS, interest relief against rental income could only be claimed if the taxpayer gave the appropriate notice under TA 1988, s 375A. The notice must be given to the Inland Revenue within 22 months of the end of the year of assessment in which the notice is to take effect. If the notice under TA 1988, s 375A covered a tax year in which MIRAS relief was given at source, the Inland Revenue would recover the MIRAS relief by raising an assessment. Interestingly both the notice under TA 1988, s 375A and the clawback of MIRAS relief fall outside the self-assessment provisions, although the notice could be given in the additional information box (white space) on the self-assessment return.

6.7 CAPITAL GAINS TAX

6.7.1 General principles

As a general rule, before 17 March 1998 the disposal of UK residential property by an expatriate during a tax year throughout which he was not resident and not ordinarily resident for UK tax purposes did not give rise to a charge to CGT.

FA 1998 introduced significant changes in the CGT regime for temporary non-residents (Taxation of Chargeable Gains Act 1992 (TCGA 1992), s 10A). Expatriates who were not resident and not ordinarily resident before 17 March 1998 are outside the scope of the new rules (but see below the changes to ESC D2 which affect all returning expatriates).

Expatriates who become not resident and not ordinarily resident on or after 17 March 1998 remain within the scope of UK CGT unless they are neither resident nor ordinarily resident for at least five complete tax years. By way of example, an expatriate leaving the United Kingdom on 31 December 1999 will only fall out of the UK CGT regime if he is neither resident nor ordinarily resident until 6 April 2005. If the expatriate is not resident for five full tax years then gains and losses accruing to him whilst overseas are treated as chargeable to CGT in the year of return.

The new rules do not apply to individuals unless they have been resident or ordinarily resident in the United Kingdom for some part of at least four out of seven tax years prior to the date of departure. Also, generally, gains or losses from assets acquired in the period of non-residence are not taxed in the year of return (but again regard must be had to ESC D2). The legislation excludes from the latter rule assets acquired from a person's spouse.

For the tax year of return to the United Kingdom all expatriates need to be aware of ESC D2 which was amended on 17 March 1998 and provides that:

> 'An individual who comes to live in the UK and is treated as resident here for any year of assessment from the date of arrival is charged to capital gains tax only in respect of chargeable gains from disposals made after arrival, provided that the individual has not been resident or ordinarily resident in the UK at any time during the five years of assessment immediately preceding the year of assessment in which he or she arrived in the UK.'

However, Extra-Statutory Concessions will not be given in any case where an attempt is made to use them for tax avoidance, and after the judgment in *R v IRC, ex p Fulford Dobson* [1987] STC 344, care should be taken in respect of any transaction involving a chargeable gain undertaken in the period from 6 April to the date of arrival in the United Kingdom. For expatriates who left the United Kingdom before 17 March 1998 and who will not meet the requirements of being not resident or not ordinarily resident for five complete tax years following the year of departure, it will usually be preferable to make disposals before 6 April preceding the return.

Clearly the legislation contained in TCGA 1992, s 10A must be carefully considered whenever expatriates are thinking of disposing of a UK residential property. The timing of the disposal may be critical.

6.7.2 Principal private residence

Expatriates who retain their home in the United Kingdom during their period of absence overseas should carefully consider the conditions to be satisfied after returning to the United Kingdom for exemption from CGT on a subsequent sale. These conditions are as follows:

(1) The property must be the individual's only or main residence throughout the period of ownership except for all or any part of the last 36 months of ownership. This period could very easily be reduced by the government if they are so inclined. If the property has been an only or main residence for part of the period of ownership the gain is apportioned between the exempt and non-exempt periods.

(2) The exemption applies to dwelling houses and land comprising garden and ground which are for the occupation and enjoyment of the main residence up to the permitted area. The permitted area is defined as 0.5 of a hectare, being approximately 1.25 acres (inclusive of the site of the dwelling house), although in any particular case the permitted area may be a larger area as the 'Commissioners may determine, if satisfied that, regard being had to the size and the character of the dwelling house, that larger area is required for the reasonable enjoyment of it as a residence'. (TCGA 1992, s 222 (3).)

(3) Certain periods of absence from the dwelling are treated as periods of residence provided the dwelling house was the only property eligible for relief and was occupied as such both before *and after* the periods of absence. These periods which can be used on a cumulative basis are:

  (a) any period or periods of absence which do not in total exceed three years; and

  (b) any period of absence throughout which the individual worked in an employment or office all the duties of which were performed outside the United Kingdom; and

  (c) any period or periods of absence not exceeding four years in total throughout which the individual was prevented from residing in the dwelling house in consequence of the situation of his place of work or because his employer required him to live elsewhere so that his duties of employment could be effectively carried out.

Working expatriates need to pay close attention to condition (b). It is clear that all duties of employment must be performed outside the United Kingdom. This is in contrast to income tax rules where incidental duties performed in the United Kingdom may be disregarded under the provisions of TA 1988, s 335. The performance of such incidental UK duties could inadvertently jeopardise the CGT relief. The condition is also framed in terms of employment or office and does not cover self-employment.

The requirements as to occupation of the property both before and after the period of absence are of considerable significance. If the expatriate returns to the United Kingdom and does not occupy his former main residence because he owns another property, then a chargeable gain may arise on disposal. ESC D4 provides assistance to the expatriate where he is unable to resume residence in his previous home because the terms of his employment require him to work elsewhere.

The concession deems the condition of reoccupation after the period of absence to be satisfied.

Where an expatriate has sold his UK home during his overseas absence, consideration needs to be given to whether any disclosure of the disposal will need to be made in the tax year of return following the changes in legislation from 17 March 1998 (see **6.7.1**). If the expatriate has purchased another property which is to be occupied on his return to the United Kingdom, the gain attributable to the period of time from purchase to actual occupation may be chargeable to CGT on disposal. This arises if the property has not been occupied as the main or only residence on purchase, even though it replaces a former main residence occupied as such, before leaving the United Kingdom. Such transactions can present an unfortunate tax pitfall for the expatriate, although the legislation contains specific relief for expatriates who live in job-related accommodation overseas. This is defined as where it is necessary for the proper performance of the duties of the employment that the employee should reside in that accommodation.

Another point to consider carefully is that for the principal private residence exemption to apply, the expatriate must have no other property available as a main residence throughout the period of absence. This creates a difficulty, as the expatriate will usually have an overseas residence – whether owned or rented. In these circumstances the expatriate should consider submitting to the Inland Revenue an election under TCGA 1992, s 222(5) that the UK property is the expatriate's only or main residence to satisfy the statutory requirements. There is a two-year time limit from acquisition of the interest in the additional property to make the election.

If part of the gain on a principal private residence is in charge to CGT and the property has been wholly or partly let as residential accommodation during the period of ownership a further relief is available. The relief is the lesser of £40,000 and the gain otherwise exempt under the general rules referred to above (TCGA 1992, s 223(4)). For a working expatriate, this relief is unlikely to be relevant unless the overseas assignment exceeds four years and there are duties in the United Kingdom. See also **7.5** regarding homes acquired partly for the purpose of realising a gain on disposal.

6.8 INHERITANCE TAX

Non-resident, UK domiciled individuals remain liable to inheritance tax (IHT) on their worldwide estate. A UK will should specifically cover the disposition of all UK properties. Where a UK domiciled person is married to a non-UK domiciled person, property transactions can be structured to minimise the exposure to IHT. Professional advice should be sought at the time the property is acquired, particularly if an offshore company or trust is being considered. Additionally, the relevant tax and legal issues should be reconsidered on a regular basis in the light of changes in legislation.

6.9 STAMP DUTY

Stamp duty is a significant cost for the purchaser of UK property. Successive Finance Acts have seen increases in the rate of stamp duty levied on UK land transactions. The rates from 28 March 2000 are:

Under £60,000	Nil
£60,001 to £250,000	1%
£250,001 to £500,000	3%
Over £500,000	4%

6.10 VALUE ADDED TAX

The standard rate of value added tax (VAT) has been 17½ per cent for many years. There is no VAT levied on the acquisition of a newly built or second-hand residential building in the United Kingdom. VAT at the standard rate is generally charged on all improvement work (including new extensions), repairs and maintenance carried out at the property. VAT is normally charged at the standard rate on the purchase of equipment (eg ovens, fridges), furniture, carpets and other items which are bought for residential property. Professional services of letting agents, surveyors, lawyers, etc will generally be subject to VAT at the standard rate as their services relate directly to UK land. 'Approved alterations' in listed residential buildings may be zero rated for VAT purposes. In this situation builders' costs need to be carefully apportioned to the approved alteration and the builder needs to be advised of the position. Advance consideration of the potential VAT savings for listed residential buildings is recommended to secure the optimum position.

For expatriates acquiring, renting or disposing of commercial property, either individually or through a company, careful consideration should always be given at an early stage to the VAT implications of the transaction.

7

CAPITAL GAINS TAX

7.1 RESIDENCE

The Taxation of Chargeable Gains Act 1992 (TCGA 1992), s 2 provides that an individual resident or ordinarily resident in the United Kingdom is subject to capital gains tax (CGT) on his worldwide capital gains. In order, therefore, to avoid UK CGT it is essential to cease to be ordinarily resident in the United Kingdom. This normally requires three complete tax years of non-residence or, when the individual concerned is in full-time employment overseas, one complete tax year of non-residence. Even if non-resident and non-ordinarily resident status is achieved, the provisions of TCGA 1992, s 10A will have to be considered if the departure from the United Kingdom was on or after 17 March 1998. This new charge, applying to 'temporary non-residents' is often referred to as the 're-entry charge'.

7.1.1 Re-entry charge for temporary non-residents

Gains realised by a non-resident may be treated as accruing to the taxpayer in the year of return to the United Kingdom if:

(1) he is resident or ordinarily resident in the United Kingdom during any part of a year of assessment (the year of return);
(2) he was not resident or ordinarily resident for one or more years of assessment immediately preceding the year of return but he had been resident or ordinarily resident previously;
(3) there are fewer than five years of assessment falling between the year of departure and the year of return; and
(4) he was resident or ordinarily resident during any part of four out of the seven years of assessment immediately preceding the year of departure.

All chargeable gains (and losses) which would otherwise have been exempt in an intervening year of non-residence, plus any gains deemed to have accrued in that period under TCGA 1992, s 13 or s 86, less any losses which would have been allowable under TCGA 1992, s 13(8) are treated as gains or losses accruing in the year of return.

In considering whether or not the re-entry charge applies, someone who arrived in the United Kingdom on 4 April 2000 would have to count 1999/00 as a year in which the residence test in s 10A is satisfied, as would someone departing from the United Kingdom on 7 April 1999. There are also some important exclusions from the re-entry charge, including gains in respect of assets acquired in the year of departure or in one of the intervening years of non-residence.

Therefore there may be some scope for planning by individuals who will realise large gains during a period of temporary non-residence but the asset stands at a relatively small gain at the time of leaving the United Kingdom. If these circumstances arose, an individual might make a disposal in the year of departure and subsequently reacquire the asset. This is subject to anti-avoidance case law and also to the rules relating to the bed and breakfasting of shareholdings.

Furthermore, the re-entry charge does not apply in a case in which a capital gain in a period of non-residence has the protection of a CGT article in a double taxation treaty between the United Kingdom and the relevant jurisdiction.

7.1.2 Years of arrival and departure

Prior to 17 March 1998, Inland Revenue Extra-Statutory Concession ESC D2 applied to exempt gains realised in the period following departure from the United Kingdom to establish non-resident status and also gains in the period prior to the date of return following a period of non-residence. This concession was not available if the Inland Revenue considered that it was being claimed for tax avoidance purposes (see *R v HMIT, ex p Fulford-Dobson* (1987) 60 TC 168, as described in **7.2**).

From 17 March 1998, ESC D2 is revised so that the gains from disposals between 6 April and the date of arrival are not charged only if the individual has not been resident or ordinarily resident at any time during the five preceding years of assessment. This ties in with the test applied for the re-entry charge.

Similarly, an individual who leaves the United Kingdom on or after 17 March 1998 is treated as not resident or ordinarily resident and not charged tax on gains from disposals made after the date of departure provided that he was not resident and not ordinarily resident for the whole of at least four out of the seven years of assessment immediately preceding the year of departure.

The concession does not apply to gains on the disposal of assets situated in the United Kingdom and which are used in or for the purposes of a trade, profession or vocation carried on by the taxpayer in the United Kingdom through a branch or agency. Neither does it apply to a settlor of a settlement in relation to gains which may be visited upon him under TCGA 1992, ss 77–79 or s 86, Sched 5.

7.2 HUSBAND AND WIFE

The residence statuses of a husband and wife are determined independently. Despite this, the CGT exemption for assets transferred between spouses married and living together is none the less preserved. In *Gubay v Kington* [1984] STC 499, it was held that the transfer of a chargeable asset by a UK resident spouse to a non-resident spouse was not a chargeable event. The scope for transferring an asset from a resident to a non-ordinarily resident spouse before sale to avoid CGT may be limited as was illustrated in *R v IRC, ex p Fulford Dobson* [1987] STC 344. In this case a wife transferred a farm to her husband who went to work in Germany and the farm was sold four days after his departure. The Revenue's refusal to apply ESC D2, because an attempt had been made to use it for tax avoidance, was upheld.

7.3 EMIGRATION

A person emigrating from the United Kingdom or leaving for at least five full tax years would normally leave the disposal of his assets showing capital gains until after his departure (taking due account of his liability in the new jurisdiction). The disposal should be deferred until after the following 5 April in case the Revenue refuse to apply ESC D2, even if the concession could still apply using the test of previous residence mentioned at **7.1.2**. However, investments showing losses would normally be sold before the date of departure in order to crystallise a loss which might be of use on any future return to the United Kingdom.

If the assets in question are used in, or in connection with, a business, there are further important considerations. See **7.6**.

It should be noted that there are occasions on which emigration can crystallise CGT problems notwithstanding that there is no actual asset disposal. This may occur when the asset has been acquired by the emigrant by way of a gift which was the subject of a hold-over relief claim (eg under TCGA 1992, s 165), or in connection with shares that had been the subject of Enterprise Investment Scheme (EIS), or reinvestment relief claims (see

7.7), or possibly where there has been a company sale, corporate reorganisation or similar and shares or other corporate paper, such as loan notes, have been acquired in exchange for shares. The last circumstance in particular requires professional advice (see also **7.6**).

7.4 INDEXATION AND TAPER RELIEF

Capital gains are calculated by deducting a base cost or base value from disposal proceeds, whether actual or notional, in relation to a transaction. Base values were subject to an indexation allowance calculated by reference to the Retail Price Index for the period from March 1982 to April 1998. The indexation allowance can reduce or eliminate a gain but from 30 November 1998 it cannot create or augment a loss. Indexation no longer accrues for individuals after 6 April 1998, although companies remain eligible for indexation. Thus there may, exceptionally, be cases in which it is desirable to hold assets with a large base cost or base value in a company in order to benefit from this ongoing relief. The indexation allowance for individuals is effectively frozen at 6 April 1998 – it has no application in relation to acquisitions thereafter.

For individuals, indexation was replaced by tapering relief for 1998/99 and subsequent years (TCGA 1992, Sched A1, inserted by FA 1998, s 121(2), Sched 20). This relief reduces chargeable gains according to the length of time for which the asset has been held, commencing at 6 April 1998. The reduction for business assets for 1998/99 is 7½ per cent of the gain for each of the first ten whole years in a qualifying period, up to a maximum of 75 per cent of the gain. For non-business assets there is no reduction until the asset has been held for three whole years including the period from 17 March 1998 to 5 April 1999 as a whole year for assets held on 17 March, known as 'bonus years'. Then the reduction is 5 per cent for each whole year, up to a maximum of 40 per cent of the gain. For 1999/2000 onwards, taper relief for business assets is 12.5% for each of the first two whole years of ownership, and 25% for each of the next two, without any bonus year. Business assets, from 6 April 2000, include all shares and securities in unlisted trading assets, shares held by employees or directors of listed trading companies, or by holders of at least 5% of the votes. For assets acquired before 6 April 1998, it is the indexed gain that is tapered. Losses are set against indexed gains before applying taper relief to the net gain. This might be considered to have the effect of tapering losses. Unlike retirement relief or indexation, taper relief can never completely extinguish a gain. Taper relief is going to be of increasing importance in CGT planning with the passage of time as Table 7.1 demonstrates. A key point in capital taxation strategy is how to preserve entitlement to taper – particularly in respect of business assets.

Table 7.1

Gains on disposal of business assets

No of whole years in qualifying holding period	Percentage reduction	Percentage of gain chargeable	Percentage effective maximum tax rate (2000/01)
1	12½	87½	35
2	25	75	30
3	50	50	20
4 or more	75	25	10

Gains on disposal of non-business assets

No of whole years in qualifying holding period*	Percentage reduction	Percentage of gain chargeable	Percentage effective maximum tax rate (2000/01)
1	–	–	40
2	–	–	40
3	5	95	38
4	10	90	36
5	15	85	34
6	20	80	32
7	25	75	30
8	30	70	28
9	35	65	26
10 or more	40	60	24

*Note bonus year for assets held on 17 March 1998.

7.5 PROPERTY

Although non-residents may be exempt from CGT in respect of a disposal of most investments, it is necessary to look rather more carefully in the case of land and buildings. The Income and Corporation Taxes Act 1988 (TA 1988), s 766, provides that a capital profit from dealing or developing land directly or indirectly may be assessed to tax under Schedule D, Case VI as UK income irrespective of the residence of the owner. TA 1988, s 777(9) enables the Board to direct that basic rate income tax may be withheld from the sale proceeds, although in practice this has proved ineffective in many cases, as the Revenue have not been aware of the disposal until too late to raise the necessary direction and the non-resident has received the sale proceeds gross. Section 776 does not apply to private residences exempt from CGT as a main residence, although it should be noted that the main residence exemption cannot be relied upon if the acquisition of the house in question was made wholly or partly for the purpose of realising a gain from the disposal of it (TCGA 1992, s 224(3)).

This avoidance has far-reaching effects and applies whenever there has been an acquisition of land with the sole or main object of realising a gain from its disposal, or land is held as trading stock, or land is developed with the sole or main object of realising a gain from its disposal. In particular it applies to multiple transactions and to schemes and arrangements, and the courts have held that assessments can be raised on persons who were not necessarily party to the scheme.

Whenever there is development or improvement of land in the United Kingdom and a non-resident vendor seeks to realise a tax-free profit, TA 1988, s 776 should be considered with the benefit of professional advice.

7.6 BUSINESS GAINS

7.6.1 Sale of a business

A not uncommon spur to emigration occurs where a person resident or ordinarily resident in the United Kingdom is intending to dispose of his business, consisting either of shares in a company or the goodwill of an unincorporated business. This gives rise to a number of problems. Although under ESC D2 a person emigrating from the United Kingdom may usually, if he so qualifies, be regarded as neither resident nor ordinarily resident from the day following the day of departure this is a purely concessional treatment as, at law, a person resident for part of the tax year is resident for the entire tax year. The Revenue may refuse to apply the concession where the sums involved are substantial, so the contract for the disposal of the shares or business should be deferred until after the following 5 April. Even then the problems are not necessarily over as the Revenue or the courts might infer a prior oral contract, or prior agreement sufficient to constitute a contract, where all the terms and conditions of the sale were finalised before final sale. In this connection there is precedent for holding that correspondence between the parties before the final contract can create a binding contract (*J H & S Timber Ltd v Quirk* [1973] STC 111) and that the beneficial ownership can pass before any transfer of legal title (*Ayerst v C & K (Construction) Ltd* [1975] STC 345, *Wood Preservation Ltd v Prior* (1968) 45 TC 112). Gains in the year of departure would also be outside

ESC D2 if the business was carried on in the United Kingdom through a branch or agency.

TCGA 1992, s 28 states that the date of disposal for CGT is the time the contract was made, and if the contract is conditional it is the time when the condition is satisfied. It would, however, be hazardous to enter into arrangements designed specifically to postpone the date of disposal in order to allow time for emigration, as this might give rise to a series of transactions or a single composite transaction, the effect of which can be considered together and might result in a date of disposal before emigration (*Furniss v Dawson* [1984] STC 153). In particular Lord Bridge's comments in this case are of interest.

> 'When one moves however from a single transaction to a series of interdependent transactions designed to produce a given result it is, in my opinion, perfectly legitimate to draw a distinction between the substance and the form of the composite transaction without in any way suggesting that any of the single transactions which make up the whole are other than genuine. This has been the approach of the United States Federal Courts enabling them to develop a doctrine whereby the tax consequences of the composite transactions are dependent on its substance and not its form. I shall not attempt to review the American authorities nor do I propose a wholesale importation of the American doctrine in all its ramifications into English law. But I do suggest that the distinction between form and substance is one which can usefully be drawn in determining the tax consequences of composite transactions and one which will help to free the Courts from the shackles which have for so long been thought to be imposed on them by the Westminster case.'

The *Westminster* case held that the form of a transaction takes precedence over its substance in taxation matters (*IRC v Duke of Westminster* (1936) 19 TC 490): this applies only in the absence of a pre-ordained series of transactions or one single composite transaction. Recent decisions in the courts have cast considerable doubt on the reliability of that case as a precedent and there must also be some doubt as to whether the present day House of Lords would come to precisely the same conclusion!

This warning having been given, it is obviously possible to enter into negotiations before leaving the United Kingdom which do not amount to a contract to dispose of the shares or business and to conclude these arrangements by a contract for sale after having become neither resident nor ordinarily resident in the United Kingdom. As has been explained earlier, to acquire non-ordinary residence will normally require a period of absence from the United Kingdom of at least three complete tax years. Moreover, the re-entry charge may require absence for two further completed tax years. However, Inland Revenue booklet IR 20, paras 2.2 to 2.4 confirms that a full-time employment, or working full-time in a trade, profession or vocation, outside the United Kingdom for a period including a complete tax year results in an individual being treated as not resident and not ordinarily resident for that year. In a letter dated 10 July 1979, quoted in *Butterworth's Yellow Tax Handbook*, the Inland Revenue stated:

> 'I can confirm that where an employee left the UK on 4 April 1979 and did not return until 6 April 1980 and was on a full-time service contract throughout that period he would be regarded as not resident and not ordinarily resident in the UK throughout the year 1979/80.'

This practice is now encapsulated in IR 20 (1999), para 2.2. The meaning of full time is explained in para 2.5:

> 'There is no precise definition of when employment overseas is "full-time", and a decision in a particular case will depend on all the facts. Where your employment involves a standard pattern of hours, we will regard it as full time if the hours you work each week clearly compare with those in a typlcal UK working week. If your job has no formal structure or no fixed number of working days, we will look at the nature of the job, local conditions and practices in the particular occupation to decide if the job is full-time.

> If you have several part-time jobs overseas at the same time, we may be able to treat this as full-time employment. That might be so if, for example, you have several appointments with the same employer or group of companies, and perhaps also where you have simultaneous employment and self-employment overseas. But if you have a main employment abroad and some unconnected occupation in the UK at the same time, we will consider whether the extent of the UK activities was consistent with the overseas employment being full-time'

It is obviously dangerous to rely on a full-time service contract overseas unless this can be substantiated by the facts of the case. The Revenue will not be easily persuaded that a person who has emigrated on selling his business in the United Kingdom for several million pounds is likely to take full-time employment; and a lot more is required than a mere service contract with some offshore company ostensibly requiring full-time duties, usually of a somewhat indeterminate nature. In any event, the re-entry charge will greatly reduce the importance of this point in relation to CGT in the majority of cases, unless the year of employment is in a suitable treaty country such as Belgium.

It is no longer necessary, or indeed possible, to obtain a residence ruling under self-assessment. The taxpayer has to submit a self-assessment return claiming non-ordinary residence, which may be challenged by the Revenue through the normal enquiry procedure.

In the case of a disposal of an unincorporated business, as opposed to shares, it is important to remember that a business carried on by a non-resident through a branch or agency in the United Kingdom remains subject to UK CGT under TCGA 1992, s 10. It is therefore essential for the business to cease while the owner is still resident in the United Kingdom and for him then to depart and thereafter conclude the disposal of the business assets, including goodwill of the former business. This is not easy to do without having entered into a binding contract before leaving the United Kingdom despite what the paperwork may purport to provide. In such circumstances it might even be more practical to transfer the business into a company in exchange for shares and claim the roll-over under the provisions of TCGA 1992, s 162, then to emigrate, and then to sell the shares in the UK company. The transfer to the company should be done before entering into any negotiations with possible purchasers, otherwise this could be regarded as a series of transactions within the *Furniss v Dawson* principle. Alternatively, it might be possible to show that the purchasers required the protection of limited liability if this was the business purpose for the transfer of the business to a company. Either way, one needs to establish whether a purchaser would be prepared to acquire the business on similar terms if transferred to a company. In practice this may not necessarily be the case.

Rather than try to argue that the contract was actually entered into after leaving the United Kingdom it might well be preferable to give the intended purchaser an option enabling him to acquire the shares after the vendor has become non-resident (TCGA 1992, s 28(2)). The term 'conditional contract' refers in particular to a contract conditional on the exercise of an option and makes it clear that the date of the disposal is the date the option is *exercised*. It is tempting to consider entering into a put and call option, but the Revenue have argued strongly in the case of development land tax transactions that a put and call option is the equivalent of a contract for sale and that they are entitled to treat it as a disposal at the date the option was entered into. The Revenue are not necessarily correct but until the point is established in law it will be wise not to rely solely on this. In any case some purchasers, particularly public companies, may be unwilling to acquire options in these circumstances.

If it is not possible to postpone the date of the contract for disposal until the vendor has become non-resident it might be possible to take a large proportion of the proceeds in the form of loan stock. If it can be shown that there is a good commercial reason for the issue of loan stock a claim for roll-over relief on the disposal of the shares should be available under TCGA 1992, s 135, with clearance under s 138. If clearance is obtained it may be possible for the vendor to become non-resident and then dispose of the loan stock, thus crystallising the gain on the shares rolled into the loan stock.

The Inland Revenue specialists are now looking very carefully at these clearance applications, and are likely to refuse clearance if the vendor states any intention to emigrate. This does not necessarily mean that a tax liability is inevitable, but a refused clearance is the clearest possible signal that a tax assessment may follow. While individuals' intentions may change, it is clear that a tax clearance obtained without full disclosure of all relevant facts cannot be relied upon, and with the benefit of hindsight the Revenue will probably be sceptical about this. A vendor with loan stock may have to wait some considerable time before he can safely emigrate in these circumstances and alternative strategies might be considered.

In any event it would be unwise to arrange before departure from the United Kingdom for the loan stock immediately to be redeemed or placed with some financial institution, as the Revenue could then argue that the issue of the loan stock was merely an inserted step in what was in reality a sale for cash, again relying on *Furniss v Dawson*.

It should be noted that capital gains on Lloyd's investments as an underwriting name are basically subject to CGT as arising from a business carried on in the United Kingdom through an agent (TCGA 1992, s 10). However, syndicate investments which form part of the Lloyd's American Trust Fund and Lloyd's Canadian Trust Fund are regarded as not situated in the United Kingdom and non-UK securities in the Lloyd's sterling trust fund are also regarded as situated outside the United Kingdom. Exempt gilts held as part of a Lloyd's fund would retain their CGT exemption.

Where it is not possible to shelter a gain on going non-resident, retirement relief may be of assistance. This applies to a disposal of the whole or part of a business or shares in a personal trading company by someone reaching the age of 50 or retiring earlier on grounds of ill-health. As with so many tax reliefs, there are many detailed conditions to satisfy before relief is due and professional advice is to be recommended. The maximum retirement relief is exemption on the first £200,000 of chargeable gains and for half of the balance up to £600,000, for 1999/00. However, the relief is being phased out and these limits will reduce on a *pro rata* basis until 6 April 2003 as follows:

£150,000 and ½ × £450,000:	2000/01
£100,000 and ½ × £300,000:	2001/02
£50,000 and ½ × £150,000:	2002/03
(Nil from 6 April 2003)	

(TCGA 1992, ss 163, 164 and Sched 6; FA 1998, s 140(1)).

Therefore an individual who wishes to rely on retirement relief should consider accelerating rather than deferring the disposal date, perhaps by selling to an interest in possession trust. Unfortunately this has now become a complicated equation due to the introduction, in FA 1998, of taper relief (see **7.4**). As taper relief increases in value with the passing of each year of assessment whilst retirement relief does the opposite, a careful evaluation based on the precise facts of the case is necessary, and professional advice should be sought.

7.7 REINVESTMENT RELIEF

Prior to 6 April 1998, individuals and some trusts could postpone CGT on any asset (not just shares) to the extent that the gain was reinvested in qualifying unquoted shares, including Enterprise Investment Scheme shares, shares in some companies quoted on the Alternative Investment Market, and up to £100,000 per annum in Venture Capital Trusts. The provisions were complex and hedged about with many anti-avoidance provisions. Only the gain (and not the whole proceeds) needed to be reinvested, TCGA 1992, ss 164A–N.

The relief applied where the reinvestor made a disposal and acquired a qualifying investment within the qualifying period, ie a period beginning 12 months before the disposal and ending three years thereafter, subject to Inland Revenue discretion to extend this period.

The qualifying reinvestment had to be in ordinary shares, not within the business expansion scheme, in a qualifying unquoted company which carried on one or more qualifying trades or was a holding company of qualifying subsidiaries carrying on qualifying trades. Where the asset disposed of consisted of shares or securities in a company, the qualifying company could not be the same company or in the same group as that company. There was no requirement that the reinvestor was an officer or employee of the new company nor that the reinvestor held a minimum or maximum number of shares.

The reinvestment relief is clawed back if a triggering event occurs within the relevant three-year period after the acquisition of the eligible shares in the qualifying reinvestment company unless the shares have already been disposed of, or the disposal is to the reinvestor's spouse who takes over the reinvestor's position. A triggering event is the shares in the reinvestment company ceasing to be eligible or the company ceasing to be a qualifying company, or the reinvestor becoming non-resident other than on taking up a full-time employment lasting for less than three years, or if the shares are exchanged for qualifying corporate bonds under TCGA 1992, s 116. The gain will not crystallise on taking up an overseas employment as long as there is no disposal of the shares before re-establishing UK residence. Therefore the reinvestment relief could not be used to roll over a gain with a view to eliminating it by subsequently going non-resident within three years. However, subsequent emigration does not crystallise a charge. Gifts of business assets also qualify for roll-over relief under TCGA 1992, ss 165–169, but the relief is not available on a gift to a non-resident and the held-over gains would crystallise on the donee becoming non-resident within six years.

7.8 ENTERPRISE INVESTMENT SCHEME

General reinvestment investment relief was abolished from 6 April 1998 and, at the same time, restrictions attaching to EISs were relaxed – for the purposes of CGT reinvestment only. There is now a two-tier EIS with the conditions for income tax relief and ongoing CGT exemption not being the same as for CGT reinvestment relief. Many of the features of the old reinvestment relief scheme remain. There is still no limit to the amount of the gain that can be deferred. However, the EIS does contain a gross assets test that limits the amount that may be invested in any one EIS company or group. This test requires the assets of the EIS reinvestment company not to exceed £15 million immediately before the issue of the new EIS shares, nor £16 million immediately afterwards (FA 1998, ss 70–74, 141 and Sched 13.

7.9 FOREIGN TAXES

It is beyond the scope of this book to consider non-UK tax liabilities, but if a business or shares are sold after having left the United Kingdom the taxpayer may well have become resident in some other country which imposes a CGT charge or assesses capital gains as income. The general advice given with regard to UK CGT may be overruled if the effective rate of overseas tax on the chargeable gain would be greater.

Local advice should be taken before concluding the contract for disposal, as to whether there is a potential tax charge in the country of residence, and if so what, if anything, can be done about it.

7.10 TRUSTS

The UK resident and domiciled beneficiary of a non-resident trust is liable to CGT if the beneficiary is resident when the gain is distributed to him. If, however, the beneficiary is not domiciled in the United Kingdom, TCGA 1992, s 87(7) exempts him from a CGT charge. Prior to 17 March 1998, if the settlor was non-domiciled and remained so, UK resident beneficiaries could receive capital distributions from a non-resident trust free of CGT but this exemption was abolished by FA 1998, s 130. See also Chapter 9.

7.11 OFFSHORE FUNDS

Before 1984, it was possible for a UK resident to invest in certain offshore funds known as 'roll-up funds', where income to the funds was not distributed but accumulated tax free – when the investment was realised the accumulated profit, both gain and income, was subject to UK CGT only. Complicated rules were introduced to take effect from 1 January 1984 (FA 1984, ss 92–100, now incorporated into TA 1988, ss 757–764) which mean that a UK resident investor is now liable to tax on his entire gain in an offshore 'roll-up' fund as if it were income, under Schedule D, Case VI. If the investor is domiciled outside the United Kingdom the tax liability will only apply to any gain actually remitted to the United Kingdom.

In the case of a UK expatriate there will be no liability to UK tax on realisations of gain from a 'roll-up' fund, so long as he remains non-resident and non-ordinarily resident in the United Kingdom, but realisations of gain after he returns home will attract the full liability to UK income tax.

This future heavy exposure to UK taxation can be avoided by investing in offshore funds that have been granted 'distributor status'. The Finance Act 1984 (FA 1984) provided that where a fund meets certain rules – the most important is that the fund must distribute at least 85 per cent of the income received – the investor will be taxed on his income and gain in the normal way, ie Schedule D, Case VI in respect of the income distribution and CGT in respect of realised growth.

The Inland Revenue have attacked offshore roll-up funds which take the form of personal bonds, where the investor appoints the investment adviser, as a transfer of assets subject to tax on the income of the bond as it arises under TA 1988, s 739. In *IRC v Willoughby* [1995] STC 143 the Court of Appeal held that such bonds were not tax-avoidance devices and were protected by TA 1988, s 741. They also held that a transferor (investor) would only fall under TA 1988, s 739 if he were ordinarily resident in the United Kingdom at the time of the transfer. This residence condition has since been overruled by legislation in FA 1997. The Special Commissioner in this case held that a tax deferral was a tax advantage and it seems that TA 1988, s 740 could apply to assess benefits from investments to a UK resident even where the investment was made while abroad if the escape route for *bona fide* commercial transactions not designed to avoid tax in TA 1988, s 741 did not apply. The House of Lords upheld the decision of the Court of Appeal, and the published decision is important in the wider context of the s 739 anti-avoidance provisions and not just in relation to roll-up funds. In relation to personal portfolio bonds, the Revenue were quick to introduce additional rules to discourage their use by UK residents following the *Willoughby* case (see **5.5**).

7.12 GIFTS FROM NON-RESIDENTS

If an asset given by a non-resident to a UK resident is subsequently disposed of by the donee, the donee is treated as acquiring the asset at market value at the time of the gift, and is liable to CGT only on any excess over the acquisition value.

7.13 NON-STERLING BANK ACCOUNTS

Under TCGA 1992, s 275(1) a non-sterling bank account belonging to a non-UK domiciled individual is treated as located outside the United Kingdom and therefore exempt from CGT on currency movements unless the account is held at the UK branch of a bank and the individual is resident in the United Kingdom. This is not precisely the same for IHT purposes (see **8.14**(2)).

7.14 UK INVESTMENT MANAGERS

An investment manager in the United Kingdom whose normal business it is to buy, sell and manage investments on behalf of a non-resident with whom he is not connected is normally protected from a UK tax charge by the provisions of FA 1995, s 127. There are cases where the protection can be lost, such as if the transactions can be taxed as part of a wider trade (eg insurance) carried on in the United Kingdom through the same agency. The investment manager must be acting as an independent agent or as manager of a quoted collective investment fund such as a unit trust.

8

INHERITANCE TAX

As has already been seen, the non-resident expatriate can, to a very great extent, avoid any liability to UK income tax and long-term non-resident expatriates need pay no capital gains tax (CGT). The main determinant of liability for income tax, apart from the location of the income source, is the individual's residence for tax purposes, and CGT is generally only chargeable on persons resident or ordinarily resident in the United Kingdom. This is not the case for inheritance tax (IHT).

A charge to IHT may arise whenever there is a transfer of assets, (other than lifetime gifts to an individual (or certain kinds of trust) made more than seven years before the donor's death), no matter where the assets are located, made by a person who is, or was at death, domiciled or deemed to be domiciled (see Chapter 2) in the United Kingdom. In addition, IHT may be charged on a transfer of assets located in the United Kingdom by a person not domiciled in the United Kingdom.

So far as most British expatriates are concerned, although they may be non-resident for many years, their domicile remains the United Kingdom and, in consequence, they remain liable to IHT.

What follows is a necessarily brief outline of IHT with the emphasis placed on those aspects which are likely to be of greatest interest or relevance to expatriates. More detailed information is to be found in this book's companion volume, the *Allied Dunbar Tax Handbook*.

Note:
It is important to remember that expatriates who do manage to change their legal domicile from the United Kingdom remain liable for IHT for three years following that change because of the 'deemed domicile' provisions described in Chapter 2. It is also important to note that many countries impose restrictions on how an estate may be left on death, often requiring a set proportion of the estate to be left to a surviving spouse or children, this is usually known as 'forced heirship'.

It is also important to remember that many other countries also have gifts taxes which apply to lifetime transfers and estate duty, IHT, or acquisitions tax on death. There may be limited relief for double taxation as there are relatively few double taxation agreements covering estate and gifts taxes and unilateral relief, if available, may be difficult to apply, particularly where there is an acquisitions tax in the country of residence which taxes the donee, and a chargeable transfer for UK IHT on the donor or deceased. In some countries gift and estate taxes often apply lower rates to close relatives (the United Kingdom exempts most transfers to spouses) but these might not apply to people living together who are not legally married.

8.1 CHARGEABLE TRANSFERS

IHT may be payable whenever there is a chargeable transfer of assets. In general terms, a chargeable transfer is one which reduces the value of the transferor's total assets or his estate: in general parlance, a gift or bequest. Tax is chargeable on the cumulative total of chargeable transfers made during the donor's lifetime and on the value of his estate at death. The period of accumulation is restricted to seven years, ie in year 8, the cumulative total of transfers made will be those of years 2 to 8, and transfers made in year 1 will drop out of account. Following death, the IHT due will be calculated on the value of the estate at death plus chargeable transfers made in the preceding seven years.

For transfers on or after 6 April 2000 the first £234,000 is charged at a nil rate and the excess is charged on death at 40 per cent and on lifetime transfers in the seven years before death at a reducing percentage of the 40 per cent rate, depending upon the number of years between the transfer and the death of the donor. Up to three years the full rate is payable, four years is reduced to 80 per cent, five years 60 per cent, six years 40 per cent, seven years 20 per cent and thereafter no IHT is usually due. Chargeable lifetime transfers, such as gifts to certain discretionary settlements, are taxed at the lifetime rate of 20 per cent.

Following death, chargeable transfers made within the previous seven years are reassessed and the additional tax then becomes payable, but there is no revaluation of the asset transferred at the date of death.

It is fundamental to an understanding of IHT to appreciate that the amount of tax payable is calculated by reference to the total loss to the donor, ie the amount by which his estate has been reduced by the transfer. It is not the value of the gift in isolation. In practice, this is of greatest importance in connection with unquoted shares. If a father has 55 per cent of the shares in a family company and transfers 10 per cent to a discretionary trust, those shares might be worth, say, £100 per share as a small minority interest. However, the father's shareholding has fallen from a 55 per cent controlling interest (shares worth, say, £500 each) to a 45 per cent large minority holding (shares worth, say, £300 each). If there were 10,000 shares in issue, the chargeable transfer (loss to the father's estate) would not be £100,000 (1,000 × £100) but £1,400,000 (from 5,500 × £500 to 4,500 × £300).

8.2 EXEMPTIONS AND RELIEFS

The IHT legislation contains many provisions exempting certain transfers of value from tax. The most important of these are described below.

8.3 POTENTIALLY EXEMPT TRANSFERS

A lifetime transfer by an individual to another individual is a potentially exempt transfer (PET). This means that if the transferor survives for seven years it is exempt, but if he dies within seven years it is chargeable. This also applies to transfers to an interest in possession trust, an accumulation and maintenance trust or a trust for a disabled person.

8.4 TRANSFERS BETWEEN SPOUSES

Where both spouses are domiciled in the United Kingdom any transfer of assets between them is exempt. Where the recipient spouse is not domiciled in the United Kingdom at the time of the transfer, the total exemption is restricted to £55,000 (by IHTA 1984, s 18(2)) – (see also later). Additional transfers would fall first into the usual zero-rate band. The practical effect of this is that for transfers on or after 6 April 2000, no tax is charged on the first £289,000 of the estate. The spouse exemption applies to both lifetime transfers and transfers at death. There is no similar restriction in other cases where the transferee is non-UK domiciled and the transferor is domiciled in the United Kingdom. This may give rise to opportunities for channelling gifts through a non-UK domiciled individual who subsequently settles a discretionary trust, subject to anti-avoidance provisions in IHTA 1984, s 268 and the extended definition of settlor in IHTA 1984, s 44.

8.5 ANNUAL ALLOWANCES

A person may make as many small gifts to as many people as he wishes in a year without incurring any IHT. In order to qualify for this exemption, the maximum gift to any individual in the year is £250 (IHTA 1984, s 20(1)). If the gift is greater than £250 it will be taxable unless it can be covered by one of the other exemptions described below. In addition to the small gifts allowance, there is an annual allowance of £3,000 (IHTA 1984, s 19). This allowance, to the extent that it is unused in the year, may be carried forward for one year only. However, where an annual allowance or part of that allowance is carried forward it can only be used once the annual allowance for the second year has, itself, been exhausted.

Example: Inheritance tax – annual allowance

Margaret does not expect to live long and gives £2,000 to her daughter in Year 1; she makes no other transfers in that year and therefore has an annual allowance totalling £4,000 in Year 2 (£1,000 balance of year 1 and £3,000 year 2). If, however, she only gives away £2,000 in that year, her surplus to carry forward to Year 3 is not £2,000, but £1,000 again. She has lost the amount carried forward from Year 1 because she did not fully utilise her Year 2 allowance. Had she given £3,000 in Year 2 she would have nothing to carry foward.

These annual allowances are available separately to husband and wife and the value of the gift is calculated without tax, ie it is not grossed up. These allowances are available only against lifetime transfers.

8.6 NORMAL EXPENDITURE OUT OF INCOME

A gift made during a person's lifetime will be exempt if it is shown:

(1) to be part of that person's habitual expenditure;
(2) that, taking one year with another, it is made out of income; and
(3) that, allowing for all such transfers out of income, the transferor is left with sufficient income to maintain his usual standard of living.

On the occasion of the first gift of income it will be considered as exempt if there is clear evidence of further gifts to be made, such as insurance policy premiums on a policy written in trust (IHTA 1984, s 21).

8.7 GIFTS IN CONSIDERATION OF MARRIAGE

Wedding gifts into trust or within seven years of death are exempt so far as they fall within the following limits:

(1) up to £5,000 from a parent of either party to the marriage;
(2) up to £2,500 from one party to the marriage to the other or from grandparents or remoter ancestors of either party;
(3) up to £1,000 in any other case.

As with the two previous exemptions, this one is also only available for gifts made during the donor's lifetime (Inheritance Tax Act 1984 (IHTA 1984), s 22).

8.8 DISPOSITIONS FOR MAINTENANCE OF FAMILY

This exemption applies to dispositions from one spouse to another and includes any made on the dissolution of a marriage (IHTA 1984, s 11). It also covers those made for the children of either spouse (including any illegitimate child of the transferor) until the end of the tax year in which the child attains the age of 18 or, if later, until the child finishes full-time education or training. Where any person makes a disposition to a child who has been in that person's care for a substantial period, the exemption also applies, even though the person is not the child's parent. Finally, the exemption applies for the maintenance of a dependent relative and, by concession, to a disposition from a child to his or her unmarried mother who is financially dependent on the child.

8.9 OTHER EXEMPT TRANSFERS

The previous exemptions have primarily concerned transfers to individuals which are in any case exempt if made more than seven years before death. There are several other exempt transfers of a more impersonal nature. These include transfers to charities, gifts for national purposes, to political parties and for the public benefit (IHTA 1984, ss 23–26).

Finally, no IHT is payable on the estate of anyone who dies from a wound, accident, or disease contracted while on active service (IHTA 1984, s 154). By concession, this exemption is extended to the estates of members of the Royal Ulster Constabulary where death is as a result of terrorist activities in Northern Ireland.

8.10 BUSINESS PROPERTY RELIEF

Relief is given for the transfer of certain property which is 'relevant business property' by way of a reduction in the valuation of the property under IHTA 1984, ss 103–114. Before relief can be given, there are certain conditions to be met. As well as being relevant business property, the transfer must be of property from a qualifying business (basically a business carried on for gain other than a business which is primarily concerned with dealing in land or securities or holding investments), and the property must have been owned for a period of at least two years prior to the transfer.

Relevant business property falls into five classes:

(1) unincorporated business – property comprising a business or interest in a business attracts relief of 100 per cent;
(2) unquoted shares or securities in a company attract relief at 100 per cent immediately before the transfer;
(3) quoted shares or securities in a company which gave the transferor control of the company immediately before the transfer attract relief at 50 per cent;
(4) land, buildings, machinery or plant, which was settled property in which he was entitled to an interest in possession and was owned for the purposes of a business carried on by the transferor – relief is at 50 per cent;
(5) land, buildings, machinery or plant which immediately before the transfer was used wholly or mainly for the purposes of a business carried on by a controlled company or by a partnership in which the transferor was a partner – relief is at 50 per cent.

Note:
Shares dealt with on the Alternative Investment Market are treated as unquoted securities for this purpose.

8.11 AGRICULTURAL PROPERTY RELIEF

Agricultural property in the United Kingdom, the Channel Islands or the Isle of Man attracts relief at 100 per cent under IHTA 1984, ss 115–124 where it has been occupied for the two years before the transfer by the transferor for the purposes of agriculture, or where it was owned for the seven years before the transfer but farmed by persons other than the transferor. A further condition to be satisfied for the 100 per cent relief is that the transferor must enjoy vacant possession or be entitled to it within 12 months or where a tenancy was granted by the transferor after 31 August 1995, or where the transferor has been beneficially entitled to the interest since before 10 March 1981 subject to certain conditions. In other cases the relief is restricted to 50 per cent.

8.12 POTENTIALLY EXEMPT LIFETIME TRANSFERS OF AGRICULTURAL AND BUSINESS PROPERTY

In circumstances where such transfers become taxable due to the death within seven years of the transferor, the conditions necessary for obtaining the relief must still be met at the date of death. Effectively, therefore, the recipient of such transfers must continue to own the property and continue to use it in the manner which qualifies it for relief for seven years after the transfer, or risk forfeiting the relief.

8.13 PERSONS NOT DOMICILED IN THE UNITED KINGDOM

Overseas assets owned by persons not domiciled in the United Kingdom are generally excluded property for the purposes of IHT (IHTA 1984, s 6(1)). That is, any transfer of such property will not give rise to a liability. However, where such persons own assets in the United Kingdom, then any transfer of such assets may give rise to a charge to tax. There are, as usual, several exemptions and reliefs available to offset this general rule, in addition to the general potential exemption for lifetime transfers to individuals.

Under a double taxation agreement, property may be deemed to be located abroad, thus making it excluded property (see Chapter 11). The property of members of visiting forces or of staff of allied headquarters is excluded property. Where a person holds certain UK government securities, then these will be excluded property if the holder is not domiciled and not ordinarily resident in the United Kingdom (IHTA 1984, s 6(2)). For this latter exclusion, it is legal domicile as opposed to the artificial deemed domicile which applies (IHTA 1984, s 267(2)).

Where overseas property is settled property, it will only be excluded property if at the time the settlement was made the settlor was not domiciled in the United Kingdom (IHTA 1984, s 48(3)(b)). If that is not the case then the settled property will not be excluded, regardless of any subsequent change of domicile of the settlor and regardless of the domicile of any beneficiaries. A reversionary interest in overseas settled property does not come under these rules but is determined according to the general rule which is that if the person beneficially entitled to the reversionary interest is domiciled in the United Kingdom, then it is normally excluded property (IHTA 1984, ss 48(3) and 6(1)).

8.14 LOCATION OF ASSETS

Where an asset is located has to be determined according to the laws of England and Wales, Scotland or Northern Ireland except where these are superseded by special provisions in a double taxation agreement. The more usual types of assets are normally considered to be situated as follows:

(1) cash – where physically located;
(2) bank accounts – the location of the bank or branch (note: foreign currency accounts owned by a non-UK domiciled person but held in the United Kingdom are exempt);
(3) registered securities – the location of the share register;
(4) bearer securities – the location of the title documents;
(5) land and buildings – their actual location;
(6) business assets – the place where the business is conducted;
(7) debts – the residence of the debtor (or for specialty debts, such as a life assurance policy issued under seal, the place where the document evidencing the debt is located and, for judgment debts, the country where the judgment is recorded).

8.15 THE NON-UK DOMICILED SPOUSE

Before 1 January 1974, a wife assumed her husband's domicile on marriage. When the marriage ended, either by death or divorce, the wife retained her husband's domicile unless and until she acquired a new domicile of choice. The current position of women married before 1 January 1974 is that they retain their husbands' domicile (originally a domicile of dependence) as their deemed domicile of choice until, by their own positive actions, they acquire a new domicile of choice. For marriages contracted after 1 January 1974, a wife has had complete independence of domicile and will retain her domicile of origin or any pre-marriage domicile of dependence until she chooses to acquire a new domicile of choice which may or may not be the same as her husband's domicile.

For IHT purposes, a couple of mixed domicile (where one of them is domiciled in the United Kingdom and the other is not) have to take extra care in their tax planning. Their situation does, however, offer some opportunities not available to couples where both are UK domiciled.

Dealing first of all with the restrictions, it has already been mentioned that a transfer from a spouse domiciled in the United Kingdom to one who is not so domiciled, is exempt only up to a total transfer of £55,000.

The reason behind this is obviously to prevent the avoidance of tax which would arise by simply using the non-domiciled spouse as a conduit for transfers of non-UK sited assets to other parties such as children. None the less, substantial value can still be transferred because the UK domiciled spouse will have, in addition to the £55,000 exemption, an additional amount of £234,000 which on transfer will be within the nil-rate band. Further transfers may be made using the annual allowance and any subsequent increases in the exempt allowance or the width of the nil-rate band. After seven years, the £234,000 transferred initially within the nil-rate band will fall out of account.

Where the spouse who is not domiciled in the United Kingdom makes any gifts or transfers, there will be no IHT liability so long as the property concerned is excluded property – generally property located outside the United Kingdom. One possible pitfall for the non-UK domiciled spouse arises following the family's assumption or resumption of residence in the United Kingdom. The Inland Revenue may seek to claim that the originally non-domiciled spouse has acquired a new domicile of choice in the United Kingdom. However, they cannot have it both ways. There is a great reluctance in the absence of very strong evidence to accept that a person has shed his or her UK domicile – it should follow, therefore, that there should be equal reluctance to accept that a person has shed a non-UK domicile of origin and acquired UK domicile by choice. The onus of proof regarding a change of domicile is on the party, the taxpayer or Revenue, alleging the change. The pointers to a change of domicile given earlier should be considered in this light. The Inland Revenue have found it hard to establish domicile of choice in the United Kingdom where there are links with a foreign domicile of origin and there is a reasonably foreseeable contingency upon which residence in the domicile of origin would be taken up again.

In any event, even the person accepted as not being domiciled in the United Kingdom in the legal sense, will be deemed to be so domiciled for IHT purposes after a period of 17 years' residence here. Strictly, the requirement is to have been resident in the United Kingdom in not less than 17 out of the 20 years of assessment ending with the year in which the relevant time falls (IHTA 1984, s 267).

8.16 SETTLED PROPERTY

If the IHT rules are generally seen as very complex, this is nowhere more true than when considering the question of settled property. There are several types of trusts or settlements which have a useful application for IHT mitigation and these are discussed in some detail below, in Chapter 9.

For details of the settled property provisions, reference must be made to more specialist textbooks but the following points illuminate, however briefly, some important aspects.

Generally, settlements are themselves subject to IHT at lifetime rates if, when the settlement was made, the settlor was domiciled in the United Kingdom. The settlement of any property after 26 March 1974 is a chargeable transfer by the settlor (assuming he is domiciled in the United Kingdom) unless the trust is for transfers into an interest in possession trust, an accumulation or maintenance trust or a trust for a disabled person (these are potentially exempt transfers). A person having an interest in possession in any property, is deemed to possess that property for IHT purposes so that when that interest ends, there is deemed to be a potentially exempt transfer of the value of the property, under IHTA 1984, ss 49–53. There is no chargeable or potentially exempt transfer if a person becomes absolutely entitled to the property in which he previously had an interest in possession. The special rules relating to discretionary trusts and accumulation and maintenance trusts are discussed later.

A reversionary interest in a settlement of UK property is excluded property under IHTA 1984, s 48(1) unless it was acquired for value.

8.17 INHERITANCE TAX PLANNING

For every tax, there soon springs up a tax-avoidance scheme, or many of them. This continuing game between legislators and tax consultants is as obvious in the area of IHT as anywhere else although the Revenue's success in ignoring purely fiscal moves in a composite transaction in *Furniss v Dawson* [1984] STC 153 should be noted. This success has now been supplemented by a further change in attitude marked by the decision in the case of *IRC v McGuckian* [1997] STC 908, in which the courts have shown a willingness to move away from the longstanding principle, stated by Lord Tomlin in the case of *IRC v Duke of Westminster* (1935) 19 TC 490, that 'every man is entitled, if he can, to order his affairs so that the tax attaching . . . is less than it otherwise would be'.

The *McGuckian* case indicates that where tax avoidance is involved, the courts may take a purposive rather than a literal view of the law. This decision removes a fundamental certainty from the British tax system and may well signal a run of further success for the Inland Revenue in countering tax avoidance (which although legal has been frowned upon by the courts consistently since the case of *IRC v W T Ramsay Ltd* (1981) 54 TC 101 broke new ground.

IHT is in some aspects similar to estate duty (the predecessor to CTT), which was considerably easier to avoid than the tax which replaced it. On the other hand, the ease of avoiding IHT – by simply making gifts to individuals more than seven years before death – depends on the donor's ability to make outright gifts and lose the benefit of the associated income, because it is no longer possible, as it was with CTT, to make gifts with reservation of interest, such as giving away a share in the family home, other than to a spouse, and continuing to live in it.

Basic IHT planning is very straightforward, such as simply making use of the various exemptions and reliefs, particularly the exemption for lifetime gifts to individuals. However, rather than merely disposing of cash, some thought might be given to transferring assets which might be expected to grow in value but which have a relatively low value at the time of transfer. Another frequent suggestion is the equalisation of estate between husband and wife with the first to die leaving a substantial part of his or her estate other than to the spouse. In this way maximum use can be made of each spouse's entitlement to allowances and the nil rate band.

Example: Inheritance tax – estate planning

A husband has an estate worth £409,000 and the wife £59,000; in their wills each leaves his or her estate to the other. On the second death, everything goes to the children. Under these provisions there would be no IHT payable on the first death and, assuming no previous chargeable transfers, an IHT charge of £93,600 (£468,000–£234,000 × 40%) on the second death. If, however, the husband transferred £175,000 to his wife during his lifetime and they each decided to leave £234,000 to their children with the balance to the spouse, there would still be no IHT to pay on the first death and on the second death, when the estate is £234,000, the IHT payable would be nil, a saving of £93,600.

One reason for equalising the estates rather than simply making enough available for the wife to use the nil rate band is to allow maximum flexibility on the first death following which a written variation of the will (see below) could be used in the light of prevailing circumstances. There has been much speculation that written variations will be legislated against but at the time of writing it is still possible to do this. Equalising makes life generally simpler as a government could just as easily reduce the zero-rated band as increase it, and graduated rates could easily be reintroduced (as opposed to the current flat rates). When the United Kingdom last had graduated IHT rates it was possible to demonstrate substantial savings from equalisation on even quite modest estates, even though both spouses might already have used their zero-rate bands.

The transferor should not so reduce his estate that the surviving spouse cannot sustain a required standard of living. In addition, payment of IHT should be postponed from the date of the first death to the second death by leaving the estate on the excess over the nil rate band to the surviving spouse. A discretionary will trust often has a role to play when there is doubt over the surviving spouse's requirements, as the spouse can be a beneficiary and, so long as the trust is within the nil rate band, no IHT need be paid.

Other IHT planning opportunities abound when there is a non-domiciled person in the family, particularly in relation to trusts (see Chapter 9).

8.18 INSURANCE POLICIES

To use insurance policies, the transferor or the intending transferor effects a policy on his life written in trust for his beneficiaries. The sum assured under such a policy should be the amount of the anticipated IHT which will be due on the estate passing at death. Where there is a relatively short period of liability to the tax as, for example, when a person emigrates permanently but remains deemed domiciled in the United Kingdom for three years, a three-year term policy would be the cheapest and simplest form of IHT protection. Similarly, if a major transfer of assets is made to take advantage of the lower lifetime rates of tax, it may be worth insuring for the difference between the tax paid, if any, and the tax which would become payable if death occurred within seven years of that transfer. In most circumstances however, a term policy is unlikely to be the wisest course because as the potential transferor gets older renewing the policy can become very expensive. A better solution may be to take out a whole of life policy and write it in trust at a reasonably early stage. Premiums paid by the life assured/settlor in respect of the policy in trust are, of course, transfers of value into the trust and hence can amount to either immediately chargeable transfers or potentially exempt transfers depending on whether the trust is a discretionary trust. However, the exemption for gifts out of income and where necessary, the £3,000 annual exemption can normally be applied to those transfers of premium and, where this is so, the payments will be totally exempt. These exemptions can also be applied to the premiums paid on an investment-orientated policy written in trust and this, too, can be a useful way of transferring a growing asset to others.

8.19 THE FAMILY HOME

One asset which can sometimes prove difficult to plan for effectively is the family home, and for many people this is their main asset. Normally a couple will own their house as joint tenants. On the death of one of them the deceased's share is automatically transferred to the survivor. Assuming the couple are married, and are both either UK or non-UK domiciled, there will be no IHT payable on this occasion but on the second death, the whole value of the house will be counted in calculating the tax. The effect of this is illustrated in the following example.

Example: Inheritance tax – the family home

A couple have joint net assets of £390,000, of which £300,000 represents the value of their house, the remaining £90,000 being invested to provide income. The house is owned under a joint tenancy and each holds about £45,000 of investments. Under their wills each leaves his or her estate to the other. The couple have two children who will inherit everything on the second death. Because the survivor after the first death will still require a similar income, it is not practicable to leave anything to the children on that occasion so the eventual IHT bill will be £62,400.

The bill can, however, be reduced by changing the way the house is owned. If the couple own the house as tenants in common, rather than as joint tenants, their individual shares do not automatically go to the other on death but may be dealt with in the same way as any other asset. Thus, in the previous example, although the income-producing assets could not be left to the children, a share of the house could be.

If, on the death of the first spouse his or her half-share in the house was left to the children, this would be a chargeable transfer of £150,000 with no IHT payable. The estate on the second death would be £240,000 on which the IHT would be £2,400, a saving of £60,000. Some care is needed to ensure that the surviving spouse is not considered to have an interest in the children's half of the freehold interest.

However, tenancies in common are not without their drawbacks. There must be a high degree of trust among all the parties so that the widow or widower can continue to live in the property only half of which she or he will own. There can also be a problem if the co-owner is declared bankrupt. It is very important for anyone contemplating such an arrangement to discuss it fully with his lawyer who will also give an indication of the cost of changing an existing joint tenancy to a tenancy in common, which usually requires only a simple notice of severance served on the co-owner.

More complicated schemes concerning the family home abound – a reflection of the significance of this problem for families of even modest wealth. Following the success of the taxpayers in the case concerning the estate of Lady Ingram (*Ingram and another v IRC* [1999] STC 37), FA 1999 contains further legislation regarding gifts with reservation concerning interests in land, affecting gifts on or after 9 March 1999 (FA 1986, s 102A). As with most areas of tax planning, it is wise to seek expert professional advice.

9

WILLS, SETTLEMENTS AND TRUSTS

9.1 WILLS AND ASSETS IN MORE THAN ONE JURISDICTION

Anyone whose assets are other than negligible should make a properly drawn-up and witnessed will, unless he has no concern about the disposition of those assets after his death. Anyone who dies without leaving a valid will dies intestate, and his property will be disposed of according to the laws of intestacy. This procedure will seldom coincide with the deceased's wishes. This is especially true if the deceased held assets in more than one jurisdiction. Not only that, but intestacy may also give rise to prolonged legal arguments and problems, which in some countries have been known to go on for half a century or more.

This brings out an important point for the expatriate, particularly. If he has UK domicile, he should not only have a valid UK will which allocates all his worldwide property according to his wishes, but he should also have a will covering any assets held outside the United Kingdom which is valid in the jurisdiction where those assets are held.

Under private international law, where there is a will, the passing of assets from the deceased's estate to his heirs is governed by the law of the deceased's domicile in the case of movable property (such as bank deposits or securities) and by the local law in the case of immovable property. It will often be the case, therefore, that any decision of, say, an English court relating to immovable property overseas will not be effective in the overseas jurisdiction until it has been approved by a court there. The overseas court may also insist on a local grant of probate or Letters of Administration, which can be a relatively expensive and traumatic procedure.

A further point to bear in mind about assets held overseas is that not all countries allow the testator complete freedom to dispose as he pleases. In many countries the children of the deceased are legally entitled to inherit a minimum portion of the estate, or of part of the estate. In other countries, the incidence of estate duties or inheritance tax (IHT) varies according to the kinship or other relationship of the heirs to the deceased. Even in the United Kingdom, with very liberal laws in this respect, a will may be challenged and the dispositions altered by the court if, for instance, no provision has been made for a person who was financially dependent on the deceased. A will may be challenged in the United Kingdom on several other grounds also, but such matters lie beyond the scope of the present Handbook.

It will be clear even from the above simple generalisations that the administration of an overseas estate can be an extremely complex business. But one thing is certain: the trouble and expense (in the way of legal fees payable both in the United Kingdom and elsewhere) incurred in sorting matters out properly in advance amount to a mere fraction of the trouble and expense that will be incurred by the executors or administrators if proper arrangements have not been made. Indeed, an individual with assets in more than one country owes it morally to his executors as well as his heirs to make proper arrangements, even if this means writing several wills and consulting with several lawyers in several jurisdictions.

Apart from the simple efficiency in dealing with a local estate under local law that only a locally acceptable document makes possible, there are two further important practical points. First, proper testamentary arrangements regularly reviewed are essential to IHT or estate duty planning. They are the only way to protect the heirs from the full ravages of taxation. Secondly, from the UK viewpoint, a grant of probate or Letters of Administration will not be given until any IHT has been paid. Since assets will not normally be released until the grant is made, the only way to pay the tax bill is to borrow the money. If overseas assets can be speedily released through a local probate, these can be used to pay the UK tax and thereby hasten the release of assets held in the United Kingdom.

9.2 WILL TRUSTS

A UK will may grant an absolute interest to a beneficiary or may create a will trust under which the assets are left to trustees for the benefit of various beneficiaries. The types of possible trust are discussed below. The commonest will trust is to leave the majority of the estate to the surviving spouse for her life with the remainder to the children or grandchildren. The advantage of this arrangement is that the life interest to the surviving spouse is treated for IHT purposes as her absolute interest and therefore the IHT exemption on leaving assets to a surviving spouse still applies. However, the ultimate destination of the assets is assured so that should, for example, the wife remarry and have further children by the second marriage, the deceased former husband's estate passes through to his own children and cannot be diverted to the children of the second marriage or to anyone else. It is possible to leave the reversionary interest to the grandchildren rather than to the children and so avoid IHT on the death of the children. Whether this is desirable of course depends on many things, including the children's assets and the respective ages of the parties.

9.3 INCIDENCE OF INHERITANCE TAX

It is also important to bear in mind when drafting the will the incidence of IHT. The Inheritance Act 1984 (IHTA 1984), s 211 following *Re Dougal* [1981] STC 514 makes it clear that IHT on death in respect of personal property and of real property in the United Kingdom is a general testamentary expense payable out of residue in the absence of contrary provisions in the will. If, therefore, the intention is that any legacy should bear its own share of IHT, it is important that the will makes this clear. There are complicated provisions in IHTA 1984, ss 38–42 to deal with the case where part of the residue is left on an exempt legacy, such as to the surviving spouse or to a charity, and part on a chargeable legacy such as to the children.

Overseas assets subject to IHT will normally be subject to their proportionate share of the IHT applicable thereto. For the avoidance of doubt, it is preferable to draft the will so that it is made perfectly clear which, if any, legacies are to bear their share of IHT.

As already noted, the provisions of a will can largely determine the amount of IHT which will fall due. A will can be looked upon as an IHT planning tool. However, if family circumstances at the date of death are significantly different from what was envisaged when the will was prepared, or if the will is highly inefficient in a tax-planning sense, the will provisions may be altered by a written variation. At the time of writing, if this is done within two years of death, no IHT will be charged on the variations or rearrangements if the parties concerned so elect, and the tax payable will be computed on the basis that the varied provisions were effective at death. How much longer this will be possible is uncertain and it is preferable not to rely on this device as part of the tax planning strategy, but instead to know that it is there for emergencies (and see **9.4**). Stamp duty is no longer payable on the value transferred under a written variation (Finance Act 1985 (FA 1985), s 85).

9.4 WRITTEN VARIATIONS

The problem with the written variation is that it requires any beneficiary whose share is being reduced to be legally competent (ie adult and of sound mind), as any attempts so to modify the interest of a child benefi-ciary would require the consent of the court. In practice, it is preferable to leave that part of the estate which, for example, may or may not be required by the surviving spouse to trustees of a discretionary settle-ment with the intention that the trustees would, within two years of the date of death, redistribute the assets among the various beneficiaries in accordance with their needs.

Written variations are treated for IHT purposes as a disposition on death under IHTA 1984, ss 17 and 142 and for capital gains tax (CGT) pur-poses by the Taxation of Chargeable Gains Act 1992 (TCGA 1992), s 62(6). However, for income tax purposes, the income in the period from the date of death to the date of the variation (or distribution from any dis-cretionary trust) remains that of the original beneficiaries. After the case of *Marshall v Kerr* [1994] STC 638 a variation in favour of children was argued by the Revenue to be a settlement by the original beneficiary so that, for income tax purposes, any income distributed to the child during his minority would be treated as the income of the parent under the Income and Corporation Taxes Act 1988 (TA 1988), s 660B. The deci-sion in *Marshall v Kerr* also has implications in relation to the offshore settlement provisions for CGT. A variation or two-year discretionary trust should therefore be regarded as a useful opportunity to fine tune the dispositions given by will rather than a substitute for a carefully planned will reviewed at frequent intervals, and a testamentary trust should be properly established in the will whenever possible.

Example: Inheritance tax – written variation

Mr Bird died in July 1997. His net estate was valued at £400,000 including a house worth £100,000. Apart from £25,000 to his son, the estate was left to Mr Bird's widow. When Mr Bird's will was drawn up many years previously the value of his estate was only about £150,000 with the house worth £50,000. He felt at the time that his widow would require £75,000 to provide her income and that was his rationale for the structuring of his will. Mrs Bird has personal assets of her own worth £50,000.

As it happens, in 1997, there will be no IHT to pay following Mr Bird's death (he has made no previous transfers) but there is a potential tax charge on Mrs Bird's death, assuming she leaves her estate to the son of £77,600. She and her son therefore effect a written variation whereby the son receives £220,000 instead of £25,000 and his children receive £10,000 in total. There is still no IHT payable on the estate. The potential charge on the death of Mrs Bird is reduced from £76,400 (on £425,000) to £Nil (on £195,000). The writ-ten variation has therefore saved IHT of £76,400 and leaves some scope for Mrs Bird's estate to increase before the family would suffer IHT on her death.

9.5 TRUSTS

A trust or settlement is a legal relationship which is established when a person transfers assets into the care of others for the benefit of a third party. The three parties concerned in this relationship, the settlor, trustees, and beneficiaries respectively, may all incur tax liabilities stemming from the trust in different ways. A detailed explanation of trust law is beyond the scope of this book and readers are referred to the *Allied Dunbar Tax Handbook* for further information. Trusts constitute an extremely complex area of the law and good professional advice is essential.

This chapter can only provide an outline of the major tax planning aspects of trusts as they affect, or might affect, the expatriate. It must be stressed that to establish a trust is not a job for a layman. Perhaps more than in any other field of tax planning, trust work requires the assistance of expert professional advice.

9.5.1 The residence of trusts

For most income tax purposes, a trust with a UK resident, ordinarily resident or domiciled settlor at the time of creation is resident outside the United Kingdom only if all the trustees are themselves so resident and the administration and management of the trust are carried out overseas, FA 1989, s 110 (*Kelly v Rogers* (1935) 19 TC 692, *Reid's Trustees v IRC* (1929) 14 TC 512). If there is a UK resident trustee of a trust settled by a non-UK resident and domiciled settlor which also has a foreign trustee, the UK resident trustee is deemed to be non-resident for income tax purposes (FA 1989, s 110(1)(*b*)). Similar provisions apply to personal representatives under FA 1989, s 111. For CGT purposes, TCGA 1992, s 69(1) only requires a majority of trustees to be non-UK resident. A trust which is not resident in the United Kingdom may enjoy substantial tax advantages over the domestic settlement but there are numerous provisions in the UK legislation which seek to prevent tax avoidance by the use of such vehicles by or for the benefit of persons ordinarily resident in the United Kingdom. The three main UK taxes, income tax, CGT and IHT can each have an impact on trusts and on each of the parties involved. Tax liabilities are determined not only by the residence of the trust and the individuals concerned but also by the type of trust which is involved. The following section on the taxation of trusts outlines the tax consequences which attach to each of the main types of trust with which the expatriate may be concerned.

9.5.2 Resident trusts

It may be useful to make the first distinction between types of trusts as between those where the settlor is alive and those where he is deceased. The main thrust of the anti-avoidance legislation is concerned with preventing a settlor using a trust mechanism to provide himself with a tax-sheltered 'piggy bank' for his own or his wife's benefit. To that end there are numerous provisions which seek to tax trust income as that of the settlor and these are described below. Where the settlor has died, whether the trust was set up during his lifetime or under his will, the taxation rules are somewhat less complex.

In general terms, a UK trust is liable for income tax at the savings, Schedule F or basic rates on all its income, wherever arising. Where trust income has already suffered tax at source or is accompanied by a tax credit, this will be accounted for in the trust assessment. Where the trust has overseas income which has been taxed abroad then relief for double taxation may be available either to the trustees or the beneficiaries. The income of discretionary trusts and accumulation trusts, after deducting expenses, is also liable at the 'rate applicable to trusts' (making an effective rate of 34 per cent on income other than UK dividends for 1999/00) – TA 1988, s 686. In the case of dividends from UK companies, from 6 April 1999, there is a special 'Schedule F trust rate', which for 1999/00 is 25 per cent (TA 1988, s 686(1A)). This represents a reduction of nine percentage points compared with the position prior to 6 April 1999, whereas the 'credit' which trustees can claim against this 'Schedule F trust rate' is reduced by ten percentage points on the dividend plus credit compared with the position prior to 6 April 1999.

Example

	1999/00 £		1998/99 £
Dividend	100.00		100.00
Credit 1/9	11.11	1/5	20.00
	111.11		120.00
Tax @ 25%	27.78	34%	40.80
Less: credit 10%	11.11	20%	24.00
Net additional tax	£16.67		£16.80

The income tax assessment of trusts is generally made in the name of the trustees and the tax due is payable out of the trust funds. Where trust income is distributed to beneficiaries it is treated as received net of tax at 34 per cent under TA 1988, s 687 (or at the savings, Schedule F or basic rates in the case of a beneficiary absolutely entitled to the income, that is where the trust is not a discretionary trust).

A non-resident trust is liable to UK tax on its UK income at the basic rate and, on accumulations, at the 'rate applicable to trusts' as well. See *IRC v Regent Trust Co Ltd* [1980] STC 140. In most cases the basic rate liability is deducted at source but from 6 April 1999 this is not the case for dividends (see above). The additional amount due must be collected by assessment. This is difficult for the UK Inland Revenue to enforce and in the case of savings and investments income there is no additional tax due unless there is a UK resident beneficiary, FA 1995, s 128(5). However, the benefit of credit for taxes paid by the trustees will not flow through to the beneficiaries of UK resident income, unless the trustees deal with this obligation and pay the rate applicable to trusts.

Trusts are also liable for CGT in much the same way as individuals but the annual exemption is restricted to 50 per cent of that available to individuals. For 2000/01, the trust exemption is therefore £3,600. For trusts formed after 6 June 1978, this exemption is split among all trusts with the same settlor, ie if he made ten trusts, each would be entitled to exemption on the first £360. For trusts formed before that date, the full £3,600 is allowed. Certain trusts for the mentally disabled and those in receipt of attendance allowances are entitled to the same exemption as an individual; TCGA 1992, Sched 1.

Some of the aspects of IHT and trusts are mentioned in Chapter 8. *What is perhaps of the greatest importance is to note that, for IHT purposes, the residence of the trust is largely immaterial.* A trust may incur a liability to IHT on its worldwide assets if, at the time it was set up, the settlor was domiciled in the United Kingdom (IHTA 1984, s 48(3)(*a*)). If the settlor was domiciled elsewhere, the IHT liability will be restricted to transfers of trust assets located in the United Kingdom.

9.5.3 Trusts created *inter vivos*

Where a settlement is made during the lifetime of the settlor, the taxation rules are particularly rigorous to prevent the avoidance of tax. An outline of these anti-avoidance provisions is given below.

9.5.4 Income tax

The basic rule a settlor must obey in order to avoid having the trust income assessed on him, is fully to divest himself of the assets he is transferring into the trust. If he retains an interest in either the income or the assets of the trust then any income not distributed to beneficiaries will be treated as the settlor's income (TA 1988, ss 660A–J, 677 and 678). A retained interest is widely defined but generally means that the settlor or his or her spouse is able to obtain some benefit from the income or assets of the trust at any time. Even where the income is distributed to others from a settlor-interested trust, any excess of higher rate tax over the basic or lower rate on the distribution will be charged to the settlor.

Included in retaining an interest is a power to revoke the trust. If the trust can be revoked in whole or in part, and on revocation the trust property reverts to the settlor or his spouse, then the income of the trust (or a part thereof corresponding to the partial revocation) will be treated as the income of the settlor (TA 1988, s 660A). The power of revocation may be immediate or postponed, but in the latter case, if the power cannot be used for at least six years, the income will not be treated as that of the settlor until the power becomes exercisable. Power to revoke includes a power to advance the whole of the capital, or to diminish the assets of the trust or the income receivable by beneficiaries other than the settlor or his spouse. Whether it is the settlor or another person who has the power to revoke is immaterial.

Where there is a settlement of income such as a covenant, it is essential that the payments should be capable of being made for a period of at least four years (TA 1988, s 660A) if a covenanted payment to charity (TA 1988, s 347A (7)), or it must be for *bona fide* commercial reasons, such as a payment to a former partner. Where a covenant fails on this rule, it will be treated as income of the settlor and not the payee. Nevertheless, the payment will still be deemed to have been made to the covenantee and then returned to the settlor: the settlor is then treated as receiving investment income, even if the payment was made out of earned income or capital. As a result, the settlor may find that he has more tax to pay because of a failed covenant than he would had he not instituted it in the first place (*Ang v Parish* [1980] STC 341).

Where a capital sum (which includes a loan or loan repayment) is paid by trustees to the settlor, his spouse, or a third party directly or indirectly at the settlor's direction, that sum is treated as the income of the settlor and is assessed on him under TA 1988, s 677. The assessment is restricted to the amount of undistributed income in the trust but includes income previously accumulated. The tax charge is based on the amount of undistributed income grossed up at the basic rate plus the additional rate and credit is given for tax already charged on the trust. Where the undistributed income is less than the capital sum, there is provision to carry forward the excess of the capital sum to subsequent years. The settlor will then be charged to the extent of undistributed income in those years until the capital sum is fully extinguished. For capital payments made after 5 April 1981, the period for carry forward is restricted to 11 years (capital payments made before that date are to be treated as made on that date so as to fall within the new rules, so far as they have not been charged).

Under a discretionary trust, that is, one where the trustees may apply the trust property and/or income at their discretion, the settlor and his spouse must be specifically excluded from benefit, otherwise the income will be charged on the settlor whether or not he receives it. This does not apply where the benefit may accrue to the widow or widower of the settlor.

Settlements for the benefit of the settlor's infant children do not generally provide an income tax advantage, in view of the effects of TA 1988, s 660B. Any income belonging to a minor child which is derived from a parental source is deemed to be the income of the parent for tax purposes. This applies not only to settlements made by parents but to any transfer of assets from the parent to his or her child. For example, if a parent gave his child shares in a company, any dividends paid to the child until he reached the age of majority would be treated as the parent's income. Similarly taxed too would be the interest in a child's bank account where the capital came from a parent, subject to the *de minimis* exemption where the child's income does not exceed £100, TA 1988, s 660B(5). From 6 April 2000, maintenance payments are only deductible to a limited extent when one of the former spouses is aged over 65 on 5 April 2000 (FA 1999, s 36).

The use of accumulation trusts was one way to create a settlement for the benefit of minor children. Where there is an irrevocable settlement of capital other than on a bare trust prior to 9 March 1999 (FA 1999, s 64) and the trustees are empowered or directed to accumulate the income arising from it for the ultimate benefit of the settlor's children, the settlor will not incur any income tax liability so long as the income is actually accumulated. The trust income is taxed at 34 per cent, or 25 per cent on Schedule F dividend income, in the name of the trustees. If any sums are paid to or for the benefit of the child before his or her eighteenth birthday or earlier marriage, such sums will be treated as the settlor's income. When the accumulated income is paid to adult beneficiaries, it is normally treated as capital in their hands. See also Chapter 8 and below, regarding the favourable treatment of these trusts for IHT purposes.

All of the above provisions apply generally but where the settlor is either not domiciled, not resident, or not ordinarily resident in the United Kingdom, certain other considerations come into play. Under TA 1988, s 660I(1), income arising under a settlement includes any income chargeable to income tax and any income which would have been so chargeable if it had been received in the United Kingdom by a person domiciled, resident and ordinarily resident in the United Kingdom. But where, in any year of assessment, the settlor is not resident, etc in the United Kingdom then the settlement income in that year will not include any income which would not have been chargeable on the settlor, had he been entitled to it, by reason of his non-residence, etc.

The other consideration concerns settlements for the settlor's children. Where the settlor is not taxable as a UK resident then there is no aggregation. Any income from such a settlement paid to the child will not be treated as the parent's income for any year in which the parent is not resident in the United Kingdom. Under these circumstances, the child beneficiary will be able to reclaim the tax deducted on his income from the trust up to the amount of the single person's allowance. Where tax has been deducted at 34 per cent he will also be able to reclaim the tax at the 'rate applicable to trusts' on the income beyond his personal allowance.

9.5.5 Capital gains tax

Capital gains tax (CGT) may become payable on the creation of a trust, on gains made in the trust, and on certain deemed disposals of trust assets. On the first of these the liability is likely to fall on the settlor, while on the second and third, the tax will be payable by the trustees out of the trust funds.

Whether a settlement is revocable or otherwise, a transfer into a settlement is considered to be a disposal of the entire property which becomes settled (TCGA 1992, s 70). This implies a deemed disposal by the transferor and the disposal will be treated as being made at market value. If this results in a capital gain then the transferor and transferee may elect to have the gain held over, if the asset consists of business assets (TCGA 1992, s 165) agricultural property (TCGA 1992, Sched 7) or where the transfer is chargeable to IHT (TCGA 1992, s 260) or reinvestment relief applies (TCGA 1992, ss 164A–N). If the deemed disposal shows a loss then this loss may normally only be utilised by the transferor against subsequent gains arising in his transactions with the trust (TCGA 1992, s 18(3)). Gains may only be held over where the trustees are resident in the United Kingdom (TCGA 1992, ss 166, 261).

During the administration of a trust, gains and losses will accrue to the trustees as they would to an individual managing his portfolio. Net gains are chargeable at 34 per cent at 1999/00 rates subject to the restricted exemption mentioned earlier. In the case of trusts where the settlor or settlor's spouse could receive any benefit, the gains are aggregated with the settlor's to determine the rate of tax.

When property ceases to be settled property, if, for example, it is distributed or a person becomes absolutely entitled to it, that is a deemed disposal and an occasion of charge on any gain (TCGA 1992, s 71(1)). Where property ceases to be settled on the death of a life tenant, there is also a deemed disposal but there will be no chargeable gain (TCGA 1992, s 72). If the trustees and recipient of the disposed property agree and so elect, the gain accruing on property eligible for hold-over relief may be held over provided that the recipient is resident in the United Kingdom (TCGA 1992, Sched 7). Where a life interest in settled property comes to an end, there is no charge if the property remains within the settlement, provided that the trust is resident in the United Kingdom for CGT purposes, or there is no deemed disposal.

If a trust ceases to be resident in the United Kingdom, the trustees are deemed to have sold all the trust assets and immediately reacquired them, so capitalising any CGT charge (TCGA 1992, s 80).

9.5.6 Inheritance tax

When a person creates a settlement there will be a diminution of the settlor's estate unless he settles the property on himself for life (IHTA 1984, s 3). This transfer of value may give rise to a liability for IHT. The IHT legislation treats differently settlements where there is or are interest(s) in possession, and those where there is no interest in possession.

Where a person is beneficially entitled to the interest in possession of settled property, he is treated as being beneficially entitled to the property in which the interest subsists (IHTA 1984, s 49(1)). Thus if two people had equal interests in possession of a trust worth £200,000, each would be treated as being entitled to £100,000. In most circumstances, on the death of one of these persons IHT would be payable by the trustees on the deemed transfer of £100,000 in addition to any other estate the deceased might have. Other events will also be treated as dispositions of the property by the person beneficially entitled to the interest in possession; if, for example, the interest is terminated during the life of the person or if it is disposed of by way of assignment or surrender. Where the disposal is for a consideration in money or money's worth, IHT will be charged on the value transferred less the consideration received.

There are, however, exceptions to this rule. If a person becomes absolutely entitled to the property or to another interest in possession, that will not be treated as a chargeable transfer (IHTA 1984, s 53(2)). Other exceptions include where the property reverts to the settlor or his spouse (if she, or he, is domiciled in the United Kingdom) or to the widow or widower of the settlor within two years of the death of the settlor (IHTA 1984, s 53(3)–(5)), and interests held by surviving spouses of a person who died before 13 November 1974 (where estate duty would have been paid on that death).

A reversionary interest is a future interest under a settlement, eg that of a remainderman who will inherit on the death of the life tenant. For IHT purposes, a reversionary interest is normally excluded property unless it was acquired at any time for money or money's worth (IHTA 1984, s 48(1)).

With one major exception, trusts where there is no interest in possession are treated harshly for IHT purposes. The major problem with the normal discretionary trust is the liability for the periodic charge under IHTA 1984, s 64. This charge is levied every tenth anniversary of the settlement date (falling after 31 March 1983) and is charged at 30 per cent of the rate which would be payable on a notional transfer of the value of the property in the trust at the end of the ten-year period. The rate is the lifetime rate of the settlor, currently a maximum of 6 per cent (30 per cent × 40 per cent × 50 per cent), and is calculated on the settlor's previous chargeable transfers in the ten years preceding the creation of the settlement: IHTA 1984, ss 65 and 67. For further details, see the *Allied Dunbar Tax Handbook*.

IHT is also payable on other occasions when property is distributed from the trust to beneficiaries (including the settlor and his or her spouse) in anticipation of the ten-year charge (IHTA 1984, s 65).

The exception to this highly taxed regime is the accumulation and maintenance settlement. Such settlements are greatly favoured and narrowly defined by IHTA 1984, s 71. They are settlements where one or more beneficiaries will, upon attaining a specified age not exceeding 25, become entitled to an interest in possession in the settled property; no interest in possession subsists in the settled property and the income from the property is to be accumulated in so far as it is not applied for the maintenance, education, or benefit of a beneficiary; and either not more than 25 years have elapsed since the trust was created or became an accumulation and maintenance trust, or all the persons who are or have been beneficiaries are or were grandchildren of a common grandparent.

The commonest use of such trusts is along the following lines: S creates a settlement under which his children obtain an interest in possession at age 21 and at age 35, say, or upon earlier marriage, they receive the capital. Income up to age 21 is to be accumulated apart from any payments made for the beneficiaries' maintenance. No lifetime IHT is payable on transfers into accumulation trusts, on any maintenance payment made, on the beneficiaries' acquisition of the interest in possession, or on the release of capital and accumulated income (IHTA 1984, s 71(3)). Neither is there a periodic charge on these settlements (IHTA 1984, s 58(1)(*b*)). But one point to bear in mind is that income of a trust may be treated as the income of the settlor if the settlor is the parent, under TA 1988, s 660B.

Accumulation and maintenance settlements offer one of the most tax-efficient ways of transferring capital to children and, especially, grandchildren.

9.5.7 Non-resident trusts

Non-resident trusts may have a particular appeal to the expatriate who is used to having his investments sheltered from the Inland Revenue and who wishes to retain a similar advantage on his return either for himself or for the benefit of his children. There can certainly be advantages in setting up non-resident trusts but the anti-avoidance legislation is a real minefield for the unwary. It is essential to consider this legislation most carefully before opting to place substantial sums in what can be an expensive attempt to establish shelter and then finding that it does not achieve its main aim.

As mentioned earlier in this chapter, a trust settled by a UK resident, ordinarily resident or domiciled settlor, will be treated as resident in the United Kingdom unless the general administration of the trust is carried on outside the United Kingdom and the trustees, or, for CGT purposes, a majority of them, are not resident or not ordinarily resident in the United Kingdom.

The UK income of a non-resident trust with no UK resident beneficiaries is liable to UK income tax at the rate applicable to trusts, 34 per cent, so far as it is to be accumulated or is payable under a discretion (see **9.5.4** and *IRC v Regent Trust Co Ltd* [1980] STC 140). Where there are UK resident beneficiaries, the limitation to tax deducted at source does not apply and savings income, other than on gilts, is taxed at 34 per cent less 20 per cent, ie 14 per cent, and in the case of dividends taxable under Schedule F at 25 per cent less 10 per cent. It should be noted, however, that where the income has tax deducted at source or has an accompanying tax credit, the rate applicable to trusts is charged only on the net income. For example, a non-UK resident trust receiving dividends of £900 (with tax credit of £100) would be liable for additional tax of £135

(£900 × 15 per cent) leaving net income of £765. A UK resident trust would have suffered total tax of £250 (dividend £900 plus tax credit of £100 = £1,000 × 25 per cent) leaving net income of £750.

From an income tax point of view, general principles can be applied which indicate that income paid to a beneficiary, where he is entitled to that income, will form part of his income for tax purposes. Where the trust is an accumulation trust, then accumulated income will not be taxable on the beneficiary and this may be paid to the beneficiary as capital in due course. General principles apart, there are several anti-avoidance provisions which also come into play.

The most important of these income tax provisions are contained in TA 1988, ss 739–746. Section 739 is seen as one of the most widely drawn anti-avoidance provisions. Where an individual ordinarily resident in the United Kingdom transfers assets so that someone not resident or domiciled in the United Kingdom receives any income from these assets, and that income can be used currently or at some future time by the individual who transferred the assets, then that income will be treated as income of the transferor.

What this means in the context of trusts is that if an individual has established a non-resident trust under which he may benefit, then the income of the trust will be treated as his income whether or not it is distributed. It will be similarly taxed if the settlor's spouse may benefit. Section 739 will not apply while the settlor is not ordinarily resident, but a non-resident trust established during a period of non-residence will be caught when the expatriate returns to the United Kingdom. This section relates only to income and does not, therefore, operate to tax capital gains (see later). If income from or accruing to a non-resident trust is to escape UK income tax then the settlor and his or her spouse must be totally precluded from any possible benefit, and the words 'power to enjoy' are widely construed under TA 1988, s 742(2). Alternatively, if it can be shown that the trust was established for *bona fide* commercial reasons, such as the establishment of a pension scheme, and that the avoidance of tax was no part of this reasoning, the section will not operate (TA 1988, s 741). This may be very difficult to prove especially since exchange controls (once a useful commercial reason) no longer operate in the United Kingdom, and the s 741 defence cannot be relied upon unless the claimant has shown the reason(s) in writing 'to the satisfaction of the Board' (of Inland Revenue).

On a more positive note, non-resident trusts can be established for the benefit of, for example, the settlor's children or grandchildren without any UK tax liability on the income as it arises overseas (see earlier for income arising in the United Kingdom). This is all well and good so long as the trust funds are accumulated but note that for minor unmarried children,

TA 1988, s 660B can deem the trust income to be that of the settlor. In other cases, where there is a distribution of income that income becomes chargeable on the beneficiary under TA 1988, s 740, if he or she is ordinarily resident in the United Kingdom. Where a benefit is received under the trust, that benefit will be taxed to the extent that the trust has relevant income. Where the benefit exceeds the relevant income then the excess will be taxed in later years as the trust accrues further relevant income. Relevant income is income of the trust which can be used to provide a benefit but is restricted to income which arose on or after 10 March 1981. If, for example, a non-resident trust established in 1977 accrued income at the rate of £2,000 a year, then in May 1997, the total income is £40,000, of which, say £28,000 is relevant income. During that year, £36,000 is paid to a beneficiary. The beneficiary's income tax liability in 1997/98 would be on £28,000 and, if income continues to accrue to the trust at the same rate, a further liability on £2,000 a year for the next four years. If, however, the trust also had realised capital gains accrued since 10 March 1981, then to the extent that there is insufficient relevant income in the year of distribution, the surplus or a part of it will be allocated to the accrued capital gains and taxed accordingly.

In general terms, a non-resident trust established by a UK domiciliary is not liable to UK CGT (except where it is carrying on a trade in the United Kingdom). However, where the settlor was domiciled and either resident or ordinarily resident in the United Kingdom when the trust was established, or in a relevant subsequent year, gains arising after 17 March 1998 may be assessed on the settlor unless he, his spouse, his children and grandchildren and their spouses and companies controlled by them, are all excluded from benefit. If that is not the case, gains arising in the period from 17 March 1998 to 5 April 1999 will be treated as accruing to the settlor on 6 April 1999 and will be taxed in 1999/00 (TCGA 1992, s 86, Sched 5).

In cases in which the settlor is excluded from benefit, when trust gains, or gains of companies owned by such trusts, are distributed to a UK domiciled beneficiary, those gains will be treated as accruing to the beneficiary and taxable on him (TCGA 1992, s 87). Gains of the trust are computed each year and the cumulative total of gains is treated as trust gains for the year. When a capital payment is made to beneficiaries, the trust gains will be attributed to them in proportion to the capital payment received by them up to the amount of that payment. Unattributed gains, ie where total gains are in excess of the capital payment, will be carried forward as trust gains for subsequent years. Gains are apportioned to non-UK domiciled or non-UK resident beneficiaries, but those beneficiaries should not suffer any tax liability as a result of apportionment. Gains can therefore be 'washed out' to non-resident beneficiaries if there are any and, subject to the re-entry charge for temporary non-residents, this has been a long-established means of sheltering CGT. Tax on gains apportioned to a UK resident and domiciled beneficiary after 6 April 1992 may be increased by 10 per cent per annum as if it were interest for a maximum of six years (TCGA 1992, ss 91–97). This is referred to as the 'supplementary charge'. The charge under s 87 was extended, in FA 1998, to UK resident and domiciled beneficiaries of trusts settled by non-domiciled settlors. Prior to 17 March 1998, capital payments to beneficiaries of non-resident trusts were exempt from tax if the settlor was not domiciled or not resident.

Trusts which emigrate from the United Kingdom on or after 19 March 1991 as a result of the appointment of non-resident trustees are deemed to have sold and reacquired their assets at market value immediately before emigration, which could crystallise a CGT charge on exit (TCGA 1992, s 80) unless the emigration is caused by the death of a trustee and the trust is reimported within six months (TCGA 1992, s 84). Past trustees may be made liable for the tax (TCGA 1992, s 82). Anti-avoidance provisions cover trusts benefiting from double taxation treaties, dual resident trusts and disposals of settled interests (TCGA 1992, ss 83–85).

As far as IHT is concerned, non-resident trusts are treated in very much the same way as resident trusts. The important point for the tax liability of these trusts is the domicile of the settlor at the time the trust is first established. If the settlor is not UK domiciled, then trust assets located outside the United Kingdom will be excluded from any IHT liability. Assets may be physically situated in the United Kingdom, but if owned by an underlying company, the trust assets will be the shares in the company. If these shares are bearer shares held outside the United Kingdom, or if the company holding the assets is non-resident, the trust property should still be excluded from IHT. However, in the case of certain assets, such as real estate situated in the United Kingdom, the use of an offshore holding company may involve other tax considerations. Expert professional advice should, as ever, be taken. The professional adviser may have a duty to return details of any non-resident trusts established for a UK domiciled individual under IHTA 1984, s 218.

Reference must be made to any double taxation agreement in force. Where a non-resident trust has an IHT liability, this normally falls on the trustees but if, for whatever reason, the liability is not met by them, the Inland Revenue may obtain the tax from any of the following under IHTA 1984, s 201:

(1) any person entitled to an interest in possession in the settled property;

(2) any person for whose benefit the property or income therefrom may be applied at or after the time of the transfer; or

(3) the settlor, if the transfer is made within his lifetime.

In summary, non-resident trusts can be very useful in tax planning. Where the settlor and his or her spouse are precluded from benefit, the income payable to beneficiaries may be effectively taxed on a remittance basis. The rules for capital gains are now rather complex, as summarised above, but do not affect non-domiciled settlors. Before embarking on any trust scheme, the expatriate must be totally clear on what he hopes to achieve, must understand the inevitable costs involved in any structure, must be professionally advised in order to achieve it and must accept the possibility of future changes to the current law and the potential these could have to nullify any anticipated savings.

10

OTHER UK TAXES

10.1 VALUE ADDED TAX

In the United Kingdom, value added tax (VAT) is payable at the standard rate of 17.5 per cent in respect of goods or services supplied in the United Kingdom by a registered business. Registration is compulsory where the taxable turnover exceeds £52,000 a year for 2000/01. Certain items are exempt from VAT, while others are zero-rated, eg most food, domestic fuel and power are charged at 5 per cent. So far as the expatriate is concerned, the most important VAT relief is that relating to exports of goods or services. If goods are exported from the United Kingdom the sale is zero-rated, and therefore VAT should not be charged. Certain supplies of international services are also zero-rated; eg an expatriate obtaining advice from a UK business, on his personal tax affairs, will receive a zero-rated bill if he is resident outside the EU. However, if he is resident inside the EU the charge will be standard-rated.

VAT due on imports of goods is paid at the time and place of entry or, if the importer has approval for deferment, by direct debit covered by banker's guarantee on the fifteenth of the month following the month in which the goods enter the United Kingdom. However, from 1 January 1993, businesses which import goods from EU member states only account for VAT on their next VAT return.

10.1.1 VAT exemptions and zero-rating

The main VAT exemptions are set out in the Value Added Tax Act 1994 (VATA 1994), Sched 9: the main headings are land (but see **10.1.2**), insurance, finance, education, health, burial and cremation.

Zero-rating for VAT purposes is given by VATA 1994, Sched 8, the main headings of which are food, books, news services, construction of dwellings, international services (see below), transport, caravans and houseboats designed for permanent habitation, gold, medicines, certain supplies to or by charities and children's clothing.

International services include services relating to land outside the United Kingdom, letting goods for hire outside the United Kingdom, the supply of cultural, artistic, sporting, scientific, educational or entertainment services performed outside the United Kingdom, valuation of goods outside the United Kingdom, the supply to a person in his business capacity of services listed in VATA 1994, Sched 5 to a member of the EU and in any capacity to a person belonging elsewhere, and the supply of insurance and allied services and export and transhipment services. Goods sent to the United Kingdom for repair and subsequently re-exported are also included in this heading. Schedule 5 refers to services treated as supplied where received, such as transfers and assignments of intellectual property, advertising services, professional services of consultants, engineers, lawyers, accountants, etc, banking, financial and insurance services, the supply of staff, hiring of goods and certain restrictive covenants.

If these services are supplied by a person who belongs outside the United Kingdom to a UK business registered for VAT, then the same consequences apply as if the recipient had himself supplied the services in the United Kingdom and that supply was a taxable supply, ie he would have to account for VAT on the value of that supply by the overseas person. Therefore if the UK business was partially exempt for UK VAT purposes, and these services received related to exempt supplies, it will suffer a disallowance of VAT input tax on these expenses. A UK business will therefore not obtain an advantage by using services supplied from abroad, which do not have a VAT charge on them, as opposed to services supplied in the United Kingdom which will bear VAT.

10.1.2 Property

Expatriates with property in the United Kingdom should appreciate that although the purchase price of domestic property is free of VAT, alterations as well as repairs and maintenance are subject to VAT. The construction of buildings for industrial and commercial use and in the community and civil engineering sector is standard-rated for VAT: the landlord has the option to charge VAT on rents and capital sums received on the supply of non-domestic buildings and developed land used for non-domestic purposes. By electing for this, the landlord is able to recover input tax on repairs and maintenance expenses. Therefore expatriate owners of commercially let property in the United Kingdom should consider whether or not to register for UK VAT and appointing an agent in the United Kingdom to deal with their UK VAT affairs.

10.1.3 Cars

Cars supplied in the United Kingdom other than for export are subject to VAT. The separate car tax has been abolished.

An expatriate returning to the United Kingdom and importing a car could be liable to VAT on the value of the car at the time of importation, plus import duty if the car is not of EU origin unless it qualifies under the personal belongings heading (see below). The exemption for a car on which VAT was originally paid in the United Kingdom has now been abolished.

10.2 EXCISE DUTIES

Many items imported into the United Kingdom suffer excise duties in addition to VAT. Examples include the obvious ones of alcohol and tobacco, perfume and gold and other less likely items such as cigarette lighters. Items acquired in the United Kingdom for personal export to countries outside the EU may be acquired in duty-free shops or those operating a personal export scheme under which the VAT, but not excise duty, may be recovered.

10.3 PERSONAL BELONGINGS

The importation of personal belongings is normally subject to import duty and VAT (if relevant). The value for import duty is basically the secondhand value (exclusive of VAT) in the United Kingdom of identical or similar objects. The value for VAT is the same but inclusive of import duty.

There are relieving provisions and these relate to three categories of belongings:

(1) cars, aircraft and caravans;
(2) boats; and
(3) other effects.

The appropriate customs formalities including the claiming of the reliefs must be complied with:

(1) Motor cars, motor bikes, aircraft and mobile homes can be admitted entirely tax and duty free if belonging to a person coming into the United Kingdom for a stay of at least six months which are already his personal property and have been owned and used abroad by him or his spouse for six months excluding time he has spent in the United Kingdom. Furthermore, the vehicle must be for personal use

and not sold, hired, etc for one year from importation under penalty of forfeiture. Release may be granted, if all duties and tax are paid. There is also a temporary importation relief for a visitor intending to stay less than six months in the United Kingdom, but the vehicle must be exported at the end of this period (see Customs and Excise Notice 3, and the Private Vehicle Memo).

(2) Boats are not in any case subject to import duty if more than 12 metres long. All boats designed or adapted for recreation or pleasure are subject to VAT as are other boats of less than 15 tons gross. The relieving provisions are virtually identical to those for motor cars (see Customs and Excise Notice 8A and later Customs and Excise Notice 8).

(3) Other baggage, personal and household effects (including pets) are relieved in the same way as cars, etc except that these goods need only have been owned and used in the expatriate's normal home for three months if he is returning from the EU: the six-month rule applies if he is returning from outside the EU and the goods are not disposed of for 12 months. These rules also apply to someone setting up a secondary home in the United Kingdom. Certain prohibited or restricted goods are not within this relief, eg goods bought under a tax-free scheme. The normal duty-free allowances apply in addition to this relief (see Customs and Excise Notice 3).

(4) In addition to the above reliefs, a person who is resident outside the EU and who intends to become normally resident in the United Kingdom on the occasion of his marriage can bring in, duty and VAT free, wedding gifts up to a value of £800 each provided that they are from non-residents. Personal and household effects need not have been used abroad, but the goods should be imported within two months before, or four months after, the wedding.

10.4 STAMP DUTY

Stamp duty on the conveyance of UK stocks and shares is chargeable at $\frac{1}{2}$ per cent. In the case of property the charge is nil up to £60,000; 1 per cent up to £250,000; 3 per cent up to £500,000 and 4 per cent above £500,000. The 3 and 4 per cent bands apply to transfers on or after 28 March 2000 (excluding transfers made in pursuance of contracts existing at that time). There is no longer any stamp duty on gifts.

Of particular interest to expatriates is the stamp duty provision under which a stampable document signed outside the United Kingdom and kept outside the United Kingdom is normally only stampable within 30 days of being brought into the United Kingdom (Stamp Act 1891, s 15(2)(*a*)), albeit with interest on the stamp duty from the date of signing. This is another area in which expert advice is essential, as certain documents may have to be produced in the United Kingdom for particular reasons.

10.5 NATIONAL INSURANCE CONTRIBUTIONS

An employee is liable to make his share of Class 1 National Insurance contributions (NICs) if he is ordinarily resident, resident or present in the United Kingdom at the time of the employment and the employer's share is payable if the employer is resident or present or has a place of business in the United Kingdom.

Where an employee goes to work in another European Economic Area (EEA) country, he will be subject to the social security legislation of that country unless he is sent there by the UK employer and work in the other EEA country is not expected to last more than 12 months after commencement of the overseas tour and he is not sent out to replace another employee who has completed a tour of duty in that country. In such circumstances the temporary non-resident remains liable for UK NICs. If unexpectedly the tour is extended, this situation may be continued for up to a further 12 months on the employer making an appropriate application to the foreign social security authorities. If the employee has special knowledge or skills or the employer has specific objectives in another EEA country which requires the employee's services, it may be possible to continue paying UK NICs for a maximum of five years. After that the expatriate is within the foreign social security regime, although he may have paid sufficient to the UK fund to ensure a reduced pension in due course.

Similar arrangements apply in reverse for workers coming from an EEA country to work in the United Kingdom on a temporary basis, in that they are liable for employees' NICs from the start, which may be postponed on production of form E101 confirming continued liability to contributions under the social security regime of the previous country. Foreign aspects of NICs are dealt with by the IR National Insurance Contributions Office, International Services Division.

Outside the EEA there are a number of countries with whom the United Kingdom has reciprocal agreements. Under these arrangements the United Kingdom issues a certificate of continuing liability and Class 1 NICs are payable as if the employee had stayed in the United Kingdom for the period specified in the certificate. If he is sent abroad for a longer period than that allowed by a reciprocal agreement, there is no UK liability and contributions are immediately payable in the country to which he is sent to work. Conversely, under a reciprocal agreement, a worker coming to the United Kingdom may be exempt from UK NICs for the period specified in the certificate.

Where the employee is sent to work outside the EEA to a country with no reciprocal agreement, UK contributions remain payable for 52 weeks if the employer has a place of business in the United Kingdom and the employee is ordinarily resident in the United Kingdom and was so immediately prior to the commencement of the employment. Employees coming to the United Kingdom from such countries are exempt from UK NICs for the first 52 weeks, if the work is for the overseas employer and the employee did not live in the United Kingdom immediately before the temporary posting.

An employer without a place of business in the United Kingdom is only liable for secondary NICs if there is a host employer with a place of business in the United Kingdom to whom the employee is attached.

11

DOUBLE TAXATION AGREEMENTS

11.1 FISCAL RESIDENCE

The United Kingdom taxes the worldwide income of a UK resident and domiciled individual and it also taxes the income arising in the United Kingdom of a non-resident. It will be appreciated that as many other countries do likewise, it is possible to be subject to tax on overseas income both in the country of residence and in the country in which the income arises. In many cases this problem is alleviated by a bilateral double taxation agreement between the two countries involved.

The United Kingdom currently has more than 100 double taxation agreements, some of which relate only to particular types of income (see Inland Revenue booklets IR 146 and IR 6). This book is aimed at the British expatriate, and it is therefore necessary to consider in the case of income arising in the United Kingdom whether there is a double tax treaty between the United Kingdom and the taxpayer's country of residence or not. If there is such a treaty, it is then necessary to consider the taxpayer's fiscal residence under the treaty.

Consider for example the case of the expatriate who has retired to Spain, where he spends the majority of the winter, but who has retained his house in the United Kingdom where he spends the summer months. Article 4 of the Anglo-Spanish Double Tax Treaty provides that it is necessary first of all to consider residence according to the rules of the country concerned. Under UK law, if he spends an average 91 days a year or more in the United Kingdom, he is resident in the United Kingdom. As he spends some eight months of the year in Spain, he is resident in Spain for Spanish tax purposes.

It is then necessary to consider in which country he has a permanent home available to him. As he has a home in both countries, it is then necessary to consider his centre of vital interests, ie the state with which his personal and economic relations are closer. This is debatable. He spends two-thirds of his time in Spain but has by no means severed his ties with the United Kingdom. If the country in which he has his centre of vital interests cannot be determined, it is necessary to look to the country in which he has a habitual abode. But as he has such an abode in both countries it is then necessary to look to his nationality. If he is a UK national, he will be regarded as resident in the United Kingdom and non-resident in Spain and taxed accordingly. If he is a Spanish national, however, on the same facts he would be regarded as resident in Spain and not resident in the United Kingdom. If he is a national in neither the United Kingdom nor Spain, the tax authorities in each country will agree his place of residence. In the circumstances envisaged this would probably be Spain and he would therefore be regarded as not resident in the United Kingdom, notwithstanding the fact that he has a home here.

A number of the older treaties do not have this tie-breaker clause with regard to residence and it is therefore possible to be resident in both countries. This also applies where there is no double tax treaty. In this case, the tax liability must be calculated in accordance with the rules of each country and advantage taken of any remaining relief under the treaties and unilateral relief where available.

Exceptionally, the second protocol to the Anglo-US treaty (SI 1980 No 568) provides that for income tax purposes a woman with US citizenship who married a UK domiciled man before 1 January 1974 and therefore acquired a UK domicile of dependence is deemed to have married on that date and may therefore retain her US domicile of origin unless she acquires a UK domicile by choice.

In order to benefit from specific reliefs under a double taxation agreement it is usually necessary to apply to the relevant authority using prescribed forms which have to be verified by a competent authority in the other contracting state, as evidence of tax residence there. It follows that treaty benefits can usually be enjoyed only by those persons who are both resident in a treaty jurisdiction and paying tax there on the relevant income.

11.2 DIVIDENDS

A non-resident in receipt of dividends from the United Kingdom is not entitled to the tax credit that is available to a UK resident unless the appropriate treaty so provides. The treaty with Spain for example provides in Art 10, para 3 that a Spanish resident entitled to dividends from a UK company is entitled to the same tax credit as a UK resident and is subject to Spanish tax on the gross equivalent of the dividends. However, the UK authorities subject the dividend to a withholding tax of 15 per cent on the gross equivalent and this tax is allowed as a credit against the Spanish tax payable. If, therefore, a British company paid a dividend of

£80, the resident in Spain would receive £80 from the company with a UK tax credit (1/9th) of £8.88. No further UK tax will be charged. He would be regarded in Spain as having received dividends of £88.88 on which tax of £8.88 had already been paid. Article 10 of the treaty between the United Kingdom and Spain says that UK tax on dividends paid to a Spanish resident shall not exceed 15 per cent. However, this is obviously not the case in this instance. The reduction in the level of tax credit from April 1999 means that in most cases a repayment of credit under the terms of a treaty will no longer be relevant. This puts non-residents on broadly the same footing as UK residents, who can no longer claim repayment of dividend tax credits.

A resident of a non-treaty country, would be treated as receiving income of £80 and would pay such local tax on that income as would be levied by the country of residence.

To avoid having to apply to the UK Inland Revenue for the repayment of part of the tax credit, it used to be possible to arrange for the company paying the dividend to repay the appropriate part of the tax credit at the same time. This requires the consent of the company and of the Inland Revenue under the Double Taxation Relief (Taxes on Income) (General) (Dividend) Regulations, SI 1973 No 317. (Usually known as the G arrangement.) However, following the abolition of advance corporation tax and the imputation system in the United Kingdom from 6 April 1999, there will be few cases in which a claim to repayment will be worth pursuing under the terms of a treaty.

11.3 INTEREST

Interest arising in the United Kingdom to a non-resident is normally taxable in the United Kingdom under Schedule D, Case III, under the Income and Corporation Taxes Act 1988 (TA 1988), s 18(3), but the charge is limited to the tax deducted at source, if any (FA 1995, s 128). Annual interest, ie on a loan exceeding 12 months, paid to a person whose usual place of abode is outside the United Kingdom, is subject to deduction of tax at the basic rate at source under TA 1988, s 349(2)(*c*) unless it is bank or building society interest, in which case a non-resident can arrange that it is paid gross, see **5.3**.

Interest paid to a non-resident may suffer a reduced rate of withholding tax or be liable in the United Kingdom for a reduced rate of tax under the treaty. Article 11 of the Anglo-Spanish Treaty, for example, reduces the tax in the country where the interest arises to 12 per cent which would be credited against the liability in the country of residence. It is possible to arrange with the Financial Intermediaries and Claims Office (FICO) to deduct tax at the reduced treaty rate, if any, on payment of interest to a non-resident under the Double Taxation Relief (Taxes on Income) (General) Regulations, SI 1970 No 488. This applies to both interest and royalties.

11.4 ROYALTIES

Royalties paid from the United Kingdom to a non-resident are subject to a withholding tax at the basic rate of 22 per cent if they are royalties in respect of a UK patent under TA 1988, s 348(2)(*a*) or s 349(1)(*b*) or in respect of copyright, and are paid to the owner of copyright whose usual place of abode is not within the United Kingdom under TA 1988, s 536. This section refers to a usual place of abode outside the United Kingdom, not residence outside the United Kingdom, although for practical purposes this will normally be the same. It should also be noted that copyright royalties paid to an author whose normal place of abode is outside the United Kingdom are not subject to withholding tax under TA 1988, s 536 in view of a Parliamentary Answer of 10 November 1969 (*Hansard*, Vol 791, col 31).

Other royalties arising in the United Kingdom are not subject to withholding tax unless they are pure income profit where the non-resident provides no services whatsoever for the royalty received. If it is pure income profit, the tax would be withheld at source at the basic rate in the same way as for any other annual payment. Under the appropriate double tax treaty, it may be possible to reduce the rate of withholding tax and in the treaty with Spain, for example, the rate of withholding tax on royalties is reduced to 10 per cent by Art 12 of the treaty. As for interest, permission may be obtained from the FICO to pay the interest subject to this reduced rate of withholding tax.

11.5 INCOME FROM REAL PROPERTY

Income from immovable property is normally taxed in the country in which it is situated, as under Art 6 of the Anglo-Spanish Double Tax Treaty. Income from property in the United Kingdom is subject to withholding tax under TA 1988, s 43 or s 42A at the basic rate of tax where payment is made to a non-resident, although under the non-resident landlords' scheme it is normally possible to arrange with the Inland Revenue for payment to be made subject to a nil level of withholding tax where the non-resident agrees to comply with his UK tax responsibilities under self-assessment. The tenant or rent-collecting agent will be authorised to pay rents gross under TA 1988, s 42A regulations (see Chapter 6).

11.6 BUSINESSES

Business profits are normally only taxed in the country of residence unless there is a permanent establishment in the other country, eg see Art 7 of the Anglo-Spanish Double Tax Treaty. Permanent establishment is very often but not always defined by the treaty, eg in Art 5 of the double tax treaty with Spain, and includes a place of management, branch, office, factory, workshop, mine, oil well, etc and in the case of Spain, a building site which exists for more than 12 months.

If there is a permanent establishment of a non-resident in the United Kingdom, it will be subject to UK tax on the profits. The assessment may be made in the name of a UK representative, ie a branch or agent who is made responsible for the tax under FA 1995, s 126/127, and who may withhold UK tax when accounting to the non-resident. A non-resident trading *with*, as opposed to *in* the United Kingdom is not, under general law, subject to UK tax and it is specifically provided that a non-resident trading in the United Kingdom through a broker who is a general agent is not liable to UK tax in view of FA 1995, s 126/127. If he is otherwise trading in the United Kingdom but not through a permanent establishment, a treaty, if there is one, will normally protect him from UK tax. In the case of a business being carried on by a non-resident it is common for the treaty to reinforce the transfer pricing provisions of TA 1988, s 770 to ensure arm's length pricing between the United Kingdom and overseas business and in the case of Spain this is contained in Art 9 of the treaty.

11.7 CAPITAL GAINS

A non-resident is not normally liable to UK capital gains tax (CGT) except in the case of assets used for a branch or business in the United Kingdom under TCGA 1992, s 10. Article 13 of the Anglo-Spanish Double Tax Treaty would allow the United Kingdom to tax immovable property in the United Kingdom, although in fact it does not do so, except for land development profits under TA 1988, s 776.

CGT articles may be especially important in the case of temporary non-residents or those who might otherwise find themselves exposed to UK CGT – perhaps because they remain ordinarily resident in the eyes of the Revenue. Not all countries tax gains in the same way. However, under the terms of some treaties, exemption may be granted in the United Kingdom for gains on moveable and intangible assets, even though a gain would actually suffer no tax in the foreign country. In such a case, the residence tie-breaker clause under the terms of the relevant treaty will be of vital importance (see **11.1**).

11.8 INDEPENDENT PERSONAL SERVICES

The self-employed activities of a non-resident will not normally be subject to tax in the United Kingdom unless there is a fixed base in the United Kingdom, as under Art 14 of the Anglo-Spanish treaty.

Many treaties have separate articles for business profits and 'income from independent services', as in the case of Spain, and it is important to recognise under which article a claim should be made.

11.9 DEPENDENT PERSONAL SERVICES

Employment income of a non-resident from activities in the United Kingdom would normally be taxable under Schedule E, Case II although this liability may be reduced by treaty relief. For example, under Art 15 of the Anglo-Spanish treaty, if the employer is not resident in the United Kingdom, the non-resident employee is present for a period not exceeding 183 days in the fiscal year and the income is not borne by a permanent establishment in the United Kingdom, he would not be liable to UK tax under Schedule E, Case II for his work in the United Kingdom. It should be noted that for this purpose, in calculating 183 days, fractions of days (of arrival and departure) must be counted. This contrasts with the United Kingdom's domestic rule, which is normally to ignore days of arrival and departure. On the other hand, directors' fees from a UK company would be subject to tax in the United Kingdom, in the case of Spain under Art 16 of the treaty.

If an employee works in two countries and is not exempted under the dependent personal services article, double taxation may arise and he may have to rely on the elimination of double taxation article if there is one, or on unilateral relief which is given in the United Kingdom (see **11.17**).

11.10 ENTERTAINERS AND SPORTSMEN

There are often special provisions relating to the remuneration of non-resident entertainers and sportsmen whose remuneration may be very large (see **5.16**). The treaty will usually provide that they are taxable in the country in which the performance is given even though they would otherwise be protected by the treaty, see, for example, Art 17 of the Anglo-Spanish treaty, withholding tax at the basic rate from the UK earnings of non-UK-resident entertainers and sportsmen.

11.11 STUDENTS AND TEACHERS

There are often special provisions in double tax treaties relating to students and teachers. For example in the treaty with Spain, Art 20 provides that a previous resident of Spain who comes to the United Kingdom for training and who receives money for his maintenance, education or benefit is not taxable in the United Kingdom. This is obviously useful where the children of expatriates come back to the United Kingdom for the purposes of their education. Teachers, as in Art 21 of the Anglo-Spanish treaty, are often allowed a two-year period, in total, *IRC v Vas* [1990] STC 137, in another country without becoming liable to tax therein.

11.12 PENSIONS

Under most of the double taxation agreements that the United Kingdom has with other countries, pensions are normally only taxable in the country of residence. The exception is pensions which result from government service, including local authority pensions; these are normally taxable only in the country from which the pension originates unless paid to a national of the country of residence. For example, under the Anglo-Spanish treaty, a UK pension paid to a resident of Spain would be liable for tax only in Spain, by virtue of Art 18. However, if the pension resulted from service with HM Government or a local authority, it would be taxable only in the United Kingdom under Art 19(3), unless the recipient was a Spanish national in which case it would be taxable only in Spain.

Clearly the operation of the agreement is straightforward where the pension is paid gross – the return is simply made to the appropriate authority. Where the pension is normally subject to deduction of tax at source, obtaining treaty relief is a little more involved. (Those pensions subject to tax deduction at source were outlined in Chapter 5 but briefly, they are likely to be any pension other than state pensions – Retirement Pension and State Earnings Related Pension – which are paid gross.) Authority for pension or retirement annuity payments to be made gross is granted by the FICO.

The Inspector will grant permission on receipt of confirmation that the individual in question is resident for tax purposes in the other jurisdiction. There is an official confirmation form for each country with which the United Kingdom has a double taxation agreement – the form may be obtained from either tax authority and is printed in both languages. For instance, in the case of a resident of Spain form SPA may be obtained from FICO or from the local office of the *Delegación de*

Hacienda del domicilio fiscal del residente de España. In other words, this relief cannot be claimed by those who do not disclose their income in the host country.

11.12.1 UK State Retirement Pension

This is always paid gross to the recipient wherever resident and would normally be taxable in the country of residence.

11.12.2 Occupational pensions in respect of government or local authority service

These pensions, eg of civil servants, members of the armed services, state system school teachers, etc would be paid subject to deduction of tax under PAYE at the appropriate code number. If the recipient is living in a treaty country it is unlikely that there would be a local tax liability in the country of residence on this income, although this may first need to be established by filing a form with the local fiscal authorities to claim relief under the relevant treaty.

11.12.3 Occupational pensions (not government)

Occupational pensions would normally be subject to deduction of tax under PAYE. A non-resident should be able to arrange for a no tax notice of coding from his local district, if he still submits UK income tax returns, or from FICO. Such pensions will normally be taxable in the country of residence.

11.12.4 Retirement annuities and personal pensions

These are normally subject to deduction of tax at the basic rate although a non-resident should be able to obtain the appropriate authority from FICO for the annuity to be paid gross. Such income would normally be taxable in the country of residence.

11.13 OTHER INCOME

In some treaties there is an article which provides that any other income arising in the treaty country will only be taxed in the country of residence. This article could, for example, apply to maintenance payments from the United Kingdom to a non-resident who would therefore receive the income gross or be able to recover the tax from the Inland Revenue. In the treaty with Spain 'other income' is in Art 22.

11.14 NON-DISCRIMINATION

Treaties often contain what is known as a non-discrimination article which says generally that a non-resident shall not be treated worse than a resident for tax purposes. In the Anglo-Spanish treaty this is contained in Art 25. Non-discrimination clauses are very often more useful as a negotiating tool than for actual invocation.

11.15 MUTUAL AGREEMENT PROCEDURE

Most treaties also contain a mutual agreement procedure whereby a resident may ask his own tax authority to negotiate with the overseas tax authority if he considers that he is being unfairly treated, or the double taxation treaty is being ignored or misinterpreted. The mutual agreement procedure is, for example, often invoked or threatened to be invoked in negotiating with the Internal Revenue Service in the United States, who tend to have a somewhat cavalier view of the application of double tax treaties with other countries.

11.16 EXCHANGE OF INFORMATION

One of the points to watch in living in a country where there is a double tax treaty with the United Kingdom, is that the treaty will usually contain a clause overriding the normal secrecy provisions and allow the appropriate tax authorities to exchange information relating to the taxpayer's financial affairs. Inland Revenue information gathering powers may now be used on behalf of other tax authorities within the European Union (FA 1990, s 125).

Although most treaties are broadly similar in many respects being based upon the OECD models, it is extremely important to refer to the actual treaty currently in force when considering the likely taxation charge as there can be significant differences.

11.17 UNILATERAL RELIEF

Double taxation relief is often given unilaterally where there is no treaty or the treaty does not cover the income in question. A UK resident is given unilateral relief under TA 1988, s 790. Unilateral relief will normally give credit for direct overseas taxes suffered but, for example, would not normally give an individual relief for the underlying taxes on a company's profits out of which a dividend is subsequently declared. As far as possible relief is given as if there had been a double taxation treaty in force, see Statement of Practice SP 7/91.

11.18 INHERITANCE TAX

The United Kingdom has only ten double taxation treaties covering IHT and consequently they are generally not of so much importance as the income tax treaties. The countries with which agreements have been concluded are:

France	Republic of Ireland
India	Republic of South Africa
Italy	Sweden
Netherlands	Switzerland
Pakistan	United States

In some circumstances the treaties can change the fiscal domicile of an individual for IHT purposes which would obviously be of extreme importance in determining his UK IHT liability. For instance, under Art 4 of the IHT Double Taxation Treaty with South Africa, a South African national with a UK domicile who had not been ordinarily resident in the United Kingdom for seven years would be regarded as domiciled in South Africa and not in the United Kingdom. This seemingly arcane illustration is mirrored in other ways in other treaties and must serve as an example of the need to seek professional advice in situations where an individual is living in one jurisdiction and has assets in another.

Where two countries both have a claim to the same assets (for IHT purposes) the potential exists, despite the treaty, for double taxation to occur. For this reason most treaties contain a double taxation relief clause which will remove or, at the least, mitigate the double liability. Where there is no double taxation treaty between countries, unilateral relief against double taxation may be available whereby a credit for the overseas tax paid will be set against the UK IHT liability. The provisions are somewhat complex and are contained in IHTA 1984, s 159.

11.19 TREATY SHOPPING

In certain cases, it is possible to use a third country's double taxation agreement to reduce a withholding tax. For example, UK patent royalties paid from the United Kingdom to a resident of Hong Kong would normally suffer UK tax at 22 per cent. If, however, a Netherlands company were interposed, the UK royalties should be paid gross to the Netherlands under the UK-Netherlands Double Tax Treaty and 7 per cent or so of the royalties would remain in the Netherlands subject to Netherlands tax. The remaining 93 per cent would, however, be paid on to Hong Kong free of withholding tax as the Netherlands does not levy a withholding tax on royalties.

This could not, however, be done for dividends from the United Kingdom, for example, even if it would produce a similar effect, as there is a specific anti-avoidance provision in the UK-Netherlands treaty to prevent the use of the treaty by a third country resident.

Care is required, however, because, as in all tax matters, if there is first, a pre-ordained series of transactions and second, steps inserted which have no business *purpose* apart from avoidance of tax, the inserted steps may be ignored for tax purposes: see *Craven v White* [1988] STC 476.

12

THE RETURNING EXPATRIATE

The successful handling of an expatriate's financial affairs requires careful planning before he leaves the United Kingdom, continuous awareness of the taxation consequences of his actions while overseas, and, perhaps most important of all, careful planning and sound advice before his return home. It would, after all, be rather unfortunate to have spent many years building up a substantial amount of capital only to have a large slice of it taken by the Inland Revenue through a lack of foresight on return. Fortunately, much can be done to mitigate potential tax charges, but it is essential for these mitigating devices to be put in train before the expatriate comes back to the United Kingdom. Effective tax planning the day after return will, more often than not, prove to be impossible or, at least, illegal or ineffective.

This chapter, in common with the rest of the book, is concerned primarily with taxation and investment, but the returning expatriate has more to consider than this, and an indication of some of the other areas of concern is also provided.

12.1 TAX LIABILITIES ON RETURN

As already mentioned, the main determinant of a person's liability to UK income tax or capital gains tax (CGT), apart, that is, from having an income or a capital gain, is his tax residence position. The mere ending of an overseas employment or a visit to the United Kingdom need not result in a change of residence. The change from non-resident to resident will only come about if any of the following circumstances apply:

(1) the person returns to the United Kingdom intending to remain permanently or for a number of years; or
(2) he spends 183 days or more in the United Kingdom in any particular tax year;
(3) he visits the United Kingdom regularly for periods which average 91 or more days each year over a period of four consecutive tax years.

For the majority of returning expatriates, the first condition above will apply. But before going on to review the consequences of this, it is worth considering the not uncommon situation of the expatriate who returns home for a period, perhaps at the end of a contract, but with the intention of finding another overseas job at the earliest opportunity. A person in these circumstances need not become resident in the United Kingdom, if his employment covered a complete tax year, but many do under the second condition above. Unlike the majority, this temporary resident will not become resident and ordinarily resident from the date of arrival: rather, he will become resident but not ordinarily resident for that year. The tax consequences here are quite different from those pertaining to the new permanent resident.

12.1.1 Taxation on remittance basis

An individual who is resident but not ordinarily resident will be taxed on the remittance basis, ie on the income he actually brings into the United Kingdom. In some respects this can be a more onerous burden than that of the permanent resident. Income which arises in the United Kingdom will be wholly taxable; overseas investment income will be assessed on the remittances made during the current year. Any remittances from an overseas trade or profession will be charged on a current year basis. Before 6 April 1997 this was a previous year basis where the source of income arose before 6 April 1994.

The remittance of earnings in the year of return from an overseas employment will also be taxable in the year of return. Earnings arising in the year of return or previous years from a trade within Schedule D will also be assessed on amounts remitted in the year of return. This latter liability is one of the major differences between the treatment of those who become ordinarily resident, who are assessed on an arising basis unless domiciled outside the United Kingdom; and those who do not. Taxable remittances can be in cash or kind, or they can be constructive remittances arising through various debt arrangements and similar devices. An expatriate who is likely to find himself in this position would be well advised to seek professional assistance at an early date, before his return, because the degree of tax liability will be determined by many individual factors which are beyond the scope of a general treatment here.

From 6 April 1995, if the business was started on or after 6 April 1994 or 6 April 1997 in other cases there will be a deemed cessation of a business on a change of residence, at the date of arrival if concessionary treatment applies or previous 6 April if not. Remittance of past profits in the years following the year of return are not taxable because the source has ceased (income must normally have a source in the fiscal year to be taxable). For

1996/97, if the current year basis does not apply in that year, the assessment is based on half of the total remittances in 1995/96 and 1996/97. In 1997/98 and future years, where the remittance basis applies the amount assessable is the total of the remittances in the fiscal year.

So far as CGT is concerned, an individual resident but not ordinarily resident will be fully liable on any gains made worldwide unless he is not domiciled in the United Kingdom. In the case of the non-domiciled individual he will be liable in full for gains made in the United Kingdom and on any gain remitted to the United Kingdom which arose abroad.

12.1.2 Tax on worldwide income

Returning to the majority case, the erstwhile expatriate will become resident and ordinarily resident from the day of his return. From then on, he will be fully liable to UK taxes on his worldwide income and capital gains unless he has a non-UK domicile. There are, however, some important exceptions and adjustments to this general rule. The first of these concerns any earnings from the overseas employment. Because, by concession, the tax year may be split in the year of return into a resident and non-resident part, the overseas earnings before return escape tax. Subsequent payments including terminal leave pay, bonuses, gratuities, or lump sums from provident funds or in commutation of pension rights, used to be allowed tax free where they related to the overseas employment, but ceased to be from 6 April 1992, under Statement of Practice SP 18/91. Any pension which arises overseas and which is payable by reason of overseas employment is taxable in the United Kingdom (whether remitted or not) but 10 per cent of the amount received is exempted from tax under the Income and Corporation Taxes Act 1988 (TA 1988), s 196.

Where the returned expatriate has a continuing source of overseas investment income this, too, will become taxable on his return. This type of income is taxed under Schedule D, Case IV or V, and the basis of assessment is the current year basis from 1997/98 (1996/97 was a transitional year).

12.1.3 Current year basis

Income previously taxed on the preceding year basis is, from 1997/98, taxed on a current year basis, removing a number of problems on returning to the United Kingdom which were illustrated in previous editions of this Handbook.

Even on the current year basis there may be advantages in closing deposit accounts before arrival in the United Kingdom.

One point to bear in mind when contemplating the return home and what to do with bank deposits is the period of notice required for withdrawals or closure of the account. Many investors use fixed-term deposits for three, six, or 12 months and if the interest rate remains attractive at the end of the term, they simply roll the money over for a subsequent term. Breaking a fixed-term account, if it is permitted at all, will always involve a stiff penalty in interest forfeited. It is essential, therefore, to ensure that all accounts can be terminated before the return date.

Example: Capitalisation of investments

Mr Swan has been abroad for ten years; he opened a deposit account in a Channel Islands bank five years ago and for the last two years the deposit has been standing at £100,000. Interest has been, and for the purpose of illustration, will continue to be, paid at the rate of 10 per cent a year. The interest earned is paid annually on 1 June and has always been withdrawn by Mr Swan and invested elsewhere. Mr Swan's contract ends on 30 April 1999 and he intends to return to the UK on 5 May 2000. If Mr Swan did nothing about his account before coming home he would be assessed for 1999/00 on interest of £10,000 × $^{11}/_{12}$ (the portion of the year in which he is resident).

If he is taxable only at the basic rate this will mean a bill of £2,108 payable on 31 January 2001.

If, on the other hand, Mr Swan had closed his account on 1 April 1999 he would have crystallised $^{10}/_{12}$ths of the interest in 1998/99 when he is not taxable, saving tax on £8,333 of interest.

Although this is one of the simplest pieces of tax planning for the returning expatriate, it is often missed. If the expatriate has held his money on deposit in the United Kingdom he will have had no liability during his period of non-residence but in the year of return this concessionary exemption is lost completely. If nothing is done about a UK account, the full amount of interest received will be assessed as it is income arising in the United Kingdom. There is no apportionment related to the part of the year during which the investor is resident.

If the account is closed before return this will make little, if any, difference. The assessment would then be on the current year basis from the beginning of the tax year to the date of closure and on the same basis from the date of reopening until the following 5 April, ie a full year's interest. The only way around this is to close the UK account in the tax year preceding the tax year of return, transfer the money offshore then use the capitalisation procedure on that offshore account. Because of the hassle involved in this, as well as the need to know the expected return date well in advance, it is better if the expatriate stays clear of UK deposits altogether. The same or better interest rates, with the same banks, can often be obtained outside the United Kingdom.

From 1997/98 income from an overseas trade managed and controlled overseas is taxable under Schedule D, Case V on the income of the accounting year ending in the fiscal year, as is the income from a UK trade or profession under Schedule D, Cases I and II. The current year basis applies to new sources of income and new businesses from 1994/95. For existing sources 1996/97, the first year of self-assessment, was assessed on the average income of the transitional period, usually the two accounting years ending in 1996/97 or on 5 April 1997. The deemed cessation on a change of residence applies to all trades and professions and investments but losses may be carried forward through the change. Foreign partnership income remains taxable under Schedule D, Case V and UK partnership income, including partnership investment income, is taxed on the current year basis on the income of the accounting period ending in the fiscal year.

12.2 CAPITAL GAINS TAX

Turning to the question of CGT, there is now less scope than there used to be for some tax planning tactics. The basic rule is that where a person is not resident and not ordinarily resident throughout the tax year, he will have no liability to UK CGT. However, this is subject to earlier comments regarding the re-entry charge for temporary non-residents. By concession, where the tax year is split into a non-resident and resident part in the year of return, no CGT will be charged on gains made during the period of non-residence (Extra-Statutory Concession ESC D2). It is invariably advisable not to rely on the concession where any material amounts of CGT may be at stake, as there are ways of realising the gains before the 6 April preceding the date of return which, so long as the expatriate had non-resident and non-ordinarily resident status which was more than temporary (ie more than five years), should ensure that he is not taxed, even though the gains may be repatriated on return to the United Kingdom.

The returning expatriate's aim should be to realise his gains before he returns but hold on to his losses until he rejoins the UK tax system. The converse, of course, may apply if there is a local CGT regime which is more burdensome than that in the United Kingdom. Sometimes a returning expatriate may have the opportunity to realise gains having left the tax regime in the host country but before rejoining the UK tax system – perhaps by taking a short holiday in a tax haven before his return. In most cases, however, the investor will not necessarily want to dispose of his holdings. One possibility is for a non-resident investor to set up before his return to the United Kingdom a simple trust, resident in the United Kingdom, and gift his gainful assets to it. The transfer would be deemed to take place at market value and the trustees would have the market value as their acquisition cost, so that in due time, when the asset is sold, the base cost will be the market value when the trust was set up so that gains arising in the period of non-residence (and indeed before that as well) may be eliminated.

Another simple step available to married couples is the 'bed and breakfast' operation under which investments are sold and repurchased the following day by the spouse. The repurchase following the previous day's sale (theoretically, and usually in practice too, at the same price or thereabouts) crystallises any underlying gain and gives an enhanced acquisition cost against which to compute the gain on the eventual disposal. It appears from the exchange of correspondence between the Institute of Chartered Accountants and the Revenue, published on 25 September 1985 as TR 588, in para 16, that the *Furniss v Dawson* doctrine would not normally be applied to a properly executed bed and breakfast transaction. Prior to 6 April 1998, this technique was available to anyone. However, repurchases by the same taxpayer within 30 days of sale are now matched with the sale, thus eliminating the advantage. For unmarried taxpayers who are willing and able to sell and wait more than 30 days to repurchase, this approach is in theory still viable.

Bed and breakfasting can incur transaction costs and there may be other ways of achieving this uplift, such as disposal to a wholly-owned investment company, or offshore trust, if one exists. Costs of establishing such vehicles may make this unattractive, but for an unmarried person, for example, with assets that are heavy with gains but not readily marketable, this may nevertheless be desirable.

Another point to remember is that a disposal will break the holding period for the purposes of CGT tapering relief. It is quite possible that, in time, the loss of taper relief could outweigh any advantage from crystallising a gain based on current value.

Where the intention is to dispose of certain assets in the near future, perhaps to purchase a house or business, the simplest course might be to sell before return and hold the proceeds on deposit until required. If any assets are showing losses, they should be retained until after return.

So far, this chapter has illustrated ways of reducing the returning expatriate's immediate tax bills. That may be sufficient planning for some expatriates who intend to spend their capital soon after return but for many others it does not go far enough. In particular, where the returning expatriate intends to use his capital to provide an income either to supplement a lower UK salary or to provide a pension in retirement, what is required is longer-term planning and the use of a 'tax shelter' and, in this context, good advice is essential.

12.3 DANGERS OF EVASION

Many expatriates believe when they return home that so long as their money is left outside the United Kingdom they will have no UK tax liability on any income arising from that money or any capital gains made. Others believe that they will only have a liability when they remit the income to the United Kingdom. For the British expatriate returning home this is, of course, untrue. Then there are those expatriates who know this to be the case but still take the view that if they leave their money offshore and 'forget' to declare it, the Inland Revenue will never find out. That view, to say the least, is extremely inadvisable. Just one or two points might help to dissuade some expatriates from this course of action.

Assuming that the unlawful evasion goes undetected for a year or two, our evasively minded individual may decide to spend some of his cash on a new house: the Inland Revenue will receive details of the transaction and any half-awake tax inspector will ask where the balance of the purchase price came from. The claim that it was a legacy from Aunt Freda will not be accepted without sight of the probate documents.

Another myth which should be exploded concerns bank secrecy. More and more countries are co-operating with each other in the transfer of information about taxpayers of mutual interest, and there is often provision for this in double taxation agreements. Even the Swiss banks, those bastions of security where it is a criminal offence to divulge any information about a bank customer, have not proved impregnable to attacks by both the French and American tax authorities.

It should also be noted that undisclosed offshore assets cause problems for executors and heirs on the death of their owners. If executors are unaware of the existence of accounts, the offshore bankers will be happy to sit on the money indefinitely. If they are aware, such assets must be included in the estate of a UK domiciled deceased for the purposes of the inheritance tax (IHT) return. This can normally be expected to alert the Revenue to the possibility of evasion by the deceased, which is quite capable of leading to fiscal penalties equal to or even exceeding the account balance. Either way, heirs can end up with next to nothing.

Finally, an incautious word in the golf club may find its way back to the taxman and the subsequent investigation will not be a pleasant experience, quite apart from the substantial costs which will inevitably be incurred.

The Revenue have no hesitation in launching criminal proceedings in cases of tax evasion, particularly where there has been non-disclosure of overseas transactions, not only against the taxpayer (*R v Hunt* [1994] STC 819) but also his professional advisers (*R v Charlton* [1996] STC 1418; *R v Dimsey and Allen* [1999] STC 846).

12.4 MISCELLANEOUS INVESTMENTS

The steps to be taken and the points to be considered with a portfolio of conventional investments have largely been covered, but many expatriates also acquire a range of other investments, whether Persian carpets, Chinese ceramics, precious metals such as bullion, coin or jewellery, motor cars, boats and so on. Where these are wanted at home for reasons of aesthetic enjoyment as well as as an investment, the investor should be prepared to pay any necessary duty, including value added tax (VAT), incurred on importing them. If it is only their investment potential that is of interest, these charges can be avoided by importing them to the Channel Islands and depositing them there. The cost of safe storage and the high cost of insurance, however, must be taken into account.

Income from and expenditure on woodlands in the United Kingdom were taken out of the tax system with effect from 15 March 1988, subject to transitional provisions, but woodlands remain a tax efficient investment. They still attract IHT privileges and may well qualify for grants.

12.5 UNREMITTABLE OVERSEAS INCOME

Where a person has overseas investment income which cannot be remitted to the United Kingdom or otherwise released from the overseas country, any tax chargeable in the United Kingdom on the income will be held over until such time as the income is released. The unremittability of the income must be by reason of the laws of the overseas country, or executive action of that country's government, or the impossibility of obtaining foreign currency there. In addition the investor must not have realised the income outside that territory for a consideration in sterling or any other freely remittable currency. Where this relief is due it must be claimed before any assessment on the income becomes final. When the income is finally released it will become taxable at that time, and relief will be given for any overseas taxes paid. If the investor dies before the income is released, then any later release will be charged to his personal representatives.

12.6 NATIONAL INSURANCE

Some of the benefits available under the British social security system will be accessible to the returning expatriate immediately, regardless of his National Insurance record while overseas, but the major benefits such as unemployment benefit, sickness and invalidity benefit and maternity grants and allowances will only be given where there is an acceptable level of contributions.

Where the returning expatriate has been receiving a National Insurance Retirement Pension at a lower level than that currently prevailing in the United Kingdom he will be entitled to have it uprated to the full rate on his resumption of UK residence.

12.7 OTHER MATTERS

The returning expatriate must also consider various legal matters. First, he must make sure to give his tenants sufficient notice if he has let his house and wishes to resume living there. It might be considered wise to seek to terminate the tenancy a month or so before the expected date of return to give time for eviction proceedings to be pursued, should the tenants resist moving. The lost rent is unlikely to be as much as the cost of staying in hotels while the law takes its course.

Another point worth watching is the expatriate's will. It may be that he has made a will under his local legal framework while abroad – this is generally advisable. The will should be reviewed on return. It may be worth retaining the overseas will, suitably amended, in so far as it relates to property in the overseas country and to have a new will in the United Kingdom. This may assist in releasing overseas assets to the executors in order to pay any IHT required before a grant of probate on the UK will (see also Chapter 9).

Finally, in some countries a tax clearance certificate is required before an exit visa is granted. Where such a certificate is necessary, it is usually essential to apply in good time. There is not a lot of point in turning up at the airport only to be told that you first have to satisfy the local taxman that you have paid all his taxes.

13

CONSTRUCTING AN INVESTMENT PORTFOLIO

13.1 INTRODUCTION

Many expatriates find that they have significantly more money available for investment than they had when they were living and working in the United Kingdom. This may be because they are earning a higher salary than they did in the United Kingdom, or it may simply be that they are receiving their salary gross rather than net of tax. Many expatriates also find that they face a wider range of investment opportunities than they did in the United Kingdom.

The first question that an expatriate should address concerns whether or not investment is a necessary activity at all. Strictly speaking, the answer is that it is not. Surplus earnings may be spent, or they may be left to accumulate in a bank account. However, a term of expatriation offers a rare opportunity to build up wealth, and even the beginner will find that by the application of a number of simple principles, the risks of investment can be minimised, and the potential for return enhanced. Advisers suggest that even the most cautious expatriate should, at the very least, consider investing that proportion of his earnings that would have been deducted as tax in the United Kingdom.

The subject of investment is important enough to merit a book of its own, and for a comprehensive treatment the reader may like to refer to the *Allied Dunbar Investment and Savings Handbook*, which is revised annually to update such key information as stock market performance and changes in UK tax rules.

This chapter discusses the construction of an investment portfolio, and identifies the criteria that should be applied when any particular investment is considered. It also identifies the key characteristics of different investments in the context of what an investor may expect them to achieve. It begins, however, by making a number of points based on the simple premise that in constructing an investment portfolio, the early stages are crucial.

13.2 FIRST STEPS

The newcomer to expatriate life will find that the process of establishing himself overseas is expensive. There may be furniture to buy, for example, and clubs to join. Newcomers also take time to find the cheaper shops used by experienced expatriates.

It is generally sensible, therefore, for a newly-arrived expatriate not to consider investment at all for the first three months overseas. The problem is that during this time, he may come into contact with investment advisers and salesmen advising him to invest in savings schemes. Their argument will tend to be that by investing straight away, the expatriate will achieve an investment benefit from the whole of his time overseas rather than, as they will put it, wasting the first three months.

Against this, there is the consideration that the newly-arrived expatriate will not have had time to work out how much of his disposable income he may commit to investment, and he will not have been able to formulate a realistic investment strategy by reference to which he can judge the suitability of any savings scheme offered to him.

He will also not have had time to build up a contingency reserve. This is the prerequisite for any expatriate investment portfolio. A contingency reserve should be easily accessible, in an instant access bank account, and it should be sufficient to meet any unforeseen liability that might otherwise force the sale of an investment at a disadvantageous time. A contingency reserve should, for example, be sufficient to meet the cost of flights back to the United Kingdom in the event of illness or loss of employment.

13.3 STARTING TO INVEST

No investment should be undertaken except by reference to a clearly thought-out objective, and with due regard for the need for diversification. This is for a practical reason. Expatriates will tend to invest with companies based in offshore centres. Not only does the offshore world offer a wider range of investment opportunities than would be available in the United Kingdom, it is also generally the case that offshore money managers operate under fewer restrictions as to what they can do with the assets entrusted to their care.

Therefore, the offshore world is at once more hazardous to the investor, and more potentially lucrative. Formulating an objective defines the range of potentially suitable investments, while investing for diversification reduces the risk of overly narrowing the range of investments made.

The two concepts require brief elucidation.

13.3.1 Formulating an objective

Working expatriates generally have a limited time overseas, and a finite amount that they can allocate regularly to investment over that time. An investment objective should first of all be realistic in that it should take account of these two factors. The expatriate should consider his need to make such non-investment financial commitments as 'family protection' – medical insurance, etc – as well as the uses he would like to make of the proceeds of his investments.

In formulating an objective, the expatriate should take into account whether he is, to use the investment industry's terminology, a cautious, balanced or aggressive investor. An aggressive investor, who is prepared to take risks, can afford an ambitious objective. For a cautious investor, however, aiming too high will simply result in sleepless nights. Quite simply, the higher the level of risk undertaken, the higher the potential return/loss.

The reader should note that risk may be defined as the likelihood that a desired result will not occur. Cautious investors often achieve better results than aggressive investors. Note also that an investor's attitude to risk should be dictated by external factors such as whether he has dependent children.

13.3.2 The importance of diversification

If an individual's only asset is £10,000 in a bank account, he takes an unnecessary risk if he places any further money in that bank account. This is simply because bank accounts may not prove to be the best-performing investment over the term of the deposit. The individual could have used the additional money to invest in something else, and by doing so, he could have doubled his chance of achieving the best performance available.

Superficially, a simple objective, eg accumulating enough capital to buy a bigger house, may appear to be best achieved by making a single investment that will, on a current projection, deliver the required amount of money. Diversification reduces the downside risk that such an investment will not perform as expected, and because it offers greater potential for outperformance, it affords greater protection against – to stick with the same example – an unexpected rise in house prices.

13.4 BUILDING AN INVESTMENT PORTFOLIO

The expatriate who is a beginner at investment as well as at living abroad should start by taking advice on how to build an investment portfolio.

Such advice may be obtained most simply at the outset through the off-shore subsidiary of a UK bank. Other potential sources of advice for expatriates may be suggested by:

(1) their employers;
(2) property managers or estate agents who handle UK property for expatriates;
(3) specialist publications for expatriates such as *Resident Abroad* or *Investment International*;
(4) the Centre for International Briefing at Farnham Castle, Farnham, Surrey GU9 0AG (tel: +44 (0)1252 721194; fax: +44 (0)1252 711283; www.cibfarnham.com).

13.4.1 How to get good advice

The key points about advice are that:

(1) the recipient should pay for it himself, so that the adviser is liable to him for the accuracy of what he says;
(2) it should not be accompanied by a recommendation to invest money on the spot; and
(3) the recipient can ignore it if he feels so inclined.

The sign of a good adviser is that he will ask a lot of questions about an intending investor's aims, aspirations, attitudes, family background, employment history, ambitions, assets and understanding of finance before he will suggest anything. Good advice depends on knowing the individual to be advised. The advice should be delivered in writing, should include supporting literature/Key Features documents where applicable and, as with every investment decision, the expatriate should sleep on it before doing anything.

13.4.2 What is good advice?

It is likely that an expatriate will first be advised to settle his 'family protection' needs as mentioned at **13.3.1**, and then to aim for a diversified portfolio of bank deposits, bonds and equities; he will tend to invest in the latter two of these asset classes through the medium of collective investment vehicles. The primary advantage of collective investment vehicles, which are discussed at **13.8**, is that the investor gains the benefit of the professional manager's expertise in selecting investments, together with diversification over a wide range of underlying investments.

Some advisers suggest that holding investments within a life assurance policy can have tax advantages and will supply continuity of administration if the investor is too busy to look after his own portfolio. Life assurance is discussed in Chapter 14.

13.4.3 Risk and return

Here is a list of points to consider:

(1) The degree of future risk in any investment is always a matter of judgment. Mathematical measures of performance, volatility or risk hold water only when applied to the past and act only as a guide to future returns.

(2) The longer investors are prepared to tie up their money, the greater the return they will be entitled to expect.

(3) The riskier an investment appears to be, the greater the return should be.

(4) In general, the various investment media can be put on a scale of financial risk as follows:

   (a) commodities: extremely risky;
   (b) equities (shares in public companies): here the risk varies greatly from company to company, but there is also the general market risk referred to above;
   (c) corporate bonds: less risky than equity, because the capital itself is not normally at risk;
   (d) collective investments (unit trusts, mutual funds, investment trusts): less risky still, because the investment is spread among many different shares, bonds, or other media;
   (e) life assurance: may incorporate an element of collective investment. An additional risk arises if the investor is unable to keep paying the premiums, as there may be a heavy penalty for early cancellation;
   (f) bank and building society deposits: normally no risk at all, but see (g) below regarding inflation;
   (g) government stocks: such as gilts – the fixed-interest stocks issued or guaranteed by the British government. Financially the safest investment of all (but depending on the issuing government and on the investor's base currency, still subject to the risk of erosion by inflation and to currency risk).

13.4.4 Investor protection

After some notorious cases of fraud and malpractice (some of them on a vast scale) in recent years, jurisdictions all over the world are reviewing and tightening their authorisation and regulation of financial intermediaries of all kinds.

Expatriates investing in the United Kingdom, or taking advice from or in some way availing themselves of the services of a UK intermediary should make sure that the company or intermediary concerned is properly authorised to offer its service. Membership of a professional body should be confirmed with the professional body and not with the member company. A similar approach should be taken to checking the validity of any licence.

When planning to invest offshore, investors should find out which is the local authority responsible for authorisation and regulation, and then make sure that the particular investment or company they are contemplating is properly subject to this authority.

13.4.5 Currencies and time

The UK expatriate will begin and should plan to end with a sterling-denominated investment portfolio. If he invests in assets denominated in other currencies, he should take advantage of favourable exchange rate movements to move back into sterling; he should not count on the exchange rate going his way at the last moment.

Some advisers suggest that expatriates should reduce their exposure to relatively volatile equity-based investments, as their return to the United Kingdom approaches, by replacing them with a greater proportion of bonds and bank deposits.

13.4.6 The components of an expatriate investment portfolio

As a rule of thumb (and a potentially hazardous one, since any such rule must make assumptions about average needs) a classically constructed portfolio might have something in the region of 10 per cent on deposit. Of the balance, somewhere between 25 per cent and 35 per cent might be invested in government bonds, with the rest in equity-linked investments (frequently collective investments such as unit trusts or offshore funds).

The sections that follow discuss these components in greater detail.

13.5 BANK AND BUILDING SOCIETY DEPOSITS

Most expatriates are likely to need some or all of the following services from their bank:

(1) sterling current account: expatriates tend to keep higher balances

than their onshore counterparts so this should, preferably, be interest bearing;

   (2) sterling deposit account: this forms an important part in constructing a secure investment portfolio;

   (3) currency deposit account: many expatriates are paid in foreign currency and, according to their domestic arrangements, may well have this currency as their base currency giving rise to a need for appropriate deposit facilities;

   (4) currency conversion facilities;

   (5) loan facilities: expatriates may need both short- and longer-term borrowing, perhaps in the latter instance to buy a home in the United Kingdom;

   (6) standing orders;

   (7) direct debit facilities;

   (8) international money transfers;

   (9) Eurocheque facilities;

   (10) credit card payment facilities;

   (11) international money orders and drafts.

Most banks, whether in the United Kingdom or offshore, can provide these services. But apart from considerations of tax (discussed immediately below), there are other good reasons for expatriates to conduct as much of their banking business as possible offshore. In the first place, they have many particular requirements and problems that UK residents do not have, and these are more likely to be understood and catered for by an offshore bank or branch that specialises in the banking needs of expatriates.

There are two further important advantages to expatriates if their bank or branch operates from either the Channel Islands or the Isle of Man:

   (1) These offshore centres are outside the UK tax jurisdiction, but have access to the UK banking network. This means that the full facilities of a UK clearing bank, such as cheque books and credit and other plastic cards for use in the United Kingdom, can be made available.

   (2) Jersey, Guernsey, and the Isle of Man have comprehensive financial services legislation enacted which assures investors of substantially the same safeguards and protection as if they had made their financial arrangements with an institution in the United Kingdom. The Isle of Man, moreover, is the first offshore centre to operate a deposit protection scheme, which covers 75 per cent of the first £20,000 of a deposit, whether in sterling or in a foreign currency.

In the matter of bank or building society deposits taxation can often be the first question to consider. This is because interest arising on an account or deposit in a bank or building society in the United Kingdom is a UK source of income for a non-UK resident. In certain circumstances, under an Extra-Statutory Concession, this interest is not taxable for non-residents, but the rules are complex, especially as they apply to the non-resident's year of departure from and year of return to the United Kingdom. These rules are explained in full detail in Chapter 5.

There is the further point that for an investor not domiciled in the United Kingdom, a deposit in the United Kingdom is treated as a UK sited asset for purposes of inheritance tax (IHT), unless the deposit is in a currency other than sterling. This point is explained in greater detail in Chapter 8.

Many, though not all, of these UK tax problems can be avoided by non-residents if they put their bank deposits offshore. This is an area in which banks and building societies compete, and there is a very wide range of savings or deposit accounts on offer. But broadly speaking, for investment purposes, the accounts fall into three main categories:

(1) deposit or savings accounts with variable interest rates (the rates changing from time to time in line with base rates or money market rates);
(2) interest bearing cheque accounts (often money market accounts);
(3) fixed-term deposits, where interest rates are usually based on prevailing money market rates for the duration of the term, and the interest is paid at the end of the term of the deposit.

The differences between the terms offered by rival institutions relate to such matters as the minimum deposit required and the minimum notice of withdrawal (which also tend to affect the rate of interest offered), the variation between the rates of interest paid on deposits of different amounts, and the timing of crediting the account with interest. Surveys of the terms and conditions offered by offshore institutions are published from time to time in the *Financial Times* magazine for British expatriates, *Resident Abroad*.

As far as deposits are concerned, there is no difference in principle between an offshore bank or branch of a bank and an offshore branch of a UK building society. In recent years, moreover, the major UK building societies have extended their range of services to include many that previously only banks supplied, such as cheque books and plastic cards, standing order/direct debit facilities, and so on. But they may be unlikely to provide the full range of services required by the expatriate investor.

Finally, one general caveat applies to deposits, whether in a bank or a building society: this part of an investor's portfolio should not be allowed to grow out of proportion to the rest of the portfolio, because there is no possibility of growth of the original capital in the case of a deposit (as distinct from any accruals of interest that may be allowed to accumulate).

13.6 FIXED-INTEREST SECURITIES

These may be divided into four groups, as follows.

13.6.1 British government stocks

British government stocks (also known as British funds, gilts, or gilt-edged securities) are instruments used by the government to raise capital. The stocks are guaranteed by the government and consequently are totally secure. Investors can be sure that the stated rate of interest will be paid and the nominal principal returned, in accordance with the provisions of the loan.

Gilt-edged securities normally have a fixed rate of interest, known as the 'coupon', which is expressed as a percentage of the nominal value; so, for example, the holder of £100 nominal of Treasury Loan $8\frac{1}{2}$ per cent 2005 will receive £8.50 a year until that date (this can either be paid gross or subject to deduction of income tax at 20 per cent) regardless of the price at which the stock was purchased or its market value from time to time. In addition to paying interest during the life of the stock, the government also has a requirement to repay the loan at the nominal or par value of £100, on the date stated – this is known as the redemption date.

The market value at any given time will depend upon the coupon, the amount of time to run to redemption and prevailing interest rate conditions. The closer a stock is to redemption the nearer the market price will be to the nominal value. Stocks are usually classified according to the length of time to run to redemption, as follows:

(1) 'shorts': five years or less to redemption;
(2) 'mediums': between five and 15 years to redemption;
(3) 'longs': over 15 years to redemption.

In addition there are also undated or irredeemable stocks with no final date specified for redemption.

For the mediums and longs, at least, the key factor in determining their capital value from time to time is the prevailing structure of interest rates compared with the coupon on the stock. If the prevailing interest rate falls, the value of the stock will rise. This is because a larger investment is required at the new rate to give an equivalent yield. Conversely, if interest rates rise, then the capital value of the stock will fall. British government stocks are exempt from CGT, no matter how long they are held, and irrespective of the fiscal residence status of the holder.

The expatriate buying gilts directly (as distinct from via a collective investment vehicle) should generally choose from the range of so-called 'exempt' or 'approved' stocks, where the income can be paid gross (ie without the normal deduction of 20 per cent income tax at source) to an individual not ordinarily resident in the United Kingdom. Details of the stocks currently exempt and advice on the procedure needed to get the interest paid gross are given in Chapter 5 at **5.4**.

Because the investment is guaranteed by the government and the coupon and redemption value are both fixed, gilt-edged securities are ideal for the investor who places a high premium on security. If, however, a gilt-edged security is not held to maturity, the value of the stock will depend directly on prevailing interest rates and will fluctuate accordingly. The wide range of stocks on the market and the complex calculations sometimes needed to compare redemption yields make it advisable to have some expert advice before investing even in these safe securities, and for this reason many investors prefer a collective medium to direct investment.

13.6.2 Bulldog bonds

'Bulldog bonds' is an informal term used to designate sterling-denominated fixed-interest bonds issued by foreign governments and international agencies in the British domestic market. The structure of such bonds is fundamentally similar to that of the gilts issued by the British government, but they are usually priced to yield $\frac{1}{2}$–1 per cent more than the nearest equivalent gilt. The interest is paid gross on some issues.

13.6.3 Eurobonds

Eurobonds developed from the market in Eurodollars, which originated in the 1950s as claims for US dollars in the hands of banks and their clients outside the United States who did not want to transfer their money to the United States. The market gradually extended to other major currencies held by persons not living in the country of the currency concerned.

Eurobonds are now issued in most of the world's major currencies, with the Japanese yen and the euro sectors the most active. The bonds are issued by consortia of banks (the primary market) on behalf of the borrowers (mostly large corporations or governments and their agencies), and the banks may then sell them to investors (the secondary market), most of whom are institutions.

Some private individuals find Eurobonds attractive, partly because they are usually issued in bearer form, which means there is no register of holders, and ownership of them can be transferred as easily as ownership of a bank note; and partly because the interest on a Eurobond is always paid (on presentation of the coupon) without any deduction of tax.

There are three main types of Eurobond:

(1) straights: which carry a fixed-interest coupon and a fixed maturity date;
(2) floating rate notes (FRNs): which have an interest rate tied to an agreed (but fluctuating) international rate, usually the London interbank offered rate (LIBOR);
(3) convertibles: which are convertible to ordinary shares on the terms stated.

The *Financial Times* gives extensive coverage to this market on its International Capital Markets page. Its table of Eurobond prices is headed 'FT/ISMA International Bond Service'.

An individual can buy Eurobonds either through his stockbroker or his bank, but there will not be much enthusiasm on the part of his intermediary unless he is investing at least £25,000 in this medium. Another point to consider is that it is not always possible for an investor to sell his Eurobonds when he wants to, owing to illiquidity in the market resulting from the attitude of the main players in the market to such factors as currency fluctuations or even political uncertainty. On the positive side, however, for the private investor wishing to have a share of the action in Eurobonds, there are a number of offshore funds specialising in collective Eurobond investment.

13.6.4 Corporate bonds

The relatively high rate of inflation in the United Kingdom throughout most of the post-war period has caused most private individuals to prefer company shares to bonds, whereas the opposite has been true in countries with historically low rates of inflation, such as Germany and Switzerland. This historical comparison of inflation rates has narrowed significantly in recent years.

Companies issue two types of fixed-interest vehicles: debentures, which are backed by specific assets of the issuer; and loan stocks, some of which are secured while others are not. Corporate bonds offer a higher yield than gilts, because even a blue-chip company is considered riskier than the British government, but against this advantage it is not always as easy to sell corporate bonds back to the market as it is to dispose of gilts. The most convenient way to deal in corporate bonds is through a stockbroker, who will also be able to explain the pros and cons of certain special types of bond such as convertibles and deep discount bonds.

For investors in international bonds, there is one further consideration that must be taken into account – EMU.

13.6.5 International bonds, European Monetary Union (EMU) and the euro

Following the launch of the EU's planned single currency, the euro, the international bond market has been affected in a number of ways. The rate at which an international bond is issued is determined, against the central rate of interest at that time, by three main factors:

(1) the trend in the currency of issue;
(2) the credit status of the issuer; and
(3) the liquidity (disposability on the market) of the issue.

The more liquid an issue, the more highly it is regarded by potential investors, which raises its price and diminishes its yield. But this aspect of a bond issue will not be affected by EMU.

The first two factors listed above were, however, affected by the establishment of a single European currency. An investor would formerly only purchase a bond denominated in a currency he expected to depreciate if the bond offered a compensatory extra yield (a so-called 'premium') to make up for the expected currency exchange loss. This premium disappeared for bonds issued in countries joining the single currency.

Although the exchange rate was decisive before the institution of the single currency, now that it has disappeared it is the credit risk which becomes the determining factor. This means that investors will have more recourse to the international credit rating agencies, and issuers of comparatively risky bonds will have to offer a premium. Not only corporations, but countries ('sovereign borrowers') will also be exposed to this credit risk spread. For example, now that Italy has joined the single currency, the spread compared with German rates is considerably reduced (with the elimination of the currency risk), but does not disappear entirely, because, expressed as a percentage of total national output, Italy's accumulated public debt is higher than Germany's. But the differential in bond rates would be small – say 0.3 per cent on 10-year stock.

There will be other, less quantifiable, consequences for the international bond market as a result of monetary union, and the attitude to the market of both issuers and investors will change as a result of the shifting of the horizon. The now fully integrated European bond market accounts for up to 30 per cent of the global market, whereas formerly, individual European countries separately accounted for comparatively unimportant market shares. In the market for collective investments, the elimination of the currency frontiers, so to speak, between individual EU member countries has created new areas of competition between issuers of bonds in getting subscribers, while by the same token, it will open up new possibilities for investment by fund managers.

13.7 DIRECT INVESTMENT IN EQUITIES

In spite of the domination of nearly all the stock markets in the world, and certainly the major ones, by professional investors managing institutional funds, there is still scope for the private individual investor. The editor's post-bag at *Resident Abroad* shows, too, that a great many expatriates are still interested in DIY equity investment, even though they may at the same time hold units in one or other type of investment fund. The well-known investment consultant Peter Doye has a regular column in the magazine intended for such expatriate investors.

It is true that the comparatively small individual investor has high costs in the way of brokerage charges and perhaps fees for ancillary services such as advice, and that the spread between the buying and selling prices of ordinary shares is such that their market price has to rise by 6 or 7 per cent (even more in the case of some of the smaller companies) before the investor can see a profit. But similar considerations apply to investment funds, which also charge annual management fees.

Some individual investors persist down the direct route into equities for the personal satisfaction or even excitement that cannot be experienced when your only stake is in a large pool of assets being managed not only on your behalf but on behalf of perhaps hundreds of other investors. A more important consideration with some individual investors, however, is this: a collective investment by definition spreads the risk, and thereby to some extent limits the possible reward, even if at the same time it limits the possible loss. Spread as a collective investment is across a number of securities, its performance will tend to be related more closely to the market or sector average than will the performance of a particular share. In other words, it is possible if you pick the shares of the right companies to make spectacular profits (and equally astonishing losses if you pick the wrong shares), which is hardly the case even with the highest performing collective funds.

Bernard Gray, in the *Beginner's Guide to Investment*, issued by the *Investors Chronicle*, suggests other ways in which the private investor may have the edge over the professional: 'he does not have to produce quarterly figures showing his relative performance, as fund managers do. Nor does he have to remain in the market when he would sooner be out.

He can buy shares because he genuinely likes their investment prospects, not because he fears being left behind by the market. And he can buy into all but the smallest companies without moving the market price to his disadvantage'. In spite of the professional's easy access to far more information about companies and markets than is normally available to the private individual, the private individual is sometimes able, by a mixture of common sense, lateral thinking, and a modicum of luck, to pick winners that the professionals miss. One expatriate investor of our acquaintance made a considerable fortune in this way. For example, when one national motorway building programme was getting under way he reasoned, ahead of the professionals, that road sign manufacturers would have a bonanza, and he was able to buy a fair stake in such a company before his and eventually other investors' shrewdness caused it to become a favourite. But here we must put in a word of warning. Playing the stock market in this way can easily be addictive, and grow from something akin to a hobby to a full-time occupation, if not an obsession.

There are more than 50 national stock markets throughout the world, and new ones are established every year. Expatriates will probably have to be very well established in their host country before they deal on the local exchange. They are much more likely to deal through a London stockbroker or bank, possibly one with a base offshore, through whom they will be able to buy most major stocks in the world. For less adventurous trading than this they will usually be better advised to consider a unit trust or offshore fund specialising in a particular national market, rather than dealing directly.

13.8 COLLECTIVE INVESTMENT VEHICLES

These may be divided into three groups, all of which work on the same basic principle: a pooling of resources which enables small investors to participate in a professionally managed portfolio of shares, benefiting from a spread of risk that they could not achieve on their own. However, it is important to realise that you can still lose money – pooled funds do not protect you from a falling stock market.

The main differences between the various types of collective investment vehicle are related to structure, location and taxation. Offshore funds are generally recommended as the most appropriate vehicles for the expatriate investor, but there are also arguments in favour of using UK-based funds in some circumstances. However, before reviewing the pros and cons of offshore and onshore funds, it is useful to examine their workings.

13.8.1 UK investment trusts

These were the first pooled funds to be established, although they are probably the least familiar to the investing public. They are public companies, listed on The Stock Exchange, which invest in the shares of other companies in the United Kingdom and overseas. They are described as 'closed end', which means that there is a fixed number of shares in existence and the fund does not expand or contract. Unlike unit trusts, however, investment trusts are permitted to gear up their investments by borrowing.

Investment trusts offer a wide range of investment opportunities: there are general trusts with an international portfolio; specific geographic trusts covering the United Kingdom, North America, Japan, Europe, etc; trusts investing in specific industrial sectors, such as smaller companies, financial and property; trusts that invest for capital growth, and trusts that aim for a high income; plus specialist vehicles such as venture capital and split capital trusts which give the investor a choice between income shares, providing income throughout the life of the trust (usually eight to ten years), and capital shares, which pay out from the accumulated capital when the assets of the trust are eventually sold.

The prices of investment trust shares are set by the stock market and are governed by the same laws of supply and demand which affect all share prices. The stockbroker's commission payable on purchase and sale of shares is usually 1 per cent, but there is also a 0.5 per cent stamp duty on the purchase of shares. But if shares are bought through an independent financial adviser, the commission is generally 3 per cent. Note that the share price may be at a premium or a discount to the net asset value (NAV) per share, which expresses the actual value of a trust's assets after the deduction of the value of its preference shares and all its liabilities.

If the share price is at a discount to the net asset value you are buying assets at a lower cost than you would pay if you bought them directly on the stock market; if it is at a premium, you are paying more. Most investment trust shares trade at a discount.

13.8.2 UK unit trusts/OEICs

Unit trusts differ from investment trusts in being structured as trust funds rather than investment companies, in which you buy units rather than shares. They are 'open-ended', which means the managers can create or redeem units to match demand, and must increase or reduce their shareholdings depending on whether money is coming in or going out of the fund. Unit trusts are not usually quoted on the stock market.

You can buy units directly from the management companies, or through an independent financial adviser. Prices reflect the value of the assets held. Two prices are given, an *offer price* which includes the 'initial charge' you pay to buy units, which is usually between 5 and 6 per cent; and the lower *bid price* for selling. Annual management charges average 1.25 per cent. You can invest a lump sum or use a savings plan to invest smaller amounts on a regular basis. There is usually no extra charge involved in these plans.

An open-ended investment company (OEIC) is a modern version of the unit trust. This means that your money is pooled with that of a number of other individuals and you are allocated OEIC shares in the fund in proportion to the amount you invest.

However, OEICs have a company structure where individuals hold shares, not units. As with unit trusts, the price of the shares reflects the value of the underlying assets and the number of shares varies depending on investor demand. Also similarly to unit trusts, you can buy OEIC shares directly from the management companies, or through an independent financial adviser. Unlike unit trusts, OEICs operate on a single pricing basis. This means that there is one price for both buyers and sellers of shares of each fund. The initial charge for investing is paid and shown separately.

Like investment trusts, unit trusts/OEICs give you access to stock markets around the world and to specialist investment sectors, including fixed-interest and money market instruments.

Investments in unit trusts/OEICs and investment trusts receive the same tax treatment. The funds themselves do not pay capital gains tax (CGT) on any profits they make, but UK resident investors may be liable for the tax on any gains realised when they sell if they are in excess of the annual allowance. Income distributions are paid effectively net of 10 per cent tax, ie with a tax credit. Non-taxpayers cannot reclaim the amount credited.

13.8.3 Offshore funds

A fund is described as 'offshore' if it is incorporated in a low-tax financial centre such as the Isle of Man, the Channel Islands, or Luxembourg, and intended for use by non-residents of that jurisdiction. Such funds generally pay little or nothing in the way of local taxes, although they may receive dividends or interest net of withholding tax, depending on where and in which instruments they invest. They are usually structured as open-ended investment companies or unit trusts, able to issue and redeem their own shares or units. Offshore fund prices reflect the value of the underlying assets, but some funds work on a dual pricing system, quoting both an offer and a bid price, while others work on a single pricing system.

The charging structure of offshore funds is similar to that of UK unit trusts, with an initial charge of nil to 5 or 6 per cent, depending on the type of underlying investment, and an annual charge of 0.5 to 2 per cent, again varying with the type and location of a fund's holdings.

Offshore funds offer a wide choice of investment opportunities and management groups. They provide an investment route into virtually every stock market in the world, most freely exchangeable currencies, Eurobonds, government bonds, commodities, financial derivatives (futures, options and warrants), and even property. If you know which areas you want to invest in you can choose specific funds, or you can opt for an international fund where the investment decisions about which markets to go into are made by the managers.

Many offshore funds are set up as umbrella funds, which simply means that instead of running separate funds the managers run one inclusive fund split into a number of sub-funds. This offers advantages for the managers, mainly in the shape of more cost-efficient administration, and generally makes it easier and cheaper for investors to switch between different investment areas.

Some offshore funds distribute the income they earn on their investments, while others accumulate it within the fund. The latter type are often more convenient for expatriate investors, but may not be suitable if you are intending to return to the United Kingdom in the near future. This is because the tax treatment of offshore funds in the United Kingdom depends on whether the fund has distributor status or not. An investment in a fund with distributor status is taxed in the same way as a UK unit trust. But if you hold a fund without distributor status, you are liable for income tax on both the income from the fund and any capital gain you make on disposal.

Thus, investments in a non-distributor fund need to be sold during a period of non-residence, and unless you can be sure that you will be overseas for some years or that you will have the opportunity to sell your holding in a subsequent period of non-residence, it is sensible to opt for a distributor fund. Most such funds have a reinvestment facility for investors who do not want to receive dividends.

Do not assume that a fund which distributes its income automatically has distributor status. The majority do, but to be granted the status, they have to satisfy certain rules, the most important of which is that they distribute at least 85 per cent of the income earned on their investments.

The major centres for offshore funds are the Channel Islands, Luxembourg, the Isle of Man, and to a growing extent, Ireland. Also notable are Bermuda and the Cayman Islands, and Gibraltar, too, is competing for offshore fund business. You will find that some funds are incorporated in one jurisdiction but administered and managed from another, usually for tax reasons. For example, a fund based in Bermuda may be run from Jersey, with investment advice coming from London. This is of little concern to investors as far as investment performance or taxation is concerned, but could affect whether or not they are covered by a compensation scheme.

Regulation in these centres is relatively good, having been tightened considerably in recent years in response to changes in the marketplace, such as the advent of the single European market for financial services, the introduction of the Financial Services Act in the United Kingdom, and various scandals – notably the collapse of the Savings & Investment Bank in the Isle of Man and the Barlow Clowes affair.

13.8.4 Advantages of offshore funds

The main attractions of offshore funds are their freedom from tax, the confidentiality factor, and the wide range of investments they offer, including currency funds which are not available at all onshore.

Where offshore funds really score on the tax front is on the income side, as they are able to pay the investor an income from investments in instruments such as Eurobonds, deposits, and gilts without the deduction of any tax. In contrast, investors in UK fixed-interest and money market funds receive income payments net of 20 per cent tax. As a result, fixed-interest and money market funds comprise a significant proportion of the offshore funds available and are widely used by expatriates.

When it comes to investment for capital growth, however, there is little difference between offshore funds and UK unit or investment trusts in terms of tax: they all accumulate investment profits free of CGT. Whether the income and capital gains earned on offshore fund investments remain tax free in the hands of the investor obviously depends on where he is resident when he receives them.

If tax is not the deciding factor in using offshore funds, the scales may be tipped in their favour by other considerations, in particular the currency factor, which plays an important role in the financial affairs of expatriate investors. All UK pooled funds are denominated in sterling regardless of where they invest, whereas offshore funds are frequently denominated in the currency of their main investment area. Thus, North American funds are quoted in dollars, Far East funds in Hong Kong dollars or Japanese yen, and European funds in euros.

In addition to providing currency exposure in this way, offshore funds also offer a means of investing in foreign currency deposits and bonds. These funds are available either on a managed basis, where the managers make the investment decisions about which currencies to hold, or on an individual currency basis where the individual decides on the currency mix. The advantage such funds offer over using bank deposits to hold foreign currency is that they give smaller investors access to money market rates of interest.

While currencies may be attractive as an investment option, refer back to **13.4.5** for a caveat.

13.8.5 Disadvantages of offshore funds

There are few real disadvantages to using offshore funds, although some commentators maintain that if you are planning to return to the United Kingdom, it makes life simpler if you stick to UK funds. There is no question then of having to sell your investment at an inopportune moment to avoid unwelcome tax consequences on your return to the United Kingdom, as you might have to if you have any non-distributor funds in your portfolio. Many expatriates prefer to keep their investments outside the United Kingdom while they are non-resident, however, and the simplest way to avoid any tax complications with offshore funds is to make sure you invest only in funds with distributor status.

It is sometimes suggested that offshore funds tend to perform less well than UK funds, owing to a combination of higher charges and lower quality investment management. But while it is the case that offshore funds do carry slightly higher charges on average than unit trusts, this is unlikely to have a significant effect on performance. Moreover, the charge that offshore funds do not receive the same attention as a group's UK funds is difficult to prove, and one that many groups keen to earn a good reputation for investment performance on an international stage would doubtless contend.

There is no consistent statistical evidence to support the contention that UK funds are the better performers, and comparisons are in any case questionable because of the currency factor. Much depends on which currency you use to measure performance: a fund denominated in US dollars investing in the United States may look lacklustre compared with a similar vehicle valued in sterling if the pound has fallen against the dollar over the investment period.

13.8.6 How to invest in offshore funds

You can invest in an offshore fund either by contacting the managers directly or via your financial adviser. Many investment managers will run a portfolio of offshore funds for you, or you can put together your own. Some fund managers will accept only lump sum investments, but quite a few also offer a non-contractual regular savings scheme.

You can check the prices of offshore funds in the *Financial Times*, which carries listings every day. Performance figures for offshore funds are carried in specialist magazines such as *Resident Abroad*, *The International* and *Investment International*. When choosing an offshore fund or fund group, look for consistent performers rather than chart toppers. Ideally, you should select funds run by management groups that can produce above-average performance across the whole range of their funds. This is particularly important if you opt to use an umbrella fund, as you are then relying solely on the investment expertise of one group, and there are only a few that are equally good in all investment sectors.

14

LIFE ASSURANCE

14.1 INTRODUCTION

Assurance contracts may be divided into three broad types, according to the nature of the primary benefits provided:

(1) life assurance policies (including single premium bonds) pay out a lump sum on death or on the expiration of a specified period;
(2) purchased life annuities pay periodic sums as long as the annuitant is alive; and
(3) pension contracts provide pensions and other benefits and are available through an individual's work or occupation.

Within each of these categories are further subdivisions. Pensions are dealt with in detail in Chapter 15.

A life assurance policy is a contract between an individual policyholder (or policyholders, in the case of certain joint policies) and a life assurance company. The life company maintains the underlying investment funds in its own right but, depending on the nature of the policy, it undertakes to pay the policyholder either a specified sum, or a sum which is increased periodically out of the profits of the company, or one which varies from time to time with the value of that part of the underlying fund which is in effect assigned to that particular investor.

An important characteristic of the life assurance policy as an investment is that it does not produce current, taxable income, but is essentially a medium- to long-term accumulator. The income and capital gains of the underlying funds accrue to and are taxed in the hands of the insurance company, but the benefits are passed on, to a greater or lesser extent, in the growth in value of the policy. Many types of policy do, however, allow regular or irregular encashment of part of the policy to provide an income.

Naturally, all life assurance policies provide life cover – a sum assured payable upon death. Most policies, other than temporary assurances, usually also provide investment benefits – sums payable on surrender or maturity of the policy. Life assurance policies may be divided into three categories depending upon the emphasis that is placed on savings or on protection (life cover):

(1) an endowment policy has a high savings element and is one under which the benefits are payable at the end of the predetermined period (the endowment term) or on death, if earlier;
(2) a whole of life policy is one under which the benefits are in general payable on death, whenever it occurs;
(3) a term policy is a form of temporary assurance, the sum assured being paid only if death occurs within a specified period.

Term assurances are used entirely for protection against financial hardship on death and will not be considered further here.

14.2 THREE TYPES OF CONTRACT

Within the endowment and whole of life categories the life policies can be one of three different types, depending on the way in which the sums payable by the company are determined:

(1) *With profit* contracts are policies under which a minimum sum is guaranteed to be paid by the life company on certain specified events, augmented from time to time by bonuses declared by the company according to its profits. These bonuses may be reversionary (bonuses added to the sum assured, either yearly or triennially) or terminal (bonuses declared at the end of the policy as an increment to the final payment).
(2) *Without profit* contracts are policies under which the life company guarantees, on certain specified events, to pay an absolute sum and invests the premiums in such a way as to produce that sum, bearing any shortfall in the return or retaining any profit in excess of the guaranteed return.
(3) Under *unit-linked* contracts the life company maintains an underlying fund, which is divided, for accounting purposes, into 'units' and undertakes to pay to the policyholder an amount equal to the greater of any guaranteed sum and the value of the units allocated to the policy. The underlying fund might consist of specific types of investment media (such as property, equities, unit trusts, investment trusts, government securities, local authority and bank loans or deposits, or building society deposits) or the fund may consist of a combination of some or all of these ('managed' or 'mixed' funds).

Out of every premium a proportion is allocated to the purchase of units which are credited to the policy. The movement in value of the underlying fund is directly reflected in the price of the units allocated to the policy and hence in the value of the policy benefits. Many types of policies give the policyholder himself the right to transfer his policy link from fund to fund at his option, by way of a simple procedure at low cost (eg a policy that is linked to an equity fund may be switched to become linked to fixed interest securities or bank deposits).

A life company generally has full investment freedom as to the type of investments it chooses, subject only to the investment being a suitable 'match' for its liabilities. In the case of unit-linked policies, the Insurance Company Regulations permit linkage only to certain types of assets, such as those listed above. If the contract is one which incorporates a guaranteed maturity value, the investor knows that he will get at least that sum. At the same time, in the case of with profit policies, he has the advantage of having the guaranteed sum augmented from time to time by reversionary and terminal bonuses. With unit-linked contracts, the value is augmented by the movement of the value of the underlying fund (capital appreciation plus reinvested income).

14.2.1 Regular premium and single premium policy

A further broad division of life policies (of all types) depends on how premiums are payable:

(1) regular premium policies (also known as annual premium policies) are those under which premiums are payable annually, half-yearly, quarterly or monthly, either throughout the policy's duration or for a limited premium-paying period of time; and
(2) single premium policies are purchased by way of one single premium or lump sum (although such policies can usually accept further investment at any time).

14.2.2 Characteristics of regular premium policies

All endowment and whole of life policies have an investment or savings element as well as a life insurance protection element. The extent to which the policy is slanted towards investment depends on the policy's nature and duration and the relationship between the premiums payable, the age of the life assured and the extent of the life cover provided.

In general, policies that have a low sum assured relative to the premiums payable over the policy life have a high savings or investment element, and conversely, high sums assured relative to the premiums payable mean that the policy is tilted more towards life assurance cover than towards investment. In considering life policies as investments, temporary or term assurances will be excluded, as these generally do not have a surrender value and benefits are payable only on death. They are usually taken out purely for life cover protection, to provide for one's family or to cover a prospective liability such as inheritance tax (IHT).

The type of policy that an individual should take out generally depends on his circumstances and objectives, weighing up not only the required degree of investment relative to protection but also the required degree of certainty of result relative to the potential for increased gain.

In general, the incidence of inflation and the conservatism of companies in guaranteeing a long-term return has meant that without profit policies have tended to provide a relatively poor rate of return compared with with profit and unit-linked policies.

A with profit policy gives the prospect of sharing in the company's investment performance where this exceeds that needed to meet the guarantee – but the need to satisfy the guarantee may still lead the company to a more conservative investment strategy.

With no guaranteed investment return a unit-linked policy could be viewed as a little more risky but may also offer the prospect of better fund performance.

14.2.3 Characteristics of single premium policies

In the main, the relevant single premium policies for investment purposes consist of single premium 'bonds' which are whole of life assurance policies. For many years these have been, in the main, unit-linked policies often marketed as property bonds, managed bonds, equity bonds, etc by reference to the initial underlying fund to which the policy was linked. There are also single premium endowment policies, but these are less significant.

In recent years, there has been considerable business written as with profit bonds. Although these did not generally incorporate the usual guarantees on future values, they did prove to be attractive in a time of recession and stock market uncertainty.

The main investment characteristic of single premium unit-linked bonds is the high allocation of the premium to investment in the underlying fund, with relatively low life cover. Virtually the entire premium is allocated to 'units', save only for the initial management charges, resulting, in effect, in the investment of most of the premium in the chosen fund. Most companies offer a wide choice of unit funds for the bond linkage.

Subsequently, at no cost or for a small administrative charge, the policyholder may switch his investment to one or more of the other funds and is thereby entitled to select a fund which reflects his own view of market conditions. Switching does not amount to a realisation for tax purposes, which is an important investment advantage.

The income produced by the underlying fund is reinvested, net of tax and annual charges, in the fund. A bond, therefore, serves as an automatic income accumulator as well as giving the investor the benefit of the capital growth from the fund, less a deduction for the insurance company's tax on capital gains.

At various times in recent years, market conditions have also made guaranteed income bonds very attractive for both life companies and investors. They may be structured as single policies paying annual amounts as a spendable 'income' by way of part surrender; or may be a combination of policies, some providing the annual 'income' and one providing the investment return at the end of the investment period, usually five years. The Inland Revenue have challenged the efficiency of some of these arrangements, contending that the annual payments are actually Schedule D, Case III income and not part surrenders of capital, but FA 1997 confirmed the position to be that assumed by the industry.

A case decided (on the hearing of a preliminary matter) in the middle of 1994 raised the question of how much life assurance protection a single premium bond had to provide for it to qualify as a life assurance policy. At first instance the judge decided that a policy providing a death benefit equal only to the surrender value at the time of death was not a life assurance contract.

An appeal against this decision in 1996 reversed it and restored the previous industry understanding.

14.3 TAXATION OF THE POLICYHOLDER

The income tax treatment of a life policy in the hands of the policyholder depends on whether the policy is a qualifying or a non-qualifying policy. Policy provisions in standard form are usually sent to the Inland Revenue by the life company for confirmation of compliance with the qualifying rules ('pre-certification'). Generally (although the rules do vary for different types of policy) a qualifying policy is one where the premium-paying period is ten years or more and where the premiums payable in any period of 12 months do not exceed more than twice the premiums payable in any other period of 12 months or $\frac{1}{8}$ of the premiums payable over ten years. In the case of a whole of life policy, the sum assured payable on death must not be less than 75 per cent of the premiums payable until age 75; and in the case of an endowment policy, the sum assured payable on death must not be less than 75 per cent of the premiums payable during the term of the policy, but for endowments this percentage is reduced by 2 per cent for each year by which the age of the life assured, at commencement, exceeds 55. Taxation of company-owned policies is considered later.

14.3.1 Qualifying policies

Tax relief on the premiums

In the case of a qualifying policy issued before 14 March 1984, the policy-holder is eligible for tax relief on the premiums if the policy is written on his or his spouse's life, if either of them pays the premiums, and if the person paying is resident in the United Kingdom for tax purposes. The current rate of tax relief on premiums paid is $12\frac{1}{2}$ per cent. If eligible, the premiums may generally be paid to the life company net of the tax relief and the company will obtain the difference from the Inland Revenue. Tax relief is allowed to the policyholder to the extent to which the total gross premiums paid by him in the year do not exceed £1,500 or, if greater, $\frac{1}{6}$ of his taxable income after deducting charges on income but before deducting personal reliefs. Tax relief will not be available if a person other than the life assured or his spouse (such as an assignee) pays the premiums.

No life assurance premium relief is available for policies issued for contracts made after 13 March 1984. For these purposes a policy issued on or before 13 March 1984 is treated as being issued after that date if the benefits it secures are increased or its term extended (either by variation or by the exercise of an option built into the contract) after that date.

Policies intact

While the policies are held intact there is no tax charge to the policyholder.

Tax-free proceeds if kept up for minimum period

If a qualifying endowment policy has been maintained for at least three-quarters of its term or ten years, whichever is shorter, and has not been made paid-up within that period, the entire proceeds will be free of income tax in the hands of the policyholder. For a whole of life policy the appropriate period is ten years. If, however, a qualifying policy is surrendered or made paid-up within these periods, the profit ultimately made on realising the policy (whether by cashing in, death, maturity or assignment for value) is potentially subject to the higher rate of tax – but not the basic rate – as with non-qualifying policies (see **14.3.2**).

Capital gains tax

No chargeable gain arises on the disposal of either qualifying or non-qualifying policies (note that surrender and payment of the sum assured under the policy are treated as 'disposals' for these purposes) where the disposal is by the original beneficial owner or by an assignee who gave no consideration for the policy (eg received the policy by way of gift).

On the other hand, if an assignee realises a profit on a policy (or an interest under it) that he, not being the original beneficial owner, acquired for value, it is liable to capital gains tax (CGT) in the same way as other chargeable assets.

To deal with the trade in second-hand policies (which were taxed under the then more favourable CGT regime), anti-avoidance legislation was introduced in 1983 so that, broadly speaking, post-26 June 1982 policies remain in the same income tax regime despite being assigned for money or money's worth. Such policies may give a potential liability to both income tax and CGT although the Taxation of Chargeable Gains Act 1992 (TCGA 1992), s 37 prevents a double tax charge arising.

Person liable for the tax charge
See below.

14.3.2 Non-qualifying policies

Tax relief on the premiums
No life assurance premium relief is allowed on premiums paid under non-qualifying policies whether issued before or after 14 March 1984.

Policies intact
As with qualifying policies, while the policies are intact there is no tax charge on the policyholder.

Termination
On final termination of a non-qualifying policy, on death, cashing in, maturity, or sale, the only income tax charge, if any, is to higher rate income tax but not basic rate. To determine whether a charge arises, the gain – basically, the excess of the cash surrender value over the premium paid – is divided by the number of years the policy has been held ('top-slicing'). Any previous withdrawals are also taken into account. This slice is then added to the taxpayer's other income for the year (after reliefs and mortgage interest). If the slice, then treated as the upper part of the individual's income, puts him in the higher rate bracket, the average rate of tax on the slice at the higher rate less the basic rate is applied to the whole gain. If the slice does not attract the higher rate of tax, the gain is, similarly, free of tax.

It should be noted that the benefit of top-slicing does not apply for the purposes of the higher personal allowance given to those aged over 65 years. Note also that it is only the income in the year of encashment that is relevant. If no chargeable events occur during other years, the individual's income, no matter how high in those years, is irrelevant. Thus, bonds or other non-qualifying policies can be realised tax-effectively in a year when the policyholder's other income is relatively low (eg after retirement).

14.4 PURCHASED LIFE ANNUITIES

14.4.1 Legal nature

There are two broad types of purchased life annuities:

(1) immediate annuities are contracts under which, in consideration of a lump sum paid to the life company, the company undertakes to pay an annuity to the annuitant for life, or for some other term, the rate of the annual annuity depending on the age and sex of the annuitant and on the yields prevailing for fixed interest investments at the time; and

(2) deferred annuities are similar to immediate annuities except that the annuity commences at a future date.

Both annuity contracts are direct contracts with the life company. Some annuity contracts provide for a guaranteed minimum number of payments; some allow the contract to be surrendered for a cash sum that takes into account the growth in the purchase consideration and any annuity payments that have already been made. Other types of annuity contract allow for a cash sum, representing the balance of the original purchase consideration, to be paid on death.

14.4.2 Characteristics

An annuity contract represents a fixed interest investment providing either regular annual payments for the life of the annuitant (lifetime annuities) or for a fixed period (temporary annuities). These payments represent a partial return of capital plus a rate of interest on the investment. In the case of deferred annuity contracts the initial purchase consideration is accumulated at a fixed rate of interest before the annuity commences. Frequently, deferred annuity contracts are purchased with the object of taking advantage of income accumulation before the annuity commencement date and of cashing in the contract before that time (these are commonly known as 'growth bonds'). In general the life company fixes the rate of the annuity in advance, although cash surrender values may be related to yields on government securities at the time of cashing in. The actual investment yield earned by the life company is irrelevant to the annuitant, as he enjoys a guaranteed benefit.

14.4.3 **Taxation of the annuitant**

Annuities paid are divided into capital content and income content, according to actuarial tables prescribed by the Inland Revenue. For example, if a man aged 70 purchased an annuity of £1,800 per annum payable half-yearly in arrears for a consideration of £10,000, £900 of the annuity might be regarded as capital with the balance of £900 being treated as income for tax purposes. In other words, every annuity is deemed to be partly a return of the original capital invested plus a yield or interest element. The interest element of each annuity payment received by the annuitant is treated as unearned income, although since the abolition of the investment income surcharge for individuals by FA 1984 this is not currently a significant disadvantage.

Despite this treatment of payments as part capital and part income, the Inland Revenue appear to regard annuities as substantially a right to income so that they cannot be transferred between spouses to take advantage of independent taxation.

In the past, if an annuity contract was encashed or assigned for value, or any capital sum paid on death, any profit made by the annuitant over and above the purchase price of the annuity, unlike single premium bonds, was subject to basic rate tax (as the company would not have paid tax on the income of its general annuity business) and higher rates if applicable. However, as part of the change to the company's tax position, FA 1991 also brought the chargeable event regime for annuities into line with that for life policies, eg by not charging gains to basic rate income tax.

Higher rate tax is charged in much the same manner as on single premium policies. In other words, the gain element is 'top-sliced' by the number of years the annuity contract has been in existence, and the resulting slice is added to the taxpayer's other income in the year of encashment to determine whether the higher rate of tax is applicable. The rate on the slice (less the basic rate) then applies to the entire gain. In calculating the amount of the gain the capital element of any annuities paid prior to encashment (but not the interest element) is included as part of the gain.

14.5 OFFSHORE SINGLE PREMIUM BONDS

These follow the basic concept of the UK single premium bond and are normally issued by offshore-based insurance companies with UK parentage. The attraction of these bonds, especially for the expatriate, is the tax treatment of the underlying fund, which (with the exception of some withholding taxes deducted at source by certain countries) grow free of tax.

14.6 PERSONAL PORTFOLIO BONDS

These are developments of the offshore single premium bond, which gives the investor the choice of including a wide range of assets, including a portfolio of assets personal to the investor, within the bond. They were designed for the substantial investor who wants to benefit from the favourable tax treatment of an offshore bond while being able to exercise choice in the management of the underlying assets.

However, FA 1998 introduced a new tax charge on such policies by deeming a gain of 15 per cent of the total premiums paid to the end of each policy year and previous deemed policy gains. This charge was not imposed in respect of any policy year ending before 6 April 1999. This provision does not apply to 'managed portfolio bonds', which give the investor access only to generally available pooled assets. This tax charge is additional to the tax charges which normally apply to offshore bonds (see **14.7** below). UK residents who have invested in such bonds, or who are contemplating investment, are strongly advised to seek expert tax advice.

14.7 THE UK TAXATION OF OFFSHORE SINGLE PREMIUM BONDS

Offshore single premium bonds are subject to their own particular income tax rules which can, in certain circumstances, produce a liability to income tax for the UK resident bondholder, both at basic rate and higher rate. Age allowance too may be affected if a gain or excess occurs.

If the bondholder has cashed in the bond at a profit or makes a partial withdrawal which is in excess of 5 per cent of the original contribution there may be a liability to tax. A potential liability to income tax arises whenever a chargeable event occurs. Chargeable events are:

(1) the surrender of a bond (where surrender is the total encashment of the bond) or the encashment of any of the individual contracts within the bond;
(2) amounts withdrawn in a policy year in excess of the cumulative 5 per cent allowance;
(3) death of the life assured, or the last survivor, in the case of joint life bonds;
(4) the sale of a bond (ie an assignment for money or money's worth).

In each case there may be a liability to basic rate tax. Higher rate tax will also be payable if the bondholder is already paying higher rate tax or if their taxable income including the gain or excess brings them into the higher rate tax bracket (although they may benefit from 'top-slicing' relief).

14.7.1 Calculation of tax (for gains excesses)

A special tax relief (called 'top-slicing') exists for UK taxpayers if the receipt of a gain or excess from a bond would cause them to move from the basic rate tax band (currently 23 per cent) into a higher rate tax band. Top-slicing has the effect of reducing the amount of gain or excess which is taxed at the higher rate. Where individuals are higher rate taxpayers before the gain or excess is included in their taxable income, the relief does not apply.

14.7.2 Non-residence

If the bondholder has been non-UK resident while owning the bond but subsequently becomes UK resident then the chargeable gain realised while UK resident will be reduced by a fraction relating to the number of years the bondholder has been UK resident and the number of years the bond has been held.

15

PENSIONS

Pension planning is one of the more complex areas of personal finance for the British expatriate, and it is a topic that should form part of a comprehensive financial review, rather than be treated in isolation. A point of particular importance is the impact of pension arrangements on the expatriate's position regarding taxation.

In this chapter we aim to provide a basic guide to successful pension planning to two broad categories of expatriate: the employee going overseas on a long-term assignment, and the pensioner planning to spend his or her retirement abroad. We conclude the chapter with a list of useful addresses for those readers who wish to find out more about their current pension options.

15.1 EMPLOYEES

Pension planning for employees should always start with a detailed analysis of existing provision. This rule applies to everyone, and not just to expatriates, because it is only when the basic building blocks are identified and evaluated that it is possible to fill gaps in provision and plan for the future.

There are three main sources of pension in the United Kingdom and throughout most of the western world:

(1) state schemes;
(2) occupational schemes; and
(3) private plans.

While the same three pillars of pension provision can be recognised in other countries outside the United Kingdom, the emphasis between them varies considerably. For example in the United Kingdom, employees and the self-employed derive the largest proportion of their total pension from occupational schemes and private plans, whereas in Italy and France and many other countries state schemes provide virtually all of an individual's pension in retirement. In most EU member states, for instance, private individual plans are rare.

15.2 STATE PENSIONS

Many expatriates ignore their state pension on the misguided assumption that it does not apply to persons with a peripatetic lifestyle who are also often highly paid. It is true that the UK state pension is not particularly generous – certainly not in comparison with other EU countries – but it forms, nevertheless, a reliable inflation-linked element in an individual's total retirement income.

Few financial advisers fully understand the vagaries of the UK state pension system, and where the eventual pension will be drawn from several sources in different countries, it is vital for the individual to keep a good record of contributions paid and benefits due.

In the United Kingdom the state pension consists of two elements – a basic or 'old age' pension and an earnings-related pension. The full rate of the basic pension for the 2000/01 tax year is £67.50 per week for a single person. Eligibility to the basic pension depends on an individual's National Insurance Contribution (NIC) record.

National Insurance is a form of taxation, and for most employees it is levied at 'nil' per cent and at 10 per cent on earnings between the lower and upper earnings limits. These earnings limits are, respectively, £76 and £535 per week for the 2000/01 tax year.

To qualify for the top rate of pension it is necessary to have paid (or had credited) NICs for at least 90 per cent of the working lifetime – which for a man is 49 years. Where an individual has less than a full contribution record a proportion of the pension is paid. Women who have not paid enough NICs to entitle them to a pension in their own right can claim a Category B pension under their husband's contributions.

The Category B pension is paid only when the husband reaches state pension age of 65, and not when the wife reaches the state pension age which currently is 60 but will rise to 65 during the phased period from 2010 to 2020. (This will not affect women currently over age 48/49. Those currently aged between 43 and 48 will have a retirement date fixed between 60 and 65 depending on their date of birth. Women currently under 40 will retire at 65.) The Category B pension, which is worth £40.40 per week for the 2000/01 tax year, is added to the husband's single person's pension of £67.50 to give what is known as the married couple's pension, currently worth £107.90.

If a woman is entitled to a small proportion of the basic pension in her own right she can claim this from age 60. Where the Category B pension is worth more, this will be paid when her husband reaches age 65. It is important to remember that the Category B pension replaces and is not paid in addition to the earlier pension.

Women currently under 44 with a full NIC record should note that they will have to work and pay NICs for an extra five years to age 65 in order to qualify for the full state pension. Women between age 44 and 49 should check with the DSS the exact date they will be able to claim their state pension.

The second element of the state pension is known as the Additional Pension or Serps – the State Earnings Related Pension Scheme. Employees automatically belong to Serps if they are not contracted out via an occupational scheme or an 'appropriate' personal pension.

The Social Security Act 1986 reduced the Serps pension for those who retire after the end of the century. Originally under Serps, which was introduced in 1978, the maximum pension was 25 per cent of band earnings assessed over the individual's best 20 years of earnings. However, after 2000, this maximum will be reduced gradually to 20 per cent while the basis of assessment will be replaced by average band earnings over a lifetime. This means that all periods of employment, including periods of low earnings, will be taken into consideration. The overall effect will be to reduce the value of the pension. There may be further changes to Serps after 'stakeholder' pensions (see below) have been introduced. It is possible that Serps will continue for older employees and a new 'second' state pension will be introduced for younger employees. These changes are all likely to be introduced after 2002 – the proposed date for full implementation of 'stakeholder'.

Few people have a clear idea of what their state pension may be worth. However, the Department of Social Security (DSS) operates a useful pensions forecast service. For details see the contacts list at the end of this chapter.

Fortunately, in most cases, it is possible to continue to build up state retirement benefits when you work abroad. But the rules vary according to the country of employment and the nature of the social security agreement between the foreign country and the United Kingdom.

15.3 STAKEHOLDER PENSIONS

The government is proposing to introduce 'stakeholder pensions' from April 2001. At the time of writing, consultation continues with the government on key points. The main features of the scheme are as follows:

(1) it does not replace state basic or Serps pensions;
(2) it aims to provide employees with access to a low charged method of pension saving on a money purchase basis;
(3) subject to certain limits, it will be possible to have a stakeholder plan in addition to existing schemes;
(4) all employers will need to offer a 'stakeholder' facility (unless they can claim an exemption, eg employees have access to an employer's scheme providing a suitable standard of access and benefits);
(5) employees are not compelled to join;
(6) implementation is due from April 2001 and existing employer's schemes must provide full access from April 2002.

15.4 EU MULTILATERAL AGREEMENT

The EU, for example, operates the Multilateral Agreement on Social Security. This came into effect following the Treaty of Rome in 1958 which established what used to be called the European Community. Under the agreement, a UK national can work in different EU countries and continue to build up a right to a state pension from each country through the payment of local national insurance contributions. On retirement the individual can retire anywhere in the Union and draw a pension based on the total number of years worked within the EU.

Under normal circumstances an individual who works abroad would pay local national insurance automatically. There are exceptions to this rule, however: for example, where the period of employment is expected to last less than one year. In this case the individual is retained in the UK social security scheme. Occasionally this period can be extended, but this is rare.

The important feature of the Multilateral Agreement is that it allows employees to aggregate the number of contribution years built up throughout the Union in order to claim a proportion of the state pension in each country of employment. The reason for this feature is that different countries have different qualifying periods for the state pension. For example, in the United Kingdom you have to pay NICs for about ten years before you qualify for a proportion of the basic state pension, although under Serps a benefit is earned from day one. In Italy and Spain, the qualifying period is 15 years, so without the agreement an individual could work for ten years in each of these two countries and not have a right to a state pension.

Under the Multilateral Agreement a pension will be paid from each country of employment provided the *total number* of years worked in the Union exceeds the *minimum qualifying period* in each member state.

On retirement, the pensions are claimed from the relevant country and usually they are paid in the local currency. This means that the pension can be subject to currency fluctuations. Each element of the pension is subject to the annual increases applied by the relevant country. Normally the separate pensions are claimed from each member state but they can be claimed through one source, eg through the equivalent of the DSS in the country of retirement.

The Multilateral Agreement makes no allowance for the fact that different pension ages operate in different member states. This means that a woman currently can draw her UK state pension from age 60, but will not be able to draw a state pension from Germany until she is 65 and from Denmark until she is 67. Most EU countries have equalised the state pension or, like the United Kingdom, have announced the date when this will come into force.

15.5 OCCUPATIONAL PENSIONS

In the United Kingdom approved occupational schemes and private plans are the most tax-efficient method of saving for retirement. Employees and the self-employed get full tax relief on contributions (within Inland Revenue limits), while the funds themselves grow free of income tax and CGT. Moreover, part of the eventual fund can be taken as tax-free cash, although the rest must be taken as pension and is taxed as income.

It is important to bear in mind these tax advantages when considering alternative options. But it is equally important to remember that under an approved UK pension the benefits cannot be taken before age 50 at the very earliest, and for most occupational schemes the normal retirement age is 65.

15.6 RETENTION IN HOME SCHEME

Many people who work abroad are seconded by a UK employer and can be retained in the UK company's pension scheme. While the employee may not be able to pay into the scheme if there are no UK earnings, it may be possible for the employer to continue contributions. Because of the tax advantages noted above retention in the home scheme is usually the best option. The normal limit on home country scheme membership for overseas secondment is ten years. The arrangement must be approved by the Pension Schemes Office (PSO), a department of the Inland Revenue.

Where it is not practical or possible to stay in the UK company scheme, the employer should make some compensation for lost pension within the salary package. This should broadly match in value the benefits of the main company scheme.

15.7 FINAL SALARY

Many company schemes provided by large employers in the United Kingdom operate on what is known as a final salary or defined benefit basis. This means that for every year of service the employee earns a proportion of his or her final salary up to a maximum pension of two-thirds final salary (restricted in the case of some higher earners). The most common pattern is to build up a pension at the rate of $\frac{1}{60}$ of final salary for each year of service up to a maximum after 40 years of two-thirds (ie $\frac{40}{60}$ths) of final salary.

This type of pension offers a valuable hedge against inflation since the pension is linked to the employee's final salary which, under normal circumstances, can be expected to outstrip the Retail Price Index (RPI).

15.8 MONEY PURCHASE

An increasing number of schemes offer what are known as money purchase pensions. Here contributions are invested to provide a fund at retirement which is used to buy an annuity from an insurance company which, in return for the lump sum investment, guarantees to pay the investor an income for life. This means that the retirement income is dependent on the investment performance of the fund, the charges deducted by the provider, and the annuity rate – ie the income the investor can secure with the fund – at the time of retirement.

Investment performance varies considerably from company to company and annuity rates fluctuate in line with the yields on long-dated gilts – the investments insurance companies buy to back the annuity guarantees. This does not necessarily mean that money purchase is a poor alternative to final salary, but it does place more emphasis on the careful choice of pension provider and the level of contributions. Both employers and employees should seek expert help before choosing a money purchase pension. This should be done with the help of a pensions adviser.

Where an employee is retained in his or her UK company scheme it is important to examine the tax consequences. Many foreign tax authorities will regard the contributions paid by the UK employer as additional salary and will tax these contributions as income.

15.9 PERSONAL PENSIONS

Personal pensions were introduced in the United Kingdom in 1988, and allow employees to contract out of Serps on an individual basis, in addition to making extra contributions within Inland Revenue limits. Unfortunately, it is not possible to continue to pay into a personal pension plan from abroad unless there is a source of UK earned income on which contributions can be based.

If the expatriate is planning to go abroad in the near future and would like to take out a personal pension in the meantime, then he should make sure that he can reduce or stop the plan without penalty. Many people fall into the trap of setting up a monthly premium plan only to find that there is a hefty penalty when contributions have to stop.

Any planned future changes of employment status should be discussed with a qualified adviser at the outset, so that a suitably flexible plan is selected. If in doubt, it is always sensible to make pension contributions on a single premium basis rather than on a regular basis such as a monthly or annual plan. This avoids any lock-in situation where early termination penalties might apply.

15.10 PENSION OPTIONS ABROAD

15.10.1 Foreign employer's scheme

If it is necessary to leave the UK company pension scheme when going abroad it is important to investigate the pensions options available overseas. The most attractive option is likely to be to join the foreign company's pension scheme, as this will probably include the advantage of employer contributions in addition to the employee's own contributions. As in the United Kingdom, most countries award tax relief on contributions to approved pension schemes – an important consideration if an individual is paying local taxes.

However, there are circumstances when it might not be advisable to join the foreign company's scheme. For example, rather as with state pension schemes, in many countries it is necessary to work for several years before an individual has what is known as a 'vested right'. The vesting period refers to the number of years he or she has to be in a company pension scheme before becoming entitled to a preserved pension or transfer value on leaving.

A preserved pension is the pension benefit left behind in a former employer's scheme. The benefit, which cannot be drawn until retirement, builds up at a modest rate within the scheme. This pension benefit in most cases can be transferred to another scheme (see **15.12**). However, an individual who leaves before the vesting period is completed, can end up with nothing to show for his contributions.

In the United Kingdom, employees are entitled to a preserved pension after two years. If an employee leaves a company scheme before that time, all he is entitled to is a return of employee contributions (but not the employer's). Moreover, a deduction is made for back payments into Serps for that period of employment, and on top of this a deduction is made for tax to repay the tax relief on contributions.

The United Kingdom is quite lenient, however, in its vesting rules. In Belgium, for example, the vesting period is five years, while in other countries it is necessary to work for 15 years or more before earning the right to a preserved pension.

15.10.2 Individual plans

Where the foreign employer does not offer a company pension scheme or it is inappropriate to join – perhaps because the job is expected to last for just a few years – the next best choice could be a local private individual plan. The foreign equivalent to personal pensions can be a good choice particularly if contributions attract tax relief at the individual's highest marginal rate. But it is worth noting that the United Kingdom is more advanced in its private pensions market than many other countries.

In the United States and Australia similar plans to UK personal pensions are available, but in most EU countries the personal pensions market is underdeveloped. This is mainly because the combination of state and occupational schemes provides a very high level of benefit and there is no need for other types of pension.

Some countries are beginning to develop an individual pensions market in a bid to switch part of the burden of pension provision from the state to the private sector. This is essential if countries are to come to terms with the cost of state schemes as the number of elderly people claiming benefits rises and the number of workers contributing to the schemes falls.

The other point to note about an individual plan is that it may not provide the important fringe benefits that a good company scheme offers, such as death benefits and widows' and dependants' pensions. Most company schemes also offer good private medical and long-term disability insurance. If you have to go it alone, make sure your insurance policies cover these important requirements.

15.11 OFFSHORE PENSIONS

Owing to the inflexibility associated with some foreign pension schemes, many expatriates, and particularly those who are constantly on the move, prefer the idea of an offshore pension fund which can be built up from wherever the employment takes place.

Offshore pensions broadly divide into two categories, namely the employer-sponsored offshore trusts, and the individual plans sold by the offshore arms of UK and other European insurance companies.

15.11.1 Employer-sponsored offshore trust

Probably the best arrangement is the employer-sponsored offshore trust. This type of arrangement is commonly used by the large multinationals which need to provide a top-quality pensions package to their expatriate executives.

Offshore pension trusts can be tailored to meet the specific needs of the employees. They can cater, for example, for an earlier retirement age than the company's main pension scheme – an essential feature for those expatriates who spend their working lives in a highly stressful or dangerous environment or in an unpleasant climate.

The trusts are established in a suitable offshore location. United Kingdom employers tend to prefer the Channel Islands, American companies opt for Bermuda and the Caribbean, German companies go for Liechtenstein or Luxembourg, while for historical reasons the Dutch prefer Curaçao.

Provided the offshore location offers a strong regulatory environment and the services necessary to operate a pension trust, few problems should arise. From the employee's point of view, however, it is essential to have a secure contract setting out the pension benefits in detail. This is important because a pension promise, which is simply a verbal agreement to the employee that the pension will be no less than that provided by the main company scheme, can prove worthless if the company is taken over or if the employee leaves under awkward circumstances.

15.11.2 Individual offshore plans

The scope for good quality offshore individual pension plans is limited, although for the UK expatriate there is a thriving market of offshore insurance companies, based in the Channel Islands, Dublin, and the Isle of Man, that offer a range of financial products. Some of these are designed to mirror pension plans in the United Kingdom, but they should never be confused with the real article. The important point to remember with this type of policy is that it simply cannot mirror the tax advantages of an onshore, Revenue-approved UK pension plan, although some plans do offer limited tax advantages and can be transferred to a UK plan if the expatriate returns home.

There is not space here to undertake a detailed analysis of each product, but it is worth pointing out that many offshore plans used for the pensions market are based on ten-year maximum investment plans (MIPs) and commit the individual to a long period of regular contributions. If an MIP is selected it is important to check what charges are imposed if, for example, the overseas secondment is terminated early.

Expatriates interested in an individual offshore plan suitable for retirement planning should consult a reputable firm of financial advisers specialising in expatriate tax and pension planning.

For many expatriates, particularly those on short-term secondment overseas, the most sensible route to retirement planning is to opt for a mixture of offshore investments which provide flexibility and good long-term growth prospects.

15.12 TRANSFERS

So far we have dealt with current and future pension planning. But, it is equally important to consider the pension benefits built up before the individual goes overseas. There are several options for individuals who leave behind a preserved pension when they go overseas, but it must be stressed that the whole issue of pension transfers is fraught with difficulty and calls for the expertise of a professional tax or actuarial adviser.

Cash refund

Where membership of the UK company pension scheme was for less than two years, it is possible to get a cash refund of employee contributions less certain deductions for tax and back payments into Serps.

Preserved pension

In many cases the best option where a company pension is substantial is to leave it where it is and to draw a pension from this source in retirement. Before this decision can be made it is important to get a pensions expert to analyse what the former employer's scheme provides in the way of annual increases – both compulsory and discretionary – and dependants' benefits such as widows' and children's pensions.

A foreign company transfer

If the foreign employer has a pension scheme it is possible in certain circumstances to transfer the value of the UK scheme into the new scheme. This would need careful consideration to ensure that the benefits guaranteed in the new scheme were roughly equal to the benefits being given up in the old scheme. Transfers to foreign schemes are dealt with by the Pension Schemes Office and are permitted only in certain cases. This option is worth considering only where the employee intends to remain abroad and stay with the same company for a long period.

A UK personal pension or buy-out bond

If for some reason an expatriate does not want to leave their pension in a former employer's scheme it may be worth considering a transfer to a personal pension. But this is a last resort. In the late 1980s and early 1990s over half a million people were mis-sold personal plans when they would have been better off leaving their pensions in their company schemes. In some cases such a transfer may yield better results, but it is essential that a pensions expert checks all other options first. This will require a detailed knowledge of the former employer's scheme.

Foreign individual plans

As mentioned above, some countries now offer an individual personal pension option. Transfers to individual plans overseas are rare, but in special circumstances can be authorised by the overseas branch of the Pension Schemes Office.

15.13 RETIRING ABROAD

For many individuals the prospect of becoming expatriate does not arise until after retirement. In these circumstances an individual's pension planning should focus on how to get his various pensions sent to his overseas address without incurring any double taxation penalties.

British state pensions can be claimed from anywhere in the world. However, the amount payable is frozen at the date the individual leaves the United Kingdom and cost-of-living increases are paid only if the individual retires to an EU country or to one of the countries with which

Table 15.1   Countries where a state pension qualifies for the annual cost of living increase

Austria	Guernsey	Norway
Barbados	Iceland	Philippines
Belgium	Republic of Ireland	Portugal
Bermuda	Israel	Sark
Bosnia-Herzegovina	Italy	Slovenia
Croatia	Jamaica	Spain
Cyprus	Jersey	Sweden
Denmark	Liechtenstein	Switzerland
Finland	Luxembourg	Turkey
France	Macedonia	United Kingdom*
Germany	Malta	United States
Gibraltar	Mauritius	Federal Republic of
Greece	Netherlands	Yugoslavia

* Not including the Isle of Man.
Note:
No uprating agreement – pensions will be frozen if paid to any country not included in the table.

Source: *Department of Social Security*

the United Kingdom has a social security agreement which includes an uprating agreement (see Table **15.1**). This means that if the expatriate moves to Australia or New Zealand, for example, he will not receive the annual increases. Without these increases the value of the pension will rapidly erode. The only good news is that if he subsequently returns to the United Kingdom, his pension will be restored to its full current value.

Company pensions in the United Kingdom can be paid to virtually any address abroad with little difficulty. But to avoid the blow of double taxation it is necessary for the expatriate to obtain a declaration from the foreign tax authority stating that he is resident and being taxed on his worldwide income in that country. This must be sent as soon as possible to his UK tax inspector. Without this certificate the UK Inland Revenue will impose a withholding tax at the basic rate of income tax on all pension payments, although this should be repaid once the certificate is through.

The same principles apply to private plans in the United Kingdom, including annuities purchased with retirement annuity pensions (the precursor to personal pensions) and personal plans.

Table 15.2   State pension ages in the European Union

	Men	Women
Austria	65	60
Belgium(1)	65	65
Denmark(2)	67	67
Finland	65	65
France(3)	65	65
Germany(4)	65	65
Greece(5)	65	60/65
Republic of Ireland	65	65
Italy(6)	60	55
Luxembourg	65	65
Netherlands	65	65
Norway	67	67
Portugal(7)	65	62
Spain	65	65
Sweden	65	65
UK(8)	65	60/65

Note:
The ages shown assume the individual has completed the qualifying period of residence and/or contribution. In some countries earlier claims are possible.

(1)   For Belgium, the full pension builds up over 45 years for men and 40 for women. A flexible age for retirement operates between 60 and 65.
(2)   Partial and temporary retirement possible from age 60.
(3)   Early retirement on reduced pension possible from age 60.
(4)   Early retirement on full pension possible from age 63 but this will be phased out by 2011.
(5)   For employees starting work after 1 January 1993, a common retirement age of 65 is applicable.
(6)   For Italy, the pension ages shown are for the main system (INPS). Low retirement ages are being increased gradually to 65 (men) and 60 (women).
(7)   A recent draft law proposed to raise the pension age for women to 65.
(8)   Phased increase in the female retirement age to 65 to commence 2010.

Source: *Derived from statistics compiled by Watson Wyatt and William M Mercer*

15.14 USEFUL ADDRESSES

Government departments publish the following free leaflets:

NI 106   *Pensioners and widows going abroad*, published by Benefits Agency Communications and Customer Liaison Branch. Tel: +44 (0)191 225 4811

SA 29   *Your Social Security, insurance, benefits and healthcare rights in the European Community and in Iceland, Liechtenstein and Norway*

NI 38   *Social Security Abroad*, published by Inland Revenue

National Insurance Contributions Office Publications.
Tel: +44 (0)191 225 4811.
Website: www.inlandrevenue.gov.uk

For further information contact the local DSS office or telephone one of the following numbers:

Information on state pensions:	+44 (0)191 203 0203
General pension queries for people planning to live/already living abroad:	+44 (0)191 218 7777

State pensions forecast

To get an idea of the value of his future state pension, the expatriate should ask the local DSS (Benefits Agency) for the pension forecast form BR 19.

Tracing a 'lost' pension

If he has difficulty tracing his pension with a former employer, he should contact:

The Pensions Registry
PO Box 1NN
Newcastle-upon-Tyne
NE99 1NN
Tel: +44 (0)191 225 6393/6394

Pension complaints

Pension complaints initially should be put in writing to the scheme manager, trustees or provider. The next step, if the response is not satisfactory, is to contact the Occupational Pensions Advisory Service (OPAS) preferably through the local Citizens Advice Bureau. OPAS can also be contacted direct at:

11 Belgrave Road
London
SW1V 1RB
Tel: +44 (0)20 7233 8080
Fax: +44 (0)20 7233 8016

Independent advice

There is no specific organisation that lists financial advisers who specialise in expatriate pensions, but most firms of consulting actuaries would be able to give advice on this topic.

Contact:

> The Association of Consulting Actuaries (ACA)
> No 1 Wardrobe Place
> London EC4V 5AG
> Tel: +44 (0)20 7248 3163
> Fax: +44 (0)20 7236 1889

The Institute of Financial Planning operates a register of advisers with international expertise.

Contact:

> The Institute of Financial Planning
> Whitefriars Centre
> Lewins Mead
> Bristol BS1 2NT
> Tel: +44 (0)117 930 4434
> Fax: +44 (0)117 929 2214
> Website: www.financialplanning.org.uk

16

COPING WITH EXCHANGE RATE MOVEMENTS

16.1 FIXED AND FLOATING EXCHANGE RATE SYSTEMS

The enormous growth of international tourism since the 1950s has made most adults aware of the vagaries of the rates of exchange between their own national currency and those of other countries; and readers of the business pages in their daily paper know how the competitiveness of their country's exports and the cost of its imports are also affected by the relative strength or weakness of its currency. As can be seen from these two examples, exchange rate fluctuations present both threats and opportunities to individual citizens and to sovereign states. But as far as individuals are concerned, expatriates are more exposed than other people to these threats and opportunities, as they are constantly bound to be carrying out transactions in at least two different currencies. In some cases, they will be drawing a salary in one currency, meeting regular expenses in another, and putting their savings into investment vehicles denominated in a third. Expatriates living in retirement are especially vulnerable, because a fixed pension in a currency other than that of their country of residence may well be their main source of income.

Economists distinguish two fundamentally different exchange rate systems: fixed and floating. These terms are self-explanatory up to a point, but let it be said that in a fixed system, the governments of the countries concerned tie their respective currencies either to a commodity such as gold or to a leading currency such as the US dollar, or to a set of currencies usually referred to in English, at least, as a basket of currencies. Under a floating system, instead of governments a free market determines the various exchange rates according to the interaction of supply and demand for the currencies in the system.

Until 1931, when the system broke down for a number of reasons, the world operated on a fixed exchange rate system based on gold. In 1944, with the end of the Second World War in prospect, delegates from 44 nations met at Bretton Woods, New Hampshire to work out a post-war system of stable exchange rates based on the US dollar, as the United States was then overwhelmingly the most powerful country with the strongest economy in the western world. The dollar was itself based on gold at a fixed rate of US$33 per ounce, and in practice only the dollar was internationally exchangeable for gold. Other currencies were determined in terms of the dollar at a rate fixed within a narrow range.

The trouble with fixed exchange rate systems, however, is that they do not work: the world of international business is much too complex to be accommodated in such a tidy framework. Sooner or later the fixed system breaks down, and has to be replaced by a floating system. So, sure enough, it was not long before the Bretton Woods system was subject to awkward pressures. But what finally put paid to it was the cost of the Vietnam War, which weakened the dollar, which caused private demand for gold to soar, forcing the establishment of a separate free market in gold for the private sector, which had been allowed to hold gold only in the form of jewellery. In 1971 the United States suspended dollar-gold convertibility, unilaterally bringing the Bretton Woods system to an end, and after formal devaluations of the dollar against gold in 1971 and 1973, the major world currencies were allowed to float freely.

The principle of floating exchange rates is simple. The exchange rate of each currency is allowed to find its own value in the marketplace (consisting nowadays of a number of currency dealers in the world's major financial centres, all watching computer monitor screens and communicating with one another by telephone or other instantaneous electronic means; and reflecting the flows of funds between these centres in response to supply and demand). But although the market is more or less free, there is some scope for each country's central bank to use its reserves of gold and other currencies to intervene in the market with the intention of either raising or lowering the international price of its own currency. A central bank can also influence its national currency by raising or lowering interest rates; and a group of central banks may at critical moments seek to correct what they view as an undesirable trend in foreign exchange markets by reaching suitably publicised agreement on a co-ordinated course of action. But central banks are not so powerful in this respect as they once were. The seven leading industrial countries – the important operators in this field – at present command between them aggregate currency and gold reserves equivalent to about US$500 billion; but this compares with a daily turnover on world foreign exchange markets equivalent to about US$1.6 billion.

But the trouble with floating exchange rate systems is that they do not work, either. Sooner or later they allow inflation in many national economies to get out of hand or threaten to. This in turn leads to competitive currency devaluations between countries, and increasingly volatile exchange rate movements which make international transactions more and more difficult. This means that the floating system has to be replaced by some kind of fixed system, or at any rate by a hybrid system incorporating features of both the fixed and the floating systems. The so-called 'Snake in the Tunnel' rules introduced by continental European governments in 1972, and their successor, the European Monetary System (EMS) based on the Exchange Rate Mechanism (ERM), which both aimed to restrict currency fluctuations within a band centred on a fixed rate, were such hybrid arrangements.

Before returning to the subject of the EMS at **16.4.2**, however, let us look more closely at the factors driving exchange rate movements, as an understanding of these may help the expatriate reader to anticipate or avoid some of the shocks that the foreign exchange market is otherwise likely to cause him.

16.2 FACTORS DRIVING EXCHANGE RATE MOVEMENTS

When exchange rates are determined either wholly or at least to a great extent by the market, the important point is to distinguish between the relatively long-term trends of strength and weakness from movements in the shorter term. We have mentioned the interplay of supply and demand in the market, and a given country's currency is in demand when people in other countries want to buy that country's internation-ally offered goods or services or to invest in it by buying or building tangible assets in it or by buying debt or equity offered by its public or private economic entities. In the light of these considerations, the long-term trends of strength and weakness of a currency reflect economic fundamentals such as relative levels of inflation and of unemployment, and the rate of increase of productivity and in overall international com-petitiveness, but also such factors as taxation levels and political stability. Strong economies produce strong currencies; weak economies either devalue their currencies by a specific measure, or allow them to depreciate, as it were automatically. Nevertheless, there is a cycle: a strong currency tends to lead to deflation and to a trade deficit – in other words to relative economic slowdown which in turn causes the strong currency to weaken.

Short-term movements, on the other hand, which may last for only a mat-ter of months or even weeks, tend to move in a cyclical pattern of their own along the longer-term trends, and are caused by international flows of (sometimes purely speculative) capital. These cycles are driven by a mixture of movements in interest rate differentials (on government stock and corporate bonds, especially), immediate political factors, and the market operators' views of the relative dearness and cheapness of currencies, particularly with reference to their relative purchasing power in their own home market.

16.3 THE DIFFICULTY IN FORECASTING RATES

In the most basic terms, the long-term rising and falling trends of particular currencies, determined by international competitiveness, will be reflected in the tendency towards trade surpluses or trade deficits (where trade covers services, such as insurance or tourism, as well as merchandise). The shorter-term movements, which may nevertheless be quite considerable, are entirely about flows of international capital, with interest rate differentials usually being the most decisive factor. Investors are naturally attracted or held by high interest rates.

But there is also a subjective or judgemental factor at play, because it is not only actual high interest rates that attract investors, but also the expectation of high rates or the belief that present high interest rates will not decline. The foreign exchange market is thus, like stock markets, influenced by investors' views and opinions, which constitute what is often referred to as 'market sentiment'. Expectations of future trends are more volatile than the fundamental factors at work in the market, and it is these expectations that make it difficult to forecast exchange rates or control them.

An even greater difficulty, however, is caused by the sheer number of currencies (and national economies) involved. Not only are economic forecasts for a single country notoriously prone to error, but in the global foreign exchange market these currencies and economies are all the time interacting in highly complex ways. Even such a notoriously successful currency speculator as Mr George Soros has on occasion misread the signs; and a consensus of specialist foreign exchange analysts can still get things wrong: thus in the first quarter of 1997, for example, the US dollar climbed against other major currencies at about twice the rate that most experts had predicted.

16.4 THE WORLD'S MAJOR CURRENCIES

The *Financial Times* lists well over 200 currencies in its weekly guide to world currencies, but fortunately from the point of view of international investment only a handful of these are important. For practical purposes, the investor need pay attention to three main currencies or currency blocs besides the currencies of his country of residence and domicile:

(1) the US dollar and currencies linked to it (properly speaking, the Canadian dollar and the Hong Kong dollar);

(2) the euro and the other European currencies effectively (though not by any legal arrangement) shadowing the euro; and

(3) the Japanese yen.

Other major currencies include the British pound and the Swiss franc.

16.4.1 The US dollar

The US dollar has been the most important single currency since 1945, and it can be fairly described as a reserve currency not only for economic and financial reasons, but also by reason of its institutionally and politically strong foundations. For all that, however, it is true to say that in the course of the last 40 years the dollar has fluctuated in value against other major currencies to an astonishing extent. During the 1960s, when the Bretton Woods system of fixed exchange rates was still operating, the pound sterling was worth $2.80. Even in 1980 it was worth $2.40. But there were moments in 1984 when it looked as if the dollar would reach parity with the pound. Against the deutschemark, the dollar reached a historic high of DM4.20 in April 1957, but its all-time low against that currency was DM1.345 in April 1995 – equivalent to less than a third of its highest rate. Against the yen, the dollar has shown even greater variations – between Y363 in July 1963 and Y79.75 in 1995, the highest value being in this case more than 4.5 times the lowest.

In the five-year period 1992-1996 the United States was the strongest economy among industrially advanced countries, with annual growth of output averaging 3 per cent, unemployment well below most European levels, consumer price inflation below the OECD average, and so on. Various other factors were also making for dollar strength in mid-1997: some international investors were staying in dollar securities because of uncertainty about EU currency arrangements, and there was in any case a wide differential between dollar short- and medium-term interest rates and those of the deutschemark, the French franc and the yen, particularly, in the dollar's favour (although sterling and Italian lira rates were higher).

On the other hand, there are signs of recovery in Europe and in Japan, and tightening monetary policy in Japan and Europe could raise interest rates there. The United States is also running a large deficit on its accounts with the rest of the world, and sooner or later this will give international investors pause for thought. It was also thought that the establishment of the European single currency (the euro) as a reserve currency would weaken the dollar, as banks round the world switched from dollars into euros. This threat to the dollar is mitigated, however, by the fact that the dollar's role as a reserve currency has declined appreciably since the collapse of the Bretton Woods system, and also by the prevalent market view that the euro could be a fairly soft currency. Certainly the first nine months of the euro on official markets have not caused a major fluctuation in the value of the dollar.

16.4.2 The euro

Under the February 1992 Treaty on European Union, better known, from the Dutch city where it was signed, as the Maastricht Treaty, the then EC member states committed themselves to the establishment of a single European Central Bank on 1 January 1999, which would be responsible for the introduction of a single European currency as soon as practicable after that date. This was the programme in principle, but in order to be part of the fully-fledged economic and monetary union (EMU) that the Maastricht Treaty envisaged, the member states were required to meet certain targets regarding the containment of inflation, the stability of exchange rates, the level of long-term interest rates, and the level of government current budget deficits and accumulated debt that have come to be referred to as the 'convergence criteria'. As the 1999 deadline approached, however, member countries had varying degrees of success in meeting these criteria, which in any case, according to the small print of the Treaty, contained certain nuances and offered some (albeit limited) loopholes. At times, doubts were raised about the feasibility of the whole EMU project, with even Germany (which usually insisted on the strictest possible interpretation of the convergence criteria) not able to meet the budget deficit criterion limiting the deficit to 3 per cent of gross domestic production.

In spite of serious difficulties, however, Germany and France both (for different reasons) were determined to press ahead with EMU, and the creation of a single currency, the euro, in accordance with the Maastricht timetable, even if not every member state would participate immediately. In fact, the United Kingdom, Sweden and Denmark did not, by their own decision, join the first phase.

The euro has, by and large, entered the markets making little more than a ripple. The anticipated weakness of the dollar with the arrival of a new reserve currency has not really materialised. The euro looks as though it is here to stay and whilst it has weakened in its first nine months it is not behaving as poorly as some observers had predicted. Having said that, by late summer 1999 the euro had depreciated by nearly 9 per cent against the pound sterling and the pound, in particular, did not seem to be suffering much as a result of uncertainty over Britain's future membership, with comments from certain leading economists indicating that the City of London, at least, could continue to prosper outside EMU. On the contrary, in the short term the pound may have assumed the mantle worn by the Swiss franc as a temporary outsider in relation to the earlier ERM. Of course much of this has to do with the perceived strength of the United Kingdom's economy and the competitiveness of its markets within Europe in 1999.

The UK Labour government is still adopting what is in effect a 'wait and see' policy towards the euro. Although there are apparently many in the government who would privately like to take Britain in, this remains such a sensitive political issue, with the Conservatives taking quite a hard line against Britain's membership, that no firm government-led initiative has taken off. The Prime Minister is generally considered to be in favour of membership quite soon after the next election – on the assumption, of course, that his party will win! It will be interesting to see whether this matter finds its way into the election manifesto when the time comes. If it does, the issue could well dominate the election campaign, although the government's position is tempered by the promise of a referendum before joining EMU, the outcome of which is not yet predictable.

Meanwhile, phase one of the monetary union process has gone ahead and, unless there is a major crisis, it seems likely that full union among the participating member states will be achieved in accordance with the set timetable.

16.4.3 The Japanese yen

The Japanese yen has been the world's strongest currency since the collapse of the Bretton Woods system, partly due to a deliberate policy of limiting imports from the rest of the world. As a result, the yen has grown steadily in importance as a major world reserve currency, but no such thing as a yen bloc has developed. Outside Japan itself, the currency of reference for most countries in Asia is the US dollar, and some countries have even tied their currency to the dollar. The Japanese authorities also rule out the possibility of a monetary union along European lines, on the grounds of the cultural, religious and historical heterogeneity of Asia, which they do not even see as a region, in the sense that western Europe can be said to be a region. But it probably suits the Japanese most on grounds of economic policy to decline to be even the top power in a currency bloc: they are aware, for example, how the pound sterling's status as a reserve currency and leader of the sterling bloc greatly complicated the task of managing the economy of the United Kingdom in the post-1945 period. In the case of Japan, such a complication would be aggravated by its dedication to a species of mercantilism (the encouragement of exports and restriction of imports) in the conduct of its international trade.

The fact that the Japanese economy is managed on a different basis from that of other advanced industrial economies makes it especially difficult for outsiders to forecast future trends – something that hardly distresses the Japanese authorities.

16.5 EXCHANGE RATES AND BONDS

The market value of a particular bond is tied to the interest rate (and yield curve, or projection of interest rates over selected periods of time) of the currency in which it is denominated. When interest rates fall, the value of bonds rises, because a larger capital is now needed to yield the same return; and conversely, when interest rates rise, the value of bonds falls.

Under a regime of fixed exchange rates, the only scope for capital gains in bonds depends on the investor's ability to assess the future course of interest rates correctly. But under a system of floating exchange rates, a significant contribution to the total return, measured in the investor's own domestic currency, on investing in bonds internationally will depend on the extent to which the other currencies in which bonds are held either appreciate or depreciate. There are, besides, important links, in more than one context, between the respective movements of exchange rates and interest rates.

The main traditional relationship between exchange rates and bond markets has arisen where particular national bond markets have a large volume of foreign funds invested in them and are thus more influenced than other bond markets by the strength or weakness of the local currency. The sterling gilt market has been a classic example of this, and the strength or weakness of sterling has heavily influenced this market and the interest rates of sterling-denominated bonds generally.

But a new and potentially more important contrary relationship than that determined by local currency strength or weakness has arisen. With interest rate differentials becoming a crucial factor in driving exchange rate movements among the three main currency blocs, there is an increasing tendency for bond markets and exchange rates to move automatically in opposite directions. This is in part because geographical currency groupings reduce the relative importance of wider international financing of bond issues, especially, for example, in the context of Europe.

Broadly speaking, as the market operates at present, if the state of the domestic economy (or group of economies) is likely to lead to lower interest rates, this will drive bond markets up, but it will tend to drive the exchange rate down. Conversely, where the prospective accelerating economic growth is expected to lead to higher interest rates and weaker bond markets, this will drive up the exchange rate.

16.6 EXCHANGE RATES AND EQUITY INVESTMENT

Thanks to post-war developments in telecommunications and information technology, the world's main stock markets, like the foreign exchange markets, now operate globally, except in matters of administration. In this environment, exchange rate movements can mean the difference between profit and loss, or, in a stock market crash, the difference between a relatively small loss and a large one. Indeed, profitable international equity investment cannot be achieved unless the exchange rate factor is taken into account in the investor's calculations.

After the worldwide fall in stock markets in October 1987, US investors found that they had suffered less on their foreign investments measured in dollars than investors in other countries measuring their investments in their own currencies. Because the US dollar fell against the yen, the deutschemark and sterling, shares in the markets in Japan, Germany and the United Kingdom that had been bought with US dollars fell in value much less in dollar terms than in local currency market-value terms, to the extent that the dollar weakened against the currency in question.

Currency weakness is also generally good for the profits and share prices in their local currency terms of companies operating in international sectors (eg export-led sectors). The resulting equity gains, however, will naturally be reduced when measured in the currency of the foreign investor. The expected depreciation of the currencies in question must be included in calculations of comparative projected total investment returns.

For example, an investment in a US company in an international business sector, benefiting from future dollar weakness, may, let us say, be expected to show a 100 per cent return in dollar terms, thus attracting Japanese investors. But if the dollar depreciates by 25 per cent against the yen, the expected return in yen terms will be only 50 per cent. For equities, however, unlike cash and bonds, the positive impact (via profits) of currency depreciation on share prices is often greater for the foreign investor than the accompanying downwards adjustment due to the depreciation.

16.7 EXCHANGE RATES AND DAY-TO-DAY LIVING EXPENSES

A potential problem arises for the expatriate when his income and living expenses are in two distinct currency blocs, as might be the case, for example, for a retired United Nations official living in France and drawing a pension denominated in US dollars. If it is practical, the only route to protection here is to cover, by means of forward exchange contracts with the expatriate's bank, his known flow of income in the source currency into the currency of the country where he is living. If this is not a practical option, it may be prudent to keep a reasonable balance on deposit in the currency of the country of residence as a reserve to draw on when needed. This tactic can be particularly useful in dealing with temporary weakness in the source currency: the expatriate concerned can then postpone converting the income concerned until the currency is stronger. It should be remembered, though, that trends can take a very long time to reverse and there is no certainty that they ever will.

17

OFFSHORE FINANCIAL CENTRES

17.1 INTRODUCTION

The term 'offshore' is not legally defined, but in the context of banking and insurance it has come to be applied to operations carried out in a jurisdiction at least one remove from the company, institution, or individual initiating or carrying out those operations. The term no doubt arose in the United Kingdom, and it implies an insular vantage point. But the United Kingdom is itself 'offshore' to many individuals and companies not domiciled (though they may be resident) there; and the term is properly applied to a number of jurisdictions, such as Luxembourg or Liechtenstein that have no shores.

If the term 'offshore' is not a legal one, still less is the expression 'tax haven', which is often applied to offshore centres. But this expression acknowledges the fact that the offshore centre in question does offer, and has been chosen because it offers, tax mitigation opportunities to investors (and sometimes to borrowers). Just how many tax havens there are in various parts of the world depends on the definition of a tax haven, but even a conservative estimate might be as high as 40.

The mushrooming of offshore financial centres in recent years has come about for a number of reasons:

(1) the need of the local authorities to boost income because other sources are stagnant;
(2) the need to create employment opportunities for better educated workforces; or
(3) perhaps merely the desire to jump on what appears to be a successful bandwagon.

But in fairness it should be said that the regulators in most offshore financial centres (certainly the ones to be concentrated on in this chapter) go out of their way to try to ensure that only legitimate business is transacted by the banks, insurance companies, investment groups and trust managers established in their territory.

214

17.2 THE CHANNEL ISLANDS AND THE ISLE OF MAN

The British Isles offshore centres of the Channel Islands (Guernsey and Jersey) and the Isle of Man compete for business on a worldwide scale. Geographically close competitors are Dublin and landlocked Luxembourg. Slightly farther afield, Gibraltar, Cyprus and Malta vie for offshore business. On the other side of the Atlantic, Bermuda is an established offshore financial centre while, in the Caribbean, the British dependent territories of the Cayman Islands, Turks & Caicos, Anguilla, British Virgin Islands and Montserrat all have financial sectors. Elsewhere in the world there are offshore centres in the Bahamas, Barbados, the Cook Islands, Labuan (Malaysia), Madeira, Mauritius and Vanuatu, to name just a few.

From the point of view of a British expatriate, however, there is no financial service that cannot be found in the Channel Islands or the Isle of Man. We will be concentrating on these centres. In addition, we will also be looking at Luxembourg and Dublin because both these centres are increasingly important as locations for investment funds.

Jersey is the biggest and the best known of the Channel Islands. Jersey's allegiance is to the British Crown, but the island makes its own laws and issues its own bank notes and coins. Guernsey is often thought of as just a smaller version of Jersey, and it is true that the two islands share several common features. Like its neighbour, Guernsey is responsible for making its own laws and issuing its own legal tender. Also like Jersey, Guernsey is effectively a member of the OECD on Britain's coat-tails and has designated territory status under the United Kingdom's financial services legislation. Designated territory status means that the United Kingdom has recognised that an offshore jurisdiction has equivalent investor protection legislation to that available in the United Kingdom. This equivalence makes it possible for its funds to be marketed in the United Kingdom.

The Isle of Man shares designated territory status with the Channel Islands. The Isle of Man has its own Parliament, sets its own income tax rates, and has long been a low-tax area enjoying total independence from the United Kingdom on matters of direct taxation. There is low corporate and personal tax, and no capital transfer tax or inheritance tax (IHT).

All the major British banks have subsidiaries in one or more of the British offshore centres. They offer all the usual facilities that are available in the United Kingdom, such as cheque guarantee and credit cards, automatic cash dispenser facilities and regular statements, plus the benefit of interest paid gross. Multicurrency cheque accounts and a whole range of currency funds have become increasingly popular in recent years. Several banks in Jersey, Guernsey and the Isle of Man offer multicurrency accounts which can be opened with a minimum balance of, typically, around £2,000. The key features of such accounts include money market levels of interest in all major and other currencies, free cheques, standing orders and direct debits, easy currency switching at competitive interest rates and the ability to hold balances in a multitude of currencies. It is not just the specialist banks that provide non-sterling facilities. These are available also from the offshore subsidiaries of some UK clearing banks and building societies.

It is possible to access currency investments through a wide range of umbrella funds. Such funds typically offer money funds in US dollars, sterling, yen, Swiss francs and euros, all of which provide investors with access to income at wholesale interest rates through investing in a spread of short-term deposits, certificates of deposit and other negotiable money market instruments. Some umbrella funds also offer a managed currency fund, which aims to maximise the value of liquid assets through the management and diversification of currency exposure. Umbrella funds are usually available either as distributing funds or on a roll-up basis. To qualify for distributor status under UK legislation, an offshore fund must distribute approximately 85 per cent of its income each year. Conversely, a roll-up fund, as its name suggests, is one in which the income accumulates inside the fund, with growth being reflected in the price per unit or per share.

Expatriates may also like to consider money funds which are also available in distributor or roll-up form. Money funds work like this: investors' money is pooled within the fund, and so qualifies for wholesale rates of interest available on the international money markets. These rates are often considerably higher than those available for smaller sums of money. Each currency is represented by its own class of share whose price will vary in line with underlying interest rates. A key point to remember is that investment in a managed share class or a currency other than the investor's own base currency is subject to exchange rate movements which can go up or down in relation to an investor's base currency.

As a guide, money funds are useful for investors who wish to hold cash deposits in a major, or even relatively minor, currency. Apart from their use as interest-bearing cash balances, they can be used to hold foreign currencies as an investment, for a business need, or simply to manage a holiday home. They can also act as a convenient parking place for money between equity investments. With managed money market currency funds or sub-funds of an umbrella, there is the prospect of added value if the managers get the timing on their currency switches right. If the investor's need is to deposit foreign currency cheques frequently and also to make payments in foreign currencies, he may be better served by using a multicurrency account on which he will receive interest paid without deduction of tax.

As can be seen, the range of banking services available to the expatriate is considerable. Many banks in the offshore centres also offer trust services. As an alternative to the banks, several building societies have set up offshore subsidiaries in recent years. The Isle of Man is unusual in that if offers a scheme to provide compensation to depositors of 75 per cent of the first £20,000 per individual or the foreign currency equivalent in the event of the collapse of a bank or building society. The Isle of Man has also become a recognised centre for international life insurance.

17.3 LUXEMBOURG

Although Jersey, Guernsey and the Isle of Man are the offshore centres most often used by British expatriates, Luxembourg is also important, being prominent in the fields of investment fund management and cross-border marketing of insurance and pension products.

Luxembourg was the first country in the EU to implement the EC Directive which allows open-ended collective investment funds authorised in one EU member state to be marketed freely, once they have been registered, in any other member state. Luxembourg has also introduced legislation to embrace funds investing in assets other than transferable securities. What has given the investment fund sector in Luxembourg an enormous impetus, however, has been its benign tax regime: the funds themselves are subject only to a 0.06 per cent levy on their net assets and, for non-resident investors in them, there is no withholding tax on distributions and no tax on capital gains.

Investment funds are not the only attraction of Luxembourg as a financial centre. For many of the wealthier internationally minded private investors an even greater attraction is the Luxembourg holding company. Shares in these companies may be registered in the holder's name, or be simply bearer shares, in which case they are anonymous. Another important advantage of these companies is that although quarterly returns must be filed for purposes of the low annual tax on issued capital that is payable, and an annual financial statement be submitted to the Luxembourg authorities, only a minimum amount of financial information has to be published. Apart from taking care of investments, the holding company can own and license trade marks and patents. The holding company pays no income taxes of any kind, but is excluded from Luxembourg's tax treaties with other countries, and so cannot claim relief for withholding taxes deducted at source on dividends and interest payments received in another jurisdiction.

Luxembourg, like the United Kingdom, is potentially threatened by moves to harmonise taxes across the EU. This cloud has been on the Luxembourgeois horizon for some time but it does seem that discussions regarding, for example, withholding taxes are gathering momentum and that individual states' right of veto may not survive for long in the new millennium. Consideration of Luxembourg and of other offshore centres within the geographical area that is Europe will increasingly be affected by the political climate. Indeed, some investors are already feeling uncomfortable about the future of these offshore centres.

Appendix I

CHECKLISTS OF DOs AND DON'Ts

GOING ABROAD

One of the most daunting things about going abroad to work is gathering together all the information necessary. Obviously the intending expatriate needs full details of his contract, health, visa and permit requirements and many more. On the financial front, the following are some of the most important things to consider:

(1) *Do* bring your UK tax affairs up to date;
(2) *Do* submit a P85 and claim any PAYE rebate if leaving part way through the tax year;
(3) *Do* inform the IR National Insurance Contributions Office, check if any contributions will be necessary and, if so, obtain form E101 if going to an EU state;
(4) *Do* make arrangements for offshore banking (including a current account for remaining UK commitments);
(5) *Do* open a local bank account for day-to-day living costs through your UK or offshore bank;
(6) *Do* close any building society deposit accounts (subject to impending mutualisation considerations);
(7) *Do* inform any mortgagee that the mortgaged property is being left vacant, or if it is to be let, ask their permission;
(8) *Do* check the continuing validity of all protective insurances, both life and personal effects, property, etc;
(9) *Do* take legal advice on letting property;
(10) *Do* make or revise a will;
(11) *Do* review existing investments not already mentioned;
(12) *Do* consider comprehensive insurance protection while overseas;
(13) *Do* make use of duty-free facilities in purchasing a car or household appliances if appropriate;
(14) *Do* inform bankers, solicitors, accountants and other advisers of the new address;
(15) *Do not* leave everything to the last minute;
(16) *Do not* take on any new investment commitments just before leaving;

(17) *Do not* forget that most countries are happy to let money in but may impose restrictions on taking it out again – check the rules;

(18) *Do not* leave valuables at home;

(19) *Do not* expect to have a large cash surplus, at least in the first few months;

(20) *Do* contact a colleague already overseas to find out basic information such as the price of a taxi from the airport;

(21) *Do* confirm arrival dates and times with local colleagues, and do travel with contact numbers and addresses for colleagues, hotels, and the British consulate;

(22) *Do* check inoculation requirements and the advisability and availability of private medical healthcare while abroad.

WHILE OVERSEAS

Given that earning and saving money is a prime motive in working abroad, many expatriates are very disappointed to find that after six months they have yet to amass a fortune. In retrospect it is hardly surprising. Even the fully furnished company house is usually missing much essential equipment, there can be a great deal of entertaining to be done either at home or at the club, the cost of living (until experience of local produce and markets is gained) is invariably high, and, after all, a new video and hi-fi are essential.

Usually after about six months, a regular savings or cash surplus pattern can be discerned and at that point some serious consideration can be given to investment.

(1) *Do* register with the local British consulate. This will ensure that your name is on the list for information, or, at worst, evacuation in case of emergency;

(2) *Do* invest surplus cash initially in a readily realisable form such as a very short-term bank deposit;

(3) *Do* retain an adequate cash reserve;

(4) *Do* wait until a regular pattern of surplus appears before entering into any major investment commitments;

(5) *Do* examine all investment propositions very carefully;

(6) *Do* seek independent advice on all financial matters;

(7) *Do not* be tempted by tales of massive profits just waiting to be made, at least until a reasonably secure base has been built up;

(8) *Do not* sign any investment document or part with cash as a result of a brief meeting with a salesman of whose credentials you are not absolutely certain;

(9) *Do not* make any long-term commitments based on current earning

capacity unless that capacity is extremely secure (for most expatriates, it is not);

(10) *Do* remember that *not* investing is also an option. Losing money is a bigger mistake than missing a profit;

(11) *Do not* attempt to beat currency or tax regulations, as the penalties can be extremely severe;

(12) *Do not* neglect to plan.

COMING HOME

One of the most vital occasions for tax and investment planning is in the months before returning to the United Kingdom. Much of what has been achieved in terms of savings and investment can be largely undone by a lack of forethought at this point. Amid the round of farewell parties, packing up and thinking of home, it is often very easy to forget to close a bank account or to realise accrued gains. The secret is to plan.

(1) *Do* prepare for your return to the United Kingdom as you would prepare for a new overseas posting. After several years' absence, the United Kingdom will be unfamiliar in many aspects;

(2) *Do* ask your employer for details of any repatriation programmes offered by the company;

(3) *Do* seek professional advice at least three months before the return date (or if the overseas period is unlikely to last, or to have lasted for at least five years, get advice in the tax year prior to return);

(4) *Do* check any local requirements for tax clearance before the issue of exit visas;

(5) *Do* check current exchange control regulations;

(6) *Do* close all offshore deposit accounts (and in the tax year before return close any UK bank deposit accounts);

(7) *Do* consider CGT and UK income tax liabilities on existing investments, in the tax year before returning;

(8) *Do* give notice to any tenants at home to quit;

(9) *Do* read Chapter 12 again.

Appendix II

TAX TABLES

INCOME TAX RATES FOR 2000–01 AND THE PREVIOUS SIX YEARS

Band of taxable income			
From £	*To* £	*Rate* %	*Cumulative tax* £
For 1994–95			
1	3,000	20	600
3,001	23,700	25	5,775
over	23,700	40	–
For 1995–96			
1	3,200	20	640
3,201	24,300	25	5,915
over	24,300	40	–
For 1996–97			
1	3,900	20	780
3,901	25,500	24	5,964
over	25,500	40	–
For 1997–98			
1	4,100	10	820
4,101	26,100	23	5,880
over	26,100	40	–
For 1998–99			
1	4,300	20	860
4,301	27,100	23	5,244
over	27,100	40	–
For 1999–00			
1	1,500	10	150
1,501	28,000	23	6,095
over	28,000	40	–
For 2000–01			
1	1,520	10	152
1,521	28,400	22	5,914
over	28,400	40	–

INCOME TAX: PERSONAL RELIEFS FOR 2000–01 AND THE PREVIOUS THREE YEARS (1)

	1997–98	1998–99	1999–00	2000–01
Personal (each) (s257)	£4,045	£4,195	£4,335	£4,385
Married couple (s257A)	£1,830(3)	£1,900(3)	£1,970(4)	Nil
(monthly reduction in year of marriage)	£152½	£158⅓	£164⅙	–

Age allowance
Reduced by £1 for every
£2 income over

£2 income over	£15,600	£16,200	£16,800	£17,000
65 to 74 (from 1989–90) in year:				
personal (each)	£5,220	£5,410	£5,720	£5,790
married couple	£3,185(3)	£3,305(3)	£5,125(4)	£5,185(4)
Maximum income –				
wife or single	£17,950	£18,630	£19,570	£19,810
husband	£20,660(2)	£21,440(2)	£25,880(2)	£26,180(2)
80 (to1988–89) or 75				
(from 1989–90) or over in year:				
personal (each)	£5,400	£5,600	£5,980	£6,050
married couple	£3,225(3)	£3,345(3)	£5,195(4)	£5,200(4)
Maximum income –				
wife or single	£18,310	£19,010	£20,090	£20,330
husband	£21,100	£21,900	£26,540	£26,720

Additional relief for children (s259)	£1,830(3)	£1,900(3)	£1,970(4)	Nil

Widow's bereavement (s262)	£1,830(3)	£1,900(3)	£1,970(4)	£2,000(4)

Blind persons (each) (s265)	£1,280	£1,330	£1,380	£1,400

(1) Earlier rates are given in previous editions of this Handbook.
(2) Different if wife in higher age bracket than husband.
(3) Relief restricted to 15 per cent.
(4) Relief restricted to 10 per cent.

Capital gains tax rates
Net gains added to income and taxed at income tax rates to 1998–99.

1999–00	2000–01
below higher rate threshold – 20 per cent	starting rate – 10 per cent
above higher rate threshold – 40 per cent	savings rate – 20 per cent
	higher rate – 40 per cent

	1997–98	1998–99	1999–00	2000–01
Annual exemption (TCGA 1992, s3)				
Individuals	£6,500	£6,800	£7,100	£7,200
Most trusts	£3,250	£3,400	£3,550	£3,600

Appendix III

USEFUL ADDRESSES

Inland Revenue offices

Inland Revenue Headquarters
Somerset House
Strand
London WC2R 1LB

Tel: +44 (0)20 7438 6622

Public Enquiry Room

Tel: +44 (0)20 7438 6420

Financial Intermediaries and
    Claims Office (FICO)
International Division
1st Floor
St John's House
Merton Road
Bootle
Merseyside L69 9BL

Tel: +44 (0)151 472 6000

Financial Intermediaries and
    Claims Office (FICO)
Fitzroy House
PO Box 46
Nottingham NG2 1BD

Tel: +44 (0)115 974 2000

Inland Revenue Head Office
    (Public Departments)
Foreign Section
Ty-Glas
Llanishen
Cardiff CF4 5ZD

Tel: +44 (0)29 2075 3271

Website:
www.inlandrevenue.gov.uk

National Insurance

IR National Insurance
    Contributions Office
International Services Division
Newcastle-upon-Tyne
NE98 1YX

Tel: +44 (0)191 213 5000
Website: www.dss.gov.uk

Investor protection: United Kingdom

Financial Services Authority
25 The North Colonade
Canary Wharf
London E14 5HS

Tel: +44 (0)20 7676 1000
Website: www.fsa.gov.uk

Offshore centres: supervisory authorities

The Bahamas:
Office of the Registrar General
Rodney E Bain Building
Shirley & Parliament Streets
PO Box N-532
Nassau

Tel: +1 809 322 3316

Guernsey:
Guernsey Financial Services
    Commission
La Plaiderie Chambers
La Plaiderie
St Peter Port
GY1 1WG

Tel: +44 481 712706

Website:
www.gfsc.guernseyci.com

Jersey:
Policy and Resources Department
Cyril Le Marquand House
The Parade
St Helier

Tel: +44 534 603400

Isle of Man:
Financial Supervision
    Commission
Megharaj Centre
1–4 Goldie Terrace
Douglas

Tel: +44 (0)624 692800

Other contacts

BDO Stoy Hayward and BDO
  International
8 Baker Street
London W1M 1DA

Tel: +44 (0)20 7486 5888
Fax: +44 (0)20 7487 3686
Website: www.bdo.co.uk
E-mail: andy.wells@bdo.co.uk

WJB Chiltern plc and MRI
  Moores Rowland
Sceptre House
169–173 Regent Street
London W1R 8DD
Tel: +44 (0)20 7339 9000
Fax: +44 (0)20 7571 8699
Websites: www.MRI-
  world.interliant.com.uk
  www.wjbchiltern.com
E-mail:
  eastawayn@wjbchiltern.com

Advisory and Brokerage Services
  Ltd
40–43 Chancery Lane
London WC2A 1JB

Tel: +44 (0)20 7405 8535
Fax: +44 (0)20 7831 8950
E-mail:
  a&b@advisory.demon.co.uk

INDEX

227